FAMILY
HEALTH
CARE

This book is dedicated to
Ray and Helen, my parents.

FAMILY HEALTH CARE

edited by
Russell J. Sawa

SAGE Publications
International Educational and Professional Publisher
Newbury Park   London   New Delhi

For information address:

SAGE Publications, Inc.
2455 Teller Road
Newbury Park, California 91320

SAGE Publications Ltd.
6 Bonhill Street
London EC2A 4PU
United Kingdom

SAGE Publications India Pvt. Ltd.
M-32 Market
Greater Kailash I
New Delhi 110 048 India

Printed in the United States of America

Library of Congress Cataloging-in-Publication Data

Main entry under title:

Family health care / Russell J. Sawa, editor.
  p. cm.
  Includes bibliographical references and index.
  ISBN 0-8039-4748-8 (cl).—ISBN 0-8039-4749-6 (pb)
  1. Family medicine. 2. Family—Health and hygiene.—3. Family psychotherapy. I. Sawa, Russell J.
  [DNLM: 1. Family Health. 2. Family Health Care. 3. Family Practice. WA 308 F1983]
  RC46.F33 1992
  616—dc20   92-49939
  DNLM/DLC   CIP

92 93 94 95 10 9 8 7 6 5 4 3 2 1

Sage Production Editor: Diane S. Foster

Contents

Foreword

This book may well mark a turning point in the sometimes troubled relationships among family medicine, family theory, and family therapy. It arose from the Calgary Symposium at which, perhaps for the first time, there was an opportunity for family physicians, psychiatrists, nurses, behavioral scientists, and members of other related disciplines to discuss the issues at length. The troubles become understandable if we see them against the background of scientific thought in our own century. The scientific view of the world has been transformed in our own time by quantum mechanics, information theory, systems theory, cybernetics, and nonequilibrium thermodynamics. Mainstream medicine, however, has remained largely untouched by this fundamental reorientation, basing its practice and education on nineteenth-century doctrines of specific etiology, mind/body separation, and the conceptual isolation of the patient from his or her environment. Medicine's conceptual backwardness is not without its justification. Medicine, after all, is a branch of technology, and we judge technologies not by their truth, but by their effectiveness. For much of this century, medical

technology, based on nineteenth-century ideas, has worked very well—
indeed, triumphantly. Even today it works well within its limits.

One exception to medicine's conceptual isolation has been the impact
of systems theory. As Ludwig von Bertalanffy (1969) observes in his
book *General System Theory,* psychiatry was the first branch of clinical
medicine to be influenced by systems theory, an experience it shared
with psychology and the social sciences. The impact of these ideas was
probably at its peak in the 1960s, the very time when family medicine
was becoming established as a clinical discipline in the medical school.

Family medicine was the name given in North America to the intellectual discipline based on the experience of general practitioners.
Since general practitioners had often been called family doctors, the
name seemed to fit very well with the historic role of the general
practitioner. There was also, however, the feeling that the name represented a new way of being a family doctor.

There was some truth in this. Those of us who received a conventional, mid-century medical education started out with limitations of
vision that proved difficult to overcome. On the other hand, there were
exceptions. Many general practitioners learned by experience how to
be family doctors in the full sense of the term. Dr. F. J. A. Huygen of
the Netherlands and Dr. William Pickles of England were notable
examples—notable also in that they documented and published their
work. In the United States, the new name filled the need to distinguish
general practice, conceptually, from other primary care disciplines. European countries, where academic general practice originated, did not
feel the need to change names.

One of the first tasks of academic family medicine was to develop a
conceptual framework for the discipline. What could be more natural
than that it should embrace the exciting new ideas and methods spawned
by general systems theory—such as family systems theory and family
therapy. These ideas were, and are still, of fundamental importance for
family medicine. Unfortunately, two understandable but important errors were made at this time. First, it was assumed that general practitioners had learned nothing from their long experience of caring for
patients and their families. Because this knowledge was largely at the
intuitive level and seldom articulated and published, it was thought not
to exist. Second, it was assumed that therapeutic techniques developed
for one clinical context could be transferred without modification to an
entirely different context. These errors were ironic, since they violated
two fundamental principles of ecology: a respect for traditional wisdom

and a belief in the importance of context. They were the equivalent of errors made by engineers who construct a new irrigation system without studying the local context, and without regard for the traditional wisdom of the local farmers. It was also unrealistic to think that family systems theory could provide the sole conceptual basis for family medicine. We needed, for example, a theory of the doctor-patient relationship and of the office consultation.

There were, of course, other sources of resistance to the new ideas. Paradigm shift, as Thomas Kuhn (1962) has observed, is always a painful process. Some adherents of the old paradigm are genuinely incapable of seeing their world in terms of the new one. General practitioners have, like other physicians, been educated according to the old paradigm. For part of what we do, the old paradigm serves us reasonably well. Moreover, we still live in a society based on a mechanistic, dualistic worldview. It is not surprising that progress has been slow.

I left the Calgary Symposium with the strong feeling that many of these problems are now behind us. Much good work has already been done in making connections between family theory and family medicine. The conference resulted in a solid agenda of work to be done in describing how family physicians work with families, and in developing and evaluating methods of application in family practice. I think that agenda and this book represent an important new beginning.

IAN R. McWHINNEY
The University of Western Ontario

Acknowledgments

I wish to acknowledge those who made this volume possible through their involvement and their support. The symposium that formed the foundation of this book was financially supported by the National Health and Research Development Program (Canada), the Medical Services Incorporated Foundation of Alberta, Alberta Heritage Foundation for Medical Research, the College of Family Physicians of Canada, the Calgary General Hospital, and the Department of Family Medicine, University of Calgary.

A special thanks to Dr. Yves Talbot, who was cochairman for the symposium. Participants in the symposium (in addition to the authors in this volume) included Drs. Wayne Elford, Michael Crouch, Janet Christie-Seely, and John Mackel (family medicine); Dr. Karl Tomm (family therapy); Dr. Maureen Leahey (family therapy/nursing); Ms. Michelle Nanchoff-Glatt and Ms. Ann Boerner (family therapy/nursing), and Dr. Janice Bell (nursing).

A special thanks also to Mrs. Marion Butcher for help in typing the manuscripts. Thanks also to those who gave me feedback and suggestions on my chapter "Three Ways of Thinking" at various stages of its development. This includes Jack Costello, S.J.; Dennis Galon, Ph.D.; Dr. Ian McWhinney; Dr. Jan Roberts; and Ms. Rhonda Zabrodski.

I also wish to thank my wife Nancy, for helping with editing suggestions when I got stuck and for supporting me through the process of the symposium and completion of this book.

RUSSELL J. SAWA

ONE

Paradigm Shift: Toward a New Vision of Family Medicine

RUSSELL J. SAWA

My undergraduate medical education took place in the first half of the 1970s. It was traditional. There was no clue to the paradigm shift that was beginning to unfold (see Ian McWhinney's foreword to this volume). There was never a word about systems theory, or about family therapy.

It was during my family practice residency that I recognized something was missing in the old paradigm, although I did not even know what the word meant at that time. It was my clinical experience that led to my insight. I had a following of patients over the course of my residency. One was a teenage girl who came in frequently, I didn't seem to be able to help her with her assortment of somatic complaints and eventual pregnancy out of wedlock. I couldn't understand what was going on, and felt that there were factors or clues other than those I had been taught to look for in medical school that were important in making sense of the situation. Somehow I sensed the reasons (and solutions) resided in her family.

With this case, I began my journey to discover the family in primary care. I went to this patient's home and interviewed her family on several occasions, but I had nowhere to turn for help in understanding the significance of the family dynamics I observed in terms of the health of my patient. I noticed other similar cases as I rotated through the various specialties during my residency and had the opportunity to observe other clinicians similarly stuck (see also p. 173 in this volume).

I began my training in family therapy, at McMaster University, while I was still a resident. At that time this was the only source of new skills

and information about families and the context of our patients. This
made clear my resolve to train as a family therapist in order to learn
what I could apply in my medical practice, and so I went back to
McMaster after my residency to learn family therapy. I was attracted
by a vision of medical practice that integrates into a unified whole an
understanding of the physical, relational, emotional, and spiritual dimensions of health and illness.

This vision has continued to direct me through its attraction, even to
the present time. It has been the basis of my motivation to seek out
others who share, in some way, that same vision. I have discovered that
I have not been alone in my thinking. In fact, some of the contributors
to this volume have followed very similar paths, beginning their work
at about the same time my journey began. We now collectively realize
how much primary care has to gain by opening space for a paradigm
shift, a new way of thinking. It is this vision that led to the process of
the symposium that provided the opportunity for the dialogue that has
resulted in the chapters in this volume.

The process began in 1985, when Drs. Yves Talbot, Janet Christie-Seely,
Michael Crouch, and Don Ransom joined me in teleconference to determine who should be the presenters at a symposium devoted to examining
the role of the family in primary care. We also concluded that the issue of
the family in primary care could be divided into four areas of expertise—
theory, methodology, education, and practice—and that experts should be
chosen from each area. Twelve scholars agreed to participate, three for
each of the four areas to be examined. To stimulate creativity, each group
of three had at least one participant from a divergent field of study, such
as a historian, organizational consultant, or medical anthropologist.

The organization of this almost gigantic task took the following form.
Each of the four perspectives was addressed by a group of three people.
This group of three would consult with each other, myself, and Dr.
Talbot (who agreed to be my cochairman) in teleconferencing, sharing
their ideas and expressing their concerns. By the time the first round of
teleconferencing had occurred, a framing hypothesis, that "the inclusion of the family in primary care leads to a more effective prevention,
diagnosis, management, and rehabilitation plan," was agreed upon.
Each individual would then write a paper that addressed the framing
hypothesis from his or her assigned perspective (assignments came
about through dialogue among the threesome), and the three would then
compare papers, teleconference, collaborate, rewrite their own papers,
and continue the process until they were finished.

It took more than 25 hours on the phone and several years to get the job done. The process was truly collaborative and evolutionary. After the authors in each group completed their papers, an additional four participants were chosen, one in each of the four areas, to respond to the papers.

Five years after its inception, funding was finally secured and the symposium took place: three days of paper presentations and further dialogue. This book is only one result of that process. Herein are published all the papers from the symposium, in the order in which they were presented.

In Part I, which deals with theory, Dr. Edward Shorter, a professor of the history of medicine, discusses changes in the family during the last 20 years (the postmodern era). He relates these changes to the kinds of problems primary care physicians see increasingly in their offices. Dr. Peter Steinglass uses the framing hypothesis to describe how systems theory is useful to primary care. Dr. William J. Doherty then outlines a model for categorizing the major domains of family and health research, and suggests which family theories are consistent with different aspects of families' experience of health and illness. Drs. Ian R. McWhinney and Joan Patterson respond to these chapters and outline what a family medicine-derived theory of the family-physician-patient relationship would look like. They also expand on some ideas about existing theories.

In Part II, on methodology, Dr. Maurine H. Venters discusses current ideas of the family as the center of health care. She reviews interdisciplinary research and discusses methodological issues related to indicators used to measure family care. She also discusses current attempts to measure the prevalence, determinants, and benefits of family care. Dr. Howard F. Stein discusses an ethnographic approach to family health care research, as well as the multiple meanings of *family* and how "family" is incorporated into family health care. Dr. Donald C. Ransom discusses future directions in the methodology of family-oriented health care research. He addresses the need for new conceptual units of study (i.e., persons and families) that will be more applicable and usable by practicing physicians. Dr. Walter W. Rosser discusses the implications of the contributions made by the three methodology chapters.

In Part III, on education, Dr. Diana McLain Smith, an organizational consultant, reviews the history of teaching the family in family medicine. She then describes how generative learning can be applied in family medicine's current effort to incorporate the family into everyday medical practice. Dr. John C. Rogers reviews the teaching models of family assessment and intervention currently used. He critiques these models, then discusses methods of producing "authentic" models. In my own chapter in this section, I discuss how physicians use "three ways of thinking"—the mechanical, personal, and systemic—to handle clinical situations, and how these ways of thinking can be used to integrate the psychosocial and biological aspects of medicine. I also explain how this can be applied in teaching situations. Finally in this section, Dr. Macaran A. Baird discusses how he and Doherty developed their model, and comments on the implications of the three education chapters.

In Part IV, which addresses practice, Dr. Lorne A. Becker reviews the problems inherent in integrating the family into family medicine. He discusses the principles of how innovations are diffused and how these principles can be used to integrate family interventions into the actual practice of our family physicians. Dr. William R. McFarlane discusses the psychoeducational approach to schizophrenia, and suggests that the principles of this approach might be used to develop models of intervention in family medicine. Dr. Thomas L. Campbell reviews the empirical literature on family interventions in health, discusses the implications of Dr. McFarlane's work, and looks at possible mechanisms of how families influence health. He then discusses how we might develop family interventions in health care. Dr. Reg L. Perkin, the executive director of the College of Family Physicians of Canada, reviews the history of the development of family medicine in Canada and suggests directions for further incorporation of the family into family medicine.

As a whole, the chapters presented in this volume summarize the cutting edge of our knowledge about the family in primary care/family medicine. They review the past, critique the present, and point the way to the future. They make a contribution to the form this new paradigm might take. What actually comes to be will be the result of many forces, including, and perhaps above all, what patients want from us as primary care family practitioners.

There is emerging evidence that the public wants family physicians to look after *all* the members of the family. As Perkin (1991) points out:

> Knowledge of the family provides the physician with more management options. The outcome for the patient is better, particularly in patients with chronic illness, patients who are receiving palliative care, patients who have problems with compliance with medications, patients who need hospitalization or surgery, and those with mental or emotional disorders. (p. 2536)

The present time is one of rapid changes in society and in our political structures. The existence of society's basic source of cohesiveness, the family unit, is under challenge. We must remember, however, that a time of crisis is also a time of opportunity.

I hope that this volume will be useful to all readers—whether clinicians, teachers, or researchers—especially to those who believe we can alter the future by our choices of today and through our vision of what could be if we follow our highest aspirations and most exciting wishes for the future. This volume contains within it the seeds of a vision of hope and renewed confidence in the dignity and potential of the human spirit, and a potential matrix upon which we can build a better and healthier future.

PART I

Theory

TWO

Recent Changes in Family Life
and New Challenges in Primary Care

EDWARD SHORTER

THE ADVENT OF THE POSTMODERN FAMILY

Since the 1960s, family life has been undergoing one of its periodic historic changes: a shift from one family system to an entirely different kind of system. The last such change took place at the end of the eighteenth century, as the "traditional" peasant family gave way to a historically unprecedented "modern" family (Shorter, 1975). This modern family style was destined to last for a century and a half, but in the 1960s the modern family in its turn began to disintegrate, and to be replaced by the "postmodern" family that we see taking shape about us today. This transition from modern to postmodern family life has brought with it new challenges to primary care in medicine.

A recent review pointed out some of the principal changes: In contrast with the modern family, which emphasized close affective ties between mother and adolescent children and lifelong "companionship" between the spouses, the postmodern family is characterized by a diminished parental role in child care, by the highly eroticized nature (and consequent fragility) of the tie between the spouses, and by the withdrawal of the family unit generally from generational and community ties (Shorter, 1989). In contrast with the modern couple, who tended to see the family unit as a larger social building block, the postmodern couple sees marriage as a means of extending their own self-actualization. These changes are not necessarily good or bad, but they have been occurring. One consequence of these changes has been an increase in the number of people outside of any family circle.

A significantly larger proportion of the population today lives alone, or without children, than in the past. The proportion of one- or two-person households has risen in the United States from 20% in 1900 to 54% in 1980 (Thornton, 1983). Even over the short term, the changes have been considerable: Households consisting of a single woman rose from 8% of the total in 1960 to 14% in 1983; those with a single man climbed from 5% to 9%. Most of this growth in aloneness has occurred among younger age groups (Glick, 1984).

THE INCREASE IN SINGLE PEOPLE

One factor contributing to the relative increase in the number of single persons has been the increase in the frequency of divorce. In Canada, the number of divorced individuals rose 38% from 1981 to 1986 (Devereaux, 1988). The United States saw 1,158,000 divorces in 1983. There are statistics on women available: In 1983, 1 out of every 50 married women divorced, as has been the case annually in the United States since 1975. This is triple the number of divorces in 1960 (Devereaux, 1988). These statistics indicate that in a general medical practice that includes 500 married women, 10 will divorce every year, so that after 10 years, 100 of the formerly married female patients will have become divorcees.

A second factor contributing to the rise of singleness has been the increase in one-parent families (single parents with one or more children under the age of 18). Whereas in 1970 in the United States only 1 family in 10 with children was a one-parent family, by 1984 this figure had doubled to 1 in 5. Of these one-parent families, 88% were headed by women. In 1984 one-fourth of all children under 18 lived in one-parent families, and projections show that, of those children born in 1984, nearly 60% may expect to spend some time in a one-parent family before they reach the age of 18 (Norton, 1986). Many of these children will never again experience a two-parent family. Birthrates among unmarried black teenagers have been high but stable over the last 30 years, while birthrates of unmarried white teenagers tripled over the period 1955 to 1983 (Newberger, 1986).

A third source of increased singleness is the postponement of marriage. By 1989 in the United States, the median age at first marriage for both men (26.2 years) and women (23.8 years) was at the highest peak since records were first collected in 1890. Since 1970 the median age has risen by 3 years. The proportion of never-married 20-24-year-olds, for example, rose from 36% in 1970 to 63% in 1989; of 30-34-year-olds, from 6% to 17% ("Research Note," 1991). People also postpone marriage by cohabiting. According to one U.S. study, "More than five times as many unmarried couples were cohabiting in 1989 as in 1970 (2.8 million versus 523,000)" ("Research Note," 1991). Writes demographer Paul Glick (1984), "Before 1970, the typical unmarried 'couple' consisted of an unmarried landlady in middle or old age who was renting a room to an unmarried young man; after 1970, it consisted of an unmarried young man who was sharing his living quarters with an unmarried young female partner."

Another element contributing to the postponement of marriage and the choice of alternative styles of living arrangements is the fact that millions of young women today seek careers outside the home, rather than take on the traditional role of housewife or homemaker.

Finally, the continued rise in the population of elderly people has contributed to the increase in detachment of individuals from their families. The number of people older than 65 has more than doubled in the last quarter century. It rose in the United States from 12.2 million in 1950 (8.1%) to more than 30.4 million in 1988 (12.4%) (National Center for Health Statistics, 1991). In 1900 only 29% of the elderly in the United States lived alone or with their spouses; in 1975, 79% did so. Those living with married children declined from 16% to 2% (Thornton, 1983).

As the numbers of elderly increase, their living arrangements are becoming increasingly solitary. In a U.S. survey of selected counties in the states of Iowa and Washington, 20% of the elderly men and 18% of the women had not seen any of their children in the preceding month. Elderly people in New Haven were asked, "How many friends do you see at least once a month?" A total of 48% of the white women and 41% of the white men answered either "none" or "one or two" (National Institute on Aging, 1986, p. 40). It is evident that a significant percentage of elderly people find themselves in social and familial isolation. Historically, this percentage has been increasing (Fischer, 1977).

The "family of American nostalgia," as Newberger (1986) has termed it, has indeed vanished: "This is the family of our first grade primers. Father works; mother is at home caring for their children—Dick, Jane, and Baby Sally." In 1981 this grouping accounted for only one American family in five (Newberger, 1986). In its stead is now the postmodern household, resembling more an isolated atom spinning in space than a solid social institution. Cut off from family ties, angry, anxious, and socially unconnected, the members of these households are more likely to visit their family doctors than are the members of intact families (Shorter, 1992).

ALONENESS AND
THE PRODUCTION OF SYMPTOMS

Socially isolated individuals are more likely to become symptomatic, or to somatize. Lipowski (1987) defines somatization as "a tendency to experience and communicate psychological distress in the form of somatic symptoms and to seek medical help for them." Such individuals see their doctors more frequently than do well-integrated individuals. After a review of the literature on health and loneliness, West (1986) concludes that "loneliness is linked with reported feelings of ill health, somatic distress, and visits to physicians as well as physical disease."

In a study conducted in Whitehaven, England, between 1975 and 1978, 109 frequent attenders (those who visited their doctors frequently) were compared with controls. Westhead (1985) found 12% of the male frequent attenders to be divorced, compared with none of the male controls. Of the female frequent attenders, 13% were widows, versus 7% of the control group. The frequent attenders had histories of poor health and neuroticism, although many also had bona fide physical disorders (Westhead, 1985). A study conducted in a general practice in Hamilton, Ontario, with 94 patients known to have "intrapersonal problems" discovered that 60% were widowed, separated, or divorced, compared with 46% of the controls. "Patients with interpersonal problems were found to have a significantly greater number of hospital admissions, higher rates of surgery and greater rates of visits to the family physician when compared to controls." They also had a far greater rate of inpatient psychiatric admissions (Brennan, 1981).

Lonely elderly people tend to develop many symptoms. In a review of the literature, Ryan (1987) found that "both lonely [elderly] males and females complained of multiple psychosomatic illnesses. . . . Negative self-assessments of health, fatigue, physician visits, and medication consumption were also more prevalent among the lonely."

The mechanism leading from being alone to the production of medical symptoms is not clear. Perhaps it is merely the stress of coping with being a single parent, or an elderly, housebound widow or widower afraid to venture out to shop. However, some isolated persons are also clinically depressed. Depression produces an array of medical symptoms, perhaps in a manner similar to somatization, for they both illustrate how our bodies express psychic disequilibrium. A mid-1970s U.S. study among a random sample of 2,300 people in Chicago, northwest Indiana, and surrounding suburbs found that 12% of the currently married were highly depressed, compared with 27% of the formerly married. The problem did not boil down simply to the social isolation of the divorced; many married couples were socially isolated as well, but the isolated divorcees had a depression rate twice as high. And the divorcees who were not isolated had considerably more depression (21%) compared with those who were married but not isolated (11%). Nor was the problem economic deprivation among the divorced, for 15% of the well-off unmarried were depressed, versus 9% of the well-off married (Pearlin, 1977).

It seems to be the specific role of jarred expectations in an individual's intimate life, rather than poverty or isolation, that helps produce this depression. In a probability sample of 680 American households in 1978, Ross (1983) found that "transitional" marriages, in which the wife was working but the husband had not yet resolved to help at home, demonstrated the most depression. Wives had the highest rates of depression when the husband did not share household duties regardless of whether the wife was working because she had to or simply because she wanted to. Both spouses had low rates of depression when the husband helped his spouse with the housework.

Depression, often associated with excessive concern with health, may produce much of the somatization seen in family medicine. This connection between depression and psychogenic physical symptoms has long been recognized (Blumer, 1982). Lloyd (1986) believes that affective disorders are the largest category of psychiatric illnesses that may cause somatization. However, many somatizers are not depressed.

Somatization is very common in primary care. Katon (1984), for instance, cites estimates of 25% to 75% of *all* patient visits. While these estimates sound excessive, they nonetheless suggest that all somatizers could not possibly have concurrent psychiatric diagnoses.

Whatever the mechanism, the point is that many individuals who are detached from the web of close family associations will visit their family physicians more frequently, either with somatization or with genuine organic pathology, than will individuals who are still bound closely to family ties. It must be pointed out that somatizers have symptoms in excess of medical findings, and a person may be a somatizer and still have underlying organic disease.

HOW FAMILY CHANGE AFFECTS
THE PRACTICE OF FAMILY MEDICINE

With increasing frequency, isolated, often anxious, patients seek out their family physicians for help. How is their clinical care different from that of patients in the 1950s?

Prevention

In forestalling future illness, it is crucial for the family physician to counsel patients. Family violence, for example, is on the increase, and the consequences of wife and child abuse are seen by nearly every family physician. Here a direct and obvious link exists between the new stresses of postmodern family life and violence within the family. In a recent review of the literature, Seagull (1987) found that most child abuse occurred in single-parent families, and that social isolation often led to child neglect, if not actual abuse. The doctor-patient relationship offers considerable opportunity to help struggling single parents, both by providing counseling and by helping them to connect with appropriate community supports.

Morbidity and Diagnosis

It is helpful for the family doctor to be aware that various psychogenic illnesses have an elective affinity for those who are single and isolated and for those detached from family life. Stewart (1987), in a study with a sample of 42 patients with total allergy syndrome, or "twentieth-century disease," noted a shift in the patients' views of the cause of the problem from urea foam to candidiasis, as the latter became a popular explanation of disease. Physicians' waiting rooms are now crowded with anxious patients who report symptoms or combinations of symptoms—abdominal pain, nausea, vomiting spells, back pain, dizziness, muscle weakness, joint pain, urinary retention or difficulty urinating, feeling sickly (all possible symptoms in a somatization disorder), facial pain, or burning mouth—for which a succession of previous consultants have been unable to identify a somatic cause, or which they believe to be fibromyalgia or chronic fatigue syndrome from a previous bout of Epstein-Barr virus.

Although social profiles of sufferers with all of these conditions are not yet available, at least some of these diagnoses and self-diagnoses occur preferentially in the unmarried. Salit (1985) found that, of 50 chronic fatigue patients (what was then called postinfectious neuromyasthenia, PIN) seen at the Toronto General Hospital, "most were unmarried women and at least 4 had been divorced." Their average age was 33, and 50% had had a major depression before the onset of their symptoms. Another study of PIN found that "71 percent of the . . . group met criteria for an affective disorder" (Taerk, 1987). It is true that among Brodsky's (1983) 8 patients who were "allergic to everything," 4 were married, 2 were divorced, and 2 were single, corresponding roughly to percentages in the general population. However, Stewart's (1985) study of "twentieth-century disease" described a group of young, middle-class female sufferers whose personal lives were in chaos. Of her original sample of 18 patients, Stewart (personal communication, 1991) has reported that as of the study in 1985, 7 were married, 8 were single, and 3 were divorced.

Patients with chronic fatigue syndrome, or "chronic Epstein Barr virus" (EBV), tend to be single. One study of 23 patients who had been referred to the National Institutes of Health showed that 13 had never married and 2 had separated (Straus, 1985). Indeed, chronic fatigue syndrome is becoming positively epidemic in primary care, as practitioners and patients alike dwell upon fatigue of a supposedly postviral origin. In a hospital division of general medicine in Boston, among those seeking primary care for any reason, 1 unselected patient out of 5 (21%) was "found to be suffering from a chronic fatigue syndrome consistent with . . . EBV infection" (Buchwald, 1987). The entire plague of such complaints as chronic fatigue from EBV sequelae may be thought of as a medically acceptable form of somatization (meaning that the suggestion of organicity is acceptable both to the doctor and to the patient).

A variety of evidence, anecdotal and quantitative, indicates that somatization may be on the rise (Shorter, 1992). According to Lipowski (1988), "Clinical and epidemiological studies published in the past twenty years indicate that patients presenting with symptoms lacking adequate medical basis are ubiquitous in all medical care settings, both inpatient and outpatient." It is interesting that, despite enormous advances in medical therapy, the number of people today who report having had a recent illness is much higher than in the 1930s (Shorter, 1986, p. 213). Barsky (1988) has recently described the pathological preoccupation with body states of our entire culture. This whole gamut of symptoms (mentioned above) may be traced in part to the anxiety and depression underlying new forms of family life.

The diagnosis therefore changes. Knowledge of these medical-demographic patterns may assist physicians with the differential diagnosis of today's patients. A patient presenting with long-standing multiple complaints might not have a formal somatization disorder (Briquet's syndrome), PIN, or any of a host of other psychogenic disorders. (For a more complete discussion of somatization, see Sawa, Chapter 12, this volume.) Yet if the patient is a young person who has recently separated from a marital union, or at age 33 is unhappy about facing a lifetime of singlehood, the likelihood that the physician is dealing with a movement toward a somatization disorder must be seriously weighed alongside the possibility of organic pathology. Separating out the psychogenic from the somatogenic offers a newly urgent professional challenge to family physicians.

Acute Treatment

Statistically, it is the elderly who are most often in need of acute treatment, and it is they who are most lacking in family support. The postmodern family has tended to be less involved with the elderly, so that when their elderly parents become ill, adult children are likely to be thousands of miles away or absent for other reasons. Why does this noninvolvement matter? Sick elderly people are also at risk of being depressed. It has been shown that depression scores are extremely high among the elderly. One study conducted in East Boston found that by the age of 85, only one male in five was without depressive symptomatology (National Institute on Aging, 1986, p. 49). La Rue (1985) concludes in a review of the literature that "depressions severe enough to warrant intervention are generally estimated to affect 10 to 15 percent of the geriatric population" (p. 667). Isolation in a hospital makes depression worse rather than better, thus trapping the elderly inpatient in a downward spiral of psychogenic and somatogenic illness. The absence of family support that might curtail this downward spiral is therefore of medical concern.

Even when the family is present, the elderly present additional complications for medical staff in acute care institutions. In Canada, acute care beds are increasingly backed up with elderly patients who no longer require such care but for whom placement cannot be arranged (Rachlis, 1989). Hospital staff often become resentful of such patients. As a classic psychiatry textbook states euphemistically, "Geriatric nursing has, at first sight, the appearance of being unrewarding" (Slater & Roth, 1977, p. 564). The subtle sense of impatience of the staff, however ill founded and unfair to the patient, may nonetheless be implicitly communicated to anxious family members. The families of these elderly patients awaiting placement may become angry at the brusqueness of the staff and find the "system" cold and impersonal. The family itself therefore requires management by physicians dealing with elderly patients in acute care settings.

Rehabilitation

Family support is crucial to the nursing care of rehabilitation patients of all ages. For example, spinal cord injuries in the young require many hours of patient nursing. In the 1950s and before, female family members were often available to spend days and nights at the bedsides of young quadriplegics, helping to feed them, wash them, and otherwise assist in nursing care. Cooksey (1954, p. 735), in a discussion of the physically handicapped, assumed that a mother or another female relative would be available to help out. An international survey in the early 1960s found that in many countries, including such advanced nations as the United Kingdom, the family performed activities to supplement nursing care while the patient was in the hospital (Beck, 1965).

Today these family members are in the labor force. In the United States the number of women with children under the age of 6 working at full-time jobs rose from 12% in 1950 to 54% in 1985 (Population Reference Bureau, 1987). The entire care of chronically hospitalized patients is now left to the nursing staff.

It is interesting that an article published in 1984 on the care of patients with spinal cord injuries does not even mention the role of the family (the article does include simple references to visitors) (Brackett, 1984). Feeling isolated and abandoned, many such patients come to resent the medical staff, become even more depressed, and pose greater problems of clinical management than ever before. Thus trends in postmodern family life create new dilemmas in yet another area of primary care.

We must learn to live with the postmodern family and its new challenges to the practice of medicine. Family physicians should at least be aware that they are facing issues different from those of previous generations, and use this information as they see fit.

THREE

Family Systems Theory and Medical Illness

PETER STEINGLASS

A review of the empirical literature not only supports systems theory as the best currently available framework within which to tackle the above issues related to primary care practice, but, further, shows that family systems theory is particularly salient when the questions at hand have to do with issues of variation in clinical course and organization of service delivery (including family/medical team interactions). I will point out, as another strength of family systems theory, that it offers a reasonable chance of suggesting ways in which biology can be meaningfully integrated with family dynamics in approaching primary care issues. Finally, as a "fringe benefit," systems theory also offers a metaphorical language for rethinking such issues as disease classification, or how to conceptualize service delivery in a way that allows for both family and medical professional input. I will therefore also include several examples of how systems thinkers are using this metaphorical language in productive and provocative ways.

THE EMPIRICAL LITERATURE ON FAMILY AND MEDICAL ILLNESS

A reasonable starting place for a discussion of family theory relevant to family medical practice is to look at the existing empirical literature on family factors as they relate to the onset and course of medical illness (Campbell, 1986; Steinglass & Horan, 1988b). This literature, which is by now quite voluminous, contains extensive case history reports and descriptive studies that have addressed family factors in health care from four different perspectives: as resources for individuals coping with medical illness, as contributors to the development of illness, as influences on relationships with health care delivery systems, and as determinants of differential clinical courses of specific illnesses. These perspectives are discussed in turn below.

The Family as a Resource for the Individual Coping With Medical Illness

This perspective presumes that the family may have little or no role in the onset of medical illnesses, but that its relevance lies in its capacity to serve as the primary referent and support group for family members who become medically ill (Litman, 1974). For example, families are often active participants in the initial definition of illness (in deciding whether or not a particular set of symptoms warrants medical attention), in the interpretation of information brought back by patients from their medical contacts, and in decision making about treatment options. Nursing care, economic support and quasi-social work services in arranging for health care options, and negotiating with employers and third-party reimbursers are all practical support activities that families may or may not engage in on behalf of members who have become ill. Also important in this regard is support in implementing particular medical regimens—this issue has often been pointed to as a critical component in determining successful compliance with medical treatment regimens. Finally, the empirical literature has also included discussion of the role of the family as a protective factor in shielding members from exposure to illness. Presumably, family health practice is one such vehicle for the unfolding of this process.

Role of Family Pathology as a Contributing Factor in the Development of Illness

This pathology-oriented perspective is obviously very different from the "resource" model described above. Perhaps the best known of the family pathology approaches is the "psychosomatic family" model proposed by Minuchin and his colleagues in conjunction with their

studies of children with Type I diabetics, intractable asthma, and eating
disorders (Minuchin et al., 1975; Minuchin, Rosman, & Baker, 1978).
The model suggests a common set of family characteristics that, along
with physiological vulnerability of the child, "produces" these conditions. These characteristics include enmeshment, rigidity, parental overprotectiveness, and lack of conflict resolution.

The psychosomatic family model is one of a number of models that
posit deficits or dysfunctional behavior patterns within the family as
etiologic agents in the development of medical illness in family members. These models, which have also been popular explanatory models
as regards psychiatric disorders (e.g., schizophrenia), have recently
come under increasing criticism. For example, critiques of the Minuchin
et al. model have pointed out that the concept of the psychosomatic
family has never been adequately operationalized, and its core constructs have never been placed within the frame of a body of recognized
and integrated theory (Coyne & Anderson, 1988; Kog, Vandereycken,
& Vertommen, 1985).

At the same time, the empirical literature is replete with reports that
have adopted the "family risk" approach in interpreting clinical data.
Here the emphasis is on the identification of specific structural, com-
positional, or behavioral characteristics of families that place individuals within those families at greater risk of developing medical illness.
An obvious example would be social class; a more intriguing example
might be a specific pattern of alliances within the family (Penn, 1983).

Family Characteristics as They Influence
Relationships With Health Care Delivery Systems

Here the issue is not so much family process variables as factors in
internal (within the family) management of illness, but rather the
interface between the family and health care providers (Reiss & De-Nour,
1989). Of interest have been such questions as utilization of health care
services (basically, whether or not chronic overutilization of services
can be attributed to factors within the family), overall satisfaction with
health care, and, once again, issues of treatment compliance. The
assumption in much of this work is that health care systems are themselves relatively fixed entities and variability in utilization of health
care services can therefore best be understood as attributable to either
individual or family-level characteristics.

Family Factors as Determinants of
Differential Clinical Courses of Specific Illnesses

The fourth perspective, and perhaps the one that has received the most attention, looks at the role of the differential response patterns of families to the challenges of acute and chronic illnesses as they influence the subsequent courses of those illnesses (Obetz, Swenson, McCarty, Gillchrist, & Burget, 1980; Podrasky, 1986; Steinglass, Temple, Lisman, & Reiss, 1982). For example, one interest might be in tying exacerbations of an episodic chronic condition such as multiple sclerosis or chronic back pain to vacillations in stress levels within the family.

This perspective has been particularly attractive because it is often possible to suggest links between family interactive and biological perspectives as determinants of differential clinical course (e.g., a study might look at the interrelationships among bereavement, immunological status, and cancer). Further, a number of these "clinical course" studies have been able to point to specific family process variables that prove more robust in predicting clinical course than traditional medical status variables. A particularly dramatic example here is a study by Reiss, Gonzales, and Kramer (1986) demonstrating that three family variables—which they call "family coordination in approaching joint problem-solving tasks," "family accomplishment level," and "family interconnectedness"—predicted with 100% accuracy early death of end-stage renal disease patients on chronic hemodialysis.

This brief overview of the empirical literature suggests that data (albeit of variable quality) exist to support each of the component parts of our framing hypothesis (see Sawa, Chapter 1, this volume), namely, that the inclusion of the family unit in the delivery of primary care permits implementation of a more effective prevention, diagnosis, treatment, and rehabilitation plan. If we match the above overview of the empirical research and clinical literature with the framing hypothesis, we can see that the first perspective noted above (family as resource) most closely addresses the issue of how inclusion of the family unit permits implementation of more effective prevention measures. The second perspective (family as contributing to illness) clearly addresses the issue of diagnosis, that is, patterns of morbidity. The third and fourth perspectives (family influence on relationship with health system and on course of illness), on the other hand, are clearly relevant to issues of acute treatment and rehabilitation (chronic clinical course variables).

At the same time, this way of organizing the empirical literature also suggests that the application of family theory to primary health care, if it is to take on the challenge of addressing all four aspects of prevention, diagnosis, treatment, and rehabilitation, must encompass and be relevant to each of the four perspectives noted above.

A FAMILY MEDICINE PERSPECTIVE
ON FAMILY SYSTEMS THEORY

Family systems theory, the application to family functioning of general systems theory, has emerged as the dominant theoretical model in the family therapy field. Its influence in family medicine has also been impressive, although it has served primarily as a conceptual model for understanding family functioning rather than as a guiding framework for organizing clinical practice or evaluating medical problems in clinical settings. Thus, although family physicians are customarily exposed to family systems theory in their training, and although lip service is often given to biopsychosocial models when clinical cases are discussed, family systems concepts are still largely underutilized as a theoretical base for evaluating the importance of family factors in primary health care settings. However, a number of family systems theorists have recently been extending ideas originally developed within psychiatric settings to problems emerging in both primary care and chronic medical settings, and the results of these explorations may make family systems theory more accessible to the family physician.

Although family systems theory comes in many sizes and shapes, each version is built around a vision of family life that sees families as dynamic entities, responsive to the interplay of two major forces—a morphogenetic (developmental) force that is reflected in the universal tendencies of families to become organizationally more complex over time and a morphostatic (regulatory) force reflected in the capacity of families to maintain stability, order, and internal constancy over time (Steinglass, 1987b). The dynamic component is the contention that these two forces not only are in constant interaction one with the other, but must balance each other if the family is to function in a healthy fashion. Thus one way of describing dysfunctional family dynamics (in family systems terms) is as a disruption of this development/regulation balance. That is, if families move too much in the direction of over-regulation, either of behavior or of uncontrolled growth, then the other critical element in family functioning—either overall stability or long-term growth and development—will suffer as a consequence.

Within this frame of reference a version of family systems theory that would be applicable to primary care issues would therefore have to, first, delineate a set of family regulatory mechanisms that play an important role in the family's response to medical illness and, second, propose a model of family development that helps us understand how medical illness affects family growth.

Family Regulatory Mechanisms

Although a wide-ranging series of constructs have been introduced to describe parameters of family functioning that serve to regulate family life, one can conveniently organize them into three main sets of constructs. For each set, the constructs themselves can be thought of as a set of *guidelines* or *constraints* within which family behavior patterns take shape. In this sense these constructs can together then be appropriately thought of as regulatory principles.

The first set of constructs describes ways in which families develop shared and implicit views of their social world. Perhaps the best example here is the family paradigm construct proposed by David Reiss (1981). The notion here is that families, over time, develop shared ideas (hypotheses) about how their social world operates and the rules for best coping in the face of these external environmental characteristics. One family might develop a shared view of the world as masterable, best approached with an open and continuously changing perspective, an exciting place in which to live. Another family might see the world as largely unfathomable, as potentially hostile and alien, as a place that calls for extreme caution and a steady and unchanging course based on long tradition.

This shared view of the external environment would in turn play an important role in shaping behavior whenever the family is interacting with its social world. For example, the nature of family paradigms might in turn provide the guidelines for the assumptions families bring to their interactions with health care systems. From the vantage point of the physician, these differences would then translate into whether the family is perceived as cooperative, compliant, receptive to medical information, and so on (the "good family") or suspicious, combative, unduly demanding, unappreciative, and the like (a "bad family").

A second set of constructs focuses not so much on how the family construes its environment, but on how the family sees *itself* in relation to its larger world. This has variably been called the family's identity, sense of coherence, and so forth. These constructs by and large refer to a set of attributions the family makes about itself in its attempt to articulate not only its identity, but also its shared values, its priorities, its sense of competence, and so on. In doing so, the family uses as a referent its sense of the full range of possibilities that families in its social world and community choose to follow. Thus the family is making a series of implicit statements about the kind of family it is, and also what kind it is not.

A particularly important point here is that most families tend to pick a delimited number of themes around which to organize their identities, and these themes then in turn play major roles in shaping family behavior. For purposes of this discussion, it should be underscored that many times one of the themes that families come to use as a central organizing principle for behavior is that of medical and/or psychiatric conditions, especially conditions that are chronic in their clinical course. In these instances the family not only becomes illness focused, it actually develops an identity built around illness-related experiences, demands, and priorities. When this occurs, the medical condition then becomes one of the central organizing principles for family life, and the family has become a "diabetic family," or an "alcoholic family."

What may be particularly important in adapting these notions to the situation of the family coping with medical illness is that some interplay has to be proposed between individual-level parameters (since it is still one individual within the family who has the illness) and family regulatory behaviors. Thus we need to build into an overall model a series of interactive processes that describe how individual and family characteristics influence each other, reinforce each other, modify each other, and so forth. The current trend in systems theory is to propose that such processes are *recursive* in nature; that is, they are mutually affecting each other all the time. Another term that is used frequently in this regard in *coevolution*. When a coevolutionary process is at work, the various components of the system are changing in synchronous fashion over time, such that it is impossible to understand the developmental course of one component (say, the illness in its chronic phase) as occurring independent of events simultaneously occurring in the other component (say, the family).

Family Growth and Development

Although everyone agrees that developmental perspectives are useful in assessing clinical problems and implementing treatment plans, satisfying models of family development have been hard to come by. A major problem has been the difficulty of conceptualizing a model that is not driven primarily by changes in family composition—births, deaths, and so on. My own efforts at model building in this area have relied on a construct I call *systemic maturation* (see Steinglass, Bennett, Wolin, & Reiss, 1987).

In using this term, I refer to unidirectional changes over time in the family as a unit. It is this effort to delineate concepts that apply to the family as a unit that I think is critical. For example, one can clearly see that as a group, with or without children, a family moves through predictable stages of (a) individuation as a new household or nuclear unit, where the definition of internal and external boundaries is the primary goal; (b) selection of and focus on major goals, values, and priorities; and (c) the consolidation and transmission of a unique and valued family legacy.

It is my impression that despite the current popularity of developmental perspectives, family-level developmental concepts such as systemic maturation are not widely understood. Even seasoned family researchers tend to think of development of individual members within families, individual trajectories that may be tightly or loosely linked depending on both the family and the individuals. In contrast, I think of the family itself as a unitary organism with its own developmental phases and transformations. Clearly, this development is driven in part by the biological maturation of family members, but a serious engagement of systems concepts holds that a family *unit* also goes through a predictable life history. The relationship between systems maturation and individual maturation within families is still unclear. However, we can assume that much of this relationship is reciprocal, with family transactions driving the development of individual members as much as a member's development drives changes in family structure.

The second concept that is important here is that of *developmental distortion* (Steinglass et al., 1987). This refers to the distortion of family structures that support systemic maturation. Such distortions occur when events alter family transactions in such a way that needs of the family as a group are no longer met, or revisions in family transactions necessary for the next stages of individual development cannot occur. Most frequently this occurs when the demands or needs of one family member come to dictate the pace of family life, superseding the process of systemic maturation. At this point, it is fair to say that family development has become *organized* around an individual-level developmental time course rather than the time course suited to the family as a group. A particularly important issue here is the finding, in research with both chronic medical and psychiatric illness families, that the chronic illness itself (e.g., alcoholism, traumatic physical injury) has the capacity to become such a central organizing principal for family life (Steinglass et al., 1982, 1987). When this occurs, we say that the chronic illness and its demands have secondarily produced such a developmental distortion for the family.

APPLICATIONS OF SYSTEMS THEORY
TO PRIMARY CARE PROBLEMS

Regulatory Mechanisms and Illness Typologies

One of the more interesting extensions of concepts of systemic regulation is how it alters thinking about medical diagnosis. The issue here is whether systems of medical diagnosis might be developed that are more sensitive to family-level factors. Is it possible, for example, to classify medical conditions based not only on clinical symptoms and pathophysiology, but also on the types of stresses and challenges illnesses present to families?

One such speculative way of classifying medical illnesses focuses on what has been called the "generic" approach to understanding how medical illness affects family life (Stein & Jessop, 1982). The concept here is that any medical illness poses two forms of stress for the family. The first emanates from factors specific to the biomedical aspects of the particular medical condition. An example might be the dietary restrictions of diabetes or coronary artery disease. Here the stressors are directly generated by the pathophysiology of the illness, and treatment plans are therefore illness based. However, other stresses also exist that are tied to the "generic" psychosocial challenges associated with the illness. These stresses often have more to do with clinical course characteristics of the particular condition than with biomedical factors per se.

John Rolland (1984, 1987a, 1987b) has been a particularly articulate spokesperson for this perspective. He argues that illness characteristics present families with different types of psychosocial challenges, and it

TABLE 3.1 Classification of Medical/Psychiatric Conditions

(I)	Failures of Biological Controls end-stage renal disease diabetes cancers
(II)	Failures of Behavioral Controls addictions traumatic injuries
(III)	Failures of Both Biological and Behavioral Controls cardiovascular disease (hypertension, coronary artery disease) gastric ulcers AIDS
(IV)	Failures of Environmental Controls toxicological disorders industrial pulmonary disorders

is the nature of these challenges rather than the specific illness itself that determines the ultimate impact of medical illness on family life. In this conceptualization, the biomedical parameters of the illness (e.g., the specific organ system affected) take a backseat to these illness characteristics, which Rolland argues have major psychosocial implications for family functioning. Four categories of illness characteristics are used to differentiate "psychosocial types" of illnesses: the type of disease onset (acute versus gradual), the typical illness course (progressive versus constant versus relapsing), the typical illness outcome (fatal versus shortened life span or possible sudden death versus no effect on longevity), and the degree of incapacitation typically associated with the illness (none versus mild versus moderate versus severe). The argument, then, is that two medical conditions that are comparable regarding onset, course, outcome, and degree of incapacitation characteristics would present families with fundamentally comparable psychosocial challenges and could therefore, for all intents and purposes, be considered comparable in terms of their likely impact on family life.

Rolland's typology is based on psychosocial challenges presented to families tied to illness characteristics. A second approach we might suggest is one based more directly on the concepts of family regulation and regulatory mechanisms previously discussed in this chapter (see Table 3.1). Here we might posit that medical *and* psychiatric conditions could both be classified according to the types of control mechanisms related to the conditions. For example, in certain instances illnesses can be directly tied to failure of internal biological controls—either organ failure (e.g., end-stage renal disease or diabetes) or biological regulatory failure (e.g., certain types of cancer or hormonal dysregulation). In other instances, conditions can be directly tied to some form of behavioral dysregulation, such as substance abuse and addictions or traumatic injuries secondary to risk-taking behaviors. Extending this type of scheme, one might posit additional types of control failures, for example, those having to do with both biological and behavioral controls, or those having to do with failures at the environmental or societal level.

One of the reasons for developing typologies such as the one proposed by Rolland or the "control failure" typology I have suggested above is that it is not unlikely that the family's experience of the illness condition is more closely related to the types of issues raised by these typologies than it is by more traditional biomedical issues associated with the illness. By extension, therefore, one might imagine that such models could form the basis for a wholesale redesign of "specialty clinics" in primary care settings. Here conditions would be aggregated not because of their biological similarities (a pulmonary clinic, an oncology group, or whatever), but rather because the psychosocial challenges of the conditions naturally brought families together to share ideas and concerns.

A Developmental View of Medical Illness

One of the ways of getting a feel for the potential power of a family developmental approach to medical illness is to see how it might alter the typical ways in which treatment planning is carried out for chronic illness situations. Typically, family involvement in treatment planning occurs early on in the course of the medical condition and is focused on ways in which the family might support the stabilization of the patient and compliance with the treatment plan. Little attention is paid to the concurrent needs of the family; rather, the medical condition is assumed to take precedence over any other issues the family might be dealing with. A family developmental approach, on the other hand, might see clinical course and treatment issues as follows.

During the onset or acute phase of severe illness or disability, families typically focus all available resources on meeting the demands of the emergency. All other family activities and plans are deferred until the crisis is resolved. However, when that resolution leads to a chronic phase in which the patient may still be very ill or impaired, families usually have trouble returning attention and resources to other normative family activities and needs. The illness comes to dominate family life, and families typically believe that diverting resources to other needs will be harmful to the patient.

The invasion of family life by chronic illness profoundly alters both family regulatory mechanisms and developmental processes. If an adult member becomes ill, his or her family roles are either forgone or added to the duties of other family members, often with serious implications for family life-style (as when the principal breadwinner becomes disabled). Established family routines, such as mealtimes or child-care activities, are changed or abandoned, and cherished traditions such as holiday celebrations are neglected because they can no longer be performed in the expected manner. Of particular importance to family life are the constraints imposed on the family's emotional interaction style by the medical condition. Specifically, the expression of strong affects engendered by the illness (and sometimes by the patient) is severely restricted by the sanctions that exempt those who are physically ill from the normal wear and tear of family life. Unexpressed feelings build up within individuals, resulting in increased isolation of family members from one another.

Many of these alterations in family life are adaptive during the acute or crisis phase of a serious illness. As the chronic phase wears on, however, a family typically clings to these established patterns of responding to the demands (perceived and actual) of the illness even when it becomes apparent that these modes of behavior are not working well. Family development is arrested as the family invests more and more energy in maintaining the status quo relative to the illness. Major decisions—to marry, to buy a first home, to have another child, to return to school or pursue a change of career—are postponed, usually indefinitely. At times families appear unable to establish any group or individual goals, priorities, or values other than patient care and illness management. Moreover, they feel powerless to redirect family resources to other family goals, believing, rather, that the illness or disability is dictating the constraints on their life-style.

This way of seeing the interface among patient, illness, family, and medical care team might well lead to a fundamental reframing of family behavior in the face of medical illness. For example, actions that were previously seen as noncompliance or undermining of treatment recommendations might now be seen as entirely appropriate redirecting of family energies to competing priorities. Further, the need for periodic review of treatment plans and an appreciation of the concept of "phase-specific" family coping strategies would help primary care physicians to mobilize and engage families more successfully in collaborative approaches to health care efforts.

FOUR

Linkages Between Family Theories and Primary Health Care

WILLIAM J. DOHERTY

This chapter outlines a model for categorizing the major domains of family and health research and suggests which family theories are most consistent with different aspects of families' experience with health and illness. The *family health and illness cycle* describes the phases of a family's experience with health and illness, beginning with health promotion and risk reduction and proceeding through family vulnerability and disease onset/ relapse, family illness appraisal, family acute response, and family adaptation to illness and recovery. For each phase, certain family theories are most apt in guiding family and health research.

FAMILY THEORY AND PRIMARY HEALTH CARE

Family theory and primary health care have developed separately from two quite different traditions. The roots of family science lie primarily in sociological and systems theories of the twentieth century, whereas primary health care has practice roots as old as medicine itself and scholarly roots as young as family medicine's emergence in the late 1960s. The growing relationship between the two fields represents an alliance that is historically unprecedented and potentially powerful, but still tentative and uncertain. Although primary health care has much to

30

offer family science—particularly through sharing its biopsychosocial orientation—the focus of this chapter will be on what family theories can offer the science and practice of primary health care.

I must note at the outset that there is no central, dominant family theory; rather, there is a collection of theories focusing on different aspects of family relationships (Bass, Doherty, LaRossa, Steinmetz, & Schumm, 1992). The field speaks with a wide array of theoretical "languages," which, if not quite a Tower of Babel, can at least be quite confusing for the uninitiated. Different theories, for example, focus on issues such as how families function in the larger society, how families create shared meanings, how families change over time, how families handle stress and resolve conflicts, and how families develop habitual patterns of interaction. Each of these theories represents a different intellectual heritage, and this can render dialogue difficult *within* the family science field, let alone with those outside it.

Perhaps the most important lesson from all family theories is the notion that the isolated individual devoid of social context—the proto-typical patient in medical training—does not exist in nature. Individuals in all cultures are born into families and most spend their lives interacting with family members. Even a socially isolated individual can be defined in terms of the lack of supportive family. We derive from our families of procreation our adult identities and our primary social support. Every person, then, is both a unique self and a representative of an intimate social group (Mead, 1934).

A central implication of this idea for primary health care is that families are inherent and inevitable participants in the prevention and treatment of diseases and health problems commonly viewed as belonging to individuals. Doherty and Baird (1983) have referred to the "therapeutic triangle" in all health care—the notion that the family is always a "third party" to health care encounters between individual patients and health professionals. Empirical support for this idea is abundant: Families have been found to be the primary source of health-related behavior patterns, of the initial assessment of individuals' health problems, of the decision to seek medical care, of health beliefs and attitudes influencing compliance with medical regimens, and of social support for chronic health problems (Christie-Seely, 1984a; Doherty & Campbell, 1988; Litman, 1974).

Although the powerful role of families in health care is incontrovertible, family theories have only recently been applied systematically to the family's role in prevention, treatment, and rehabilitation. The first step toward this application must be to organize the family and health literature in a theoretically meaningful way.

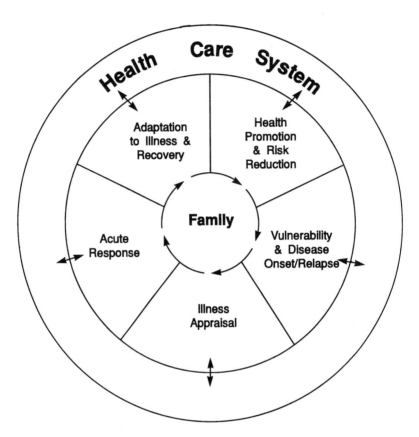

Figure 4.1. Family Health and Illness Cycle

THE FAMILY HEALTH AND ILLNESS CYCLE

I developed the family health and illness cycle as a way to organize both the family and health research literature and the family's longitudinal experience with health and illness. The version presented here is described more fully in *Families and Health* (Doherty & Campbell, 1988). The model is depicted in Figure 4.1, which can best be read by beginning with the two o'clock position and reading clockwise. The circular arrows represent the temporal flow of the family's experience; the two-way arrows represent the family's interactions with the health care system. For present purposes, the cycle can be viewed as a family health care map onto which family theory can be placed.

The category *family health promotion and risk reduction* refers to family beliefs and behavior patterns that either help family members stay healthy or put them at long-term risk for developing disease. A wide range of studies have examined families' role in dietary practices, exercise patterns, and cigarette smoking—the three life-style behavior patterns believed to have the strongest links to health and disease (Council on Scientific Affairs, 1983; National Center for Health Statistics, 1984). In addition to this emphasis on specific health practices, family health promotion and risk reduction concerns more general dimensions of family life that orient family members toward health or illness—for example, the family's cohesion and its sense that the world is coherent and predictable (Reiss, 1981). Naturally, the family never operates in isolation from the health care system and the rest of society. Families are influenced particularly by health care professionals with whom they interact and whom they encounter in the media, as well as by other families in their reference group.

The next category, *family vulnerability and disease onset/relapse,* refers to life events and experiences of the family that render family members more immediately susceptible to becoming ill or relapsing from a chronic illness. The principal body of research on this topic examines how family stress, stemming from either internal or external events, renders family members susceptible to illness. For example, Meyer and Haggerty (1962) found that strep infections in children are likely to be preceded by a stressful event in the family. Beautrais, Fergusson, and Shannon (1982) report that family stressful life events strongly predict physician visits and hospitalizations. An example of how family stress precipitates relapse from chronic disease is the well-documented impact of family "affective style" on relapse in young adult schizophrenics following hospitalization (Doane, Falloon, Goldstein, & Mintz, 1985).

Family illness appraisal refers to family beliefs about a family member's illness and to family decisions about how to deal with the illness episode. This is the family's gatekeeping function vis-à-vis the health care system. A long tradition in medical sociology and medical anthropology attests to the family's role in verifying and legitimating an individual's sickness, in explaining why the individual got sick, and in deciding whether medical advice is needed or whether the matter should be handled within the family or a lay referral network (Eisenberg & Kleinman, 1981; Gottlieb, 1976). Of course, these family decisions occur within a context of the availability and accessibility of health care. And families' appraisals are often made in interaction with—and often in conflict with—the appraisals of health professionals (Doherty & Campbell, 1988).

Family acute response refers to the immediate aftermath of illness for the family. This family experience is likely to be tied closely to family illness appraisal, since the early response to an illness episode is influenced by the family's assessment of its seriousness. An example of acute response is the adjustments a family must make in the period immediately following a heart attack or a cancer surgery. When the illness is disabling or life threatening, the family is apt to experience a crisis—a period of disorganization in which normal coping patterns are not adequate (Hill, 1958). In these circumstances, the family may assemble its extended kin network for vigils at the bedside and for support in the daily functions of meals and child care. For less serious problems, the family's acute response may be limited to someone staying home with a sick member or a period of worry about a member's health.

Family adaptation to illness and recovery refers to how a family reorganizes itself around a chronic illness or disability of a family member, and to the ways in which a family adapts to the recovery of an ill member. During this phase, the family must promote the continued recovery or stabilization of the family member's health while simultaneously maintaining its ability to nurture other family members and maintain its place in the community. In chronic illness, families also must manage long-term, complex relationships with health care professionals and other societal agents such as insurance companies and government agencies. This process of family adaptation has been the most extensively studied area in the family and health area, usually taking the form of studies of families' coping with medical illness (Patterson & McCubbin, 1983). The adaptation phase also offers serious challenges for primary health professionals who must forge positive long-term relationships with these families.

To summarize the temporal flow of the family health and illness cycle, one may begin with a long health promotion and risk reduction phase centering on family behaviors related to diet, exercise, smoking, and perhaps general family functioning in areas such as stress management and mutual support. The next, briefer phase—vulnerability and disease onset/relapse—begins when there is a pileup of physical and psychosocial stressors that precipitate an illness episode. An example might be a heart attack after a family argument. The family must then evaluate the illness symptoms and the need for medical attention, as well as appraise the diagnosis and advice of the health care professionals. While continuing this appraisal process, the family moves into the acute response phase, during which reactions, say, to a heart attack are likely to involve fear and shock, followed by mobilization of family resources. The family enters its emergency mode of operating. Finally, the patient stabilizes after the acute episode, and returns home to continue recovery and rehabilitation. Here the family faces the challenge of adapting to revised roles and responsibilities, either temporarily or permanently. The cycle can then be seen as beginning anew as the family confronts the challenges of reducing the risk of a repeated illness and promoting the health of the family member.

Before moving on to how family theories interface with this model, I want to mention several limitations of the family health and illness cycle. Because it deals with the family's experience with a particular member's illness, the framework does not capture the complex dynamics created by multiple illnesses in the family. Second, the model is more elaborated in the illness area than in the prevention and health promotion areas. Third, it does not deal explicitly with families' interactions with other important social groups beyond health professionals. Fourth, the model separates processes that may overlap or occur simultaneously in certain situations. On the other hand, the family health and illness cycle does seem to serve as an adequate vehicle to organize the hundreds of studies on families and health. Virtually all these studies can be viewed as focusing on one of the dimensions in the model.

HOW FAMILY THEORIES RELATE TO THE FAMILY AND HEALTH AND ILLNESS CYCLE

As indicated before, there is no fully comprehensive theory of the family, only partial theories with particular emphases or conceptual lenses. The following discussion attempts to overlay several prominent family theories on the dimensions of the family health and illness cycle. Criteria for inclusion were that the theory focus on the family as a unit, that its scope be reasonably broad, and that it have a substantial body of literature in the family field. My proposals are outlined in Table 4.1. Space considerations allow for only a brief summary of each theory, with the goal of a broad outline that can stimulate further refinements and elaborations.

TABLE 4.1 Family Theories and the Family Health and Illness Cycle

Family Health Dimensions	Family Theories
Health promotion and risk reduction	systems
	developmental
Vulnerability and disease onset appraisal	stress
	symbolic interactionism
	constructivist
Acute response	stress
Adaptation to illness/recovery	systems
	developmental
	constructivist
	stress and coping

Family health promotion and risk reduction would seem to be best studied from a family systems theory perspective (Bowen, 1978; Broderick & Smith, 1979; Constantine, 1986; Minuchin, 1974) and from family development theory (Aldous, 1978; Mattessich & Hill, 1987). Family systems theory focuses on the repeating patterns of interaction whereby families create stable identities. Although family systems theory has been applied most extensively to dysfunctional family dynamics, it can be applied readily to understanding the role of health behaviors in family relationships (for an extensive discussion of systems theory and health issues, see Steinglass, Chapter 3, this volume). Whitehead and Doherty (1989; Doherty and Whitehead, 1986), for example, have examined how cigarette smoking becomes a vehicle for inclusion/exclusion patterns and power/control issues in family relationships. Family systems theory goes beyond simplistic notions of "modeling" health behaviors to demonstrate how practices such as diet, exercise, and smoking are incorporated into family structures that are difficult to change with simple education and advice.

Family development theory is a useful complement to family systems theory in studying families during the health promotion and risk reduction phase. Whereas family systems theory deals primarily with the immediate interactional context of health behaviors, family development theory looks at the family longitudinally—particularly at its major transitions related to adding and losing members and the aging of family members (Aldous, 1978; Mattessich & Hill, 1987). This theory is helpful for an understanding of the particular challenges facing families in promoting health at different periods in the family life cycle. There may be times, for example, when families are particularly oriented to changing health practices, such as after the birth of a first child or the death of a family member. Similarly, difficulty in handling major family transitions such as divorce and retirement may render a family less competent in promoting health and reducing risks.

The vulnerability phase of the family health and illness cycle would seem to be best captured by family stress theory, articulated originally by sociologist Reuben Hill (1958) and more recently by Boss (1988) and McCubbin and Patterson (1983). Family stress theory describes how environmental or internal demands can extend a family beyond its ability to care for its members, leading to a crisis or breakdown in the family. It goes beyond psychological stress theory by emphasizing how stressors exert a disorganizing influence on the family, which then requires a reorganizing effort to move beyond the crisis. An obvious implication for health and illness is the role of family stress in exacerbating the vulnerability of family members to illness and injury. The famous Holmes and Rahe (1967) scale, which ranks and measures stressful life changes, includes family stress events at the top of the list: death of a family member, divorce, serious illness of a family member. Family stress theory also emphasizes the role of family resources in alleviating the negative impact of stressful events and the role of the family's definition of the situation in determining the family's response (Boss, 1988).

The appraisal phase of the cycle can be examined through two kinds of family theory: symbolic interactionism and constructivist (attribution) theories. Symbolic interactionism is a sociological theory that emphasizes how individuals and families create meanings in their environments and enact roles based on these meanings (see, e.g., Burr et al., 1979; Mead, 1934). Meanings and roles are forged through interactions among family members and through interactions with the social environment. For example, families' experiences with certain symptoms and illnesses become crystallized in symbolic images related to threat and safety, leading to idiosyncratic family actions that may be difficult for professionals to understand—as when a family that has experienced spinal meningitis subsequent to headache symptoms "overreacts" every time a child gets a headache. The self-definition of what it means to be a mother might be a powerful determinant of a woman's decision to manage her ill child at home or take the child immediately to a health professional. Families also operate from their "symbol systems" in appraising the competence and trustworthiness of health professionals. Symbolic interaction theory, then, offers potentially rich insights into family functioning around health and illness.

Family constructivist theories also deal with meanings, but focus more on total family meanings as opposed to the individual meanings emphasized by symbolic interactionism (Reiss, 1981; Steinglass et al., 1987). Family constructivist theories have emphasized how families construe their relationship to the social environment—particularly the extent to which the social environment is viewed as predictable, orderly, and trustworthy—and how families believe they should orient themselves to this environment—for example, by active, coordinated engagement or by more separate individual responses. A growing body of research from this tradition has been examining the influence of these family "constructions" on how families manage chronic illness and relate to health professionals.

The acute response phase appears to be best understood through family stress theory, described above. The family's actions will reflect the four factors outlined by Hill (1958) in his classic formulation of family stress theory: (a) the stressful event (the illness), (b) the family's resources for dealing with the event (economic, social, psychological, and so on), (c) the family's definition of the event (as catastrophic, as manageable, as potentially helpful, and so on), and (d) the degree of crisis. This theoretical framework can be applied nicely to studies of how families respond to a serious new diagnosis or the sudden onset of a life-threatening or disabling illness.

The adaptation phase can be viewed from a variety of theoretical frameworks. As mentioned before, this is the most extensively studied area in the family health and illness cycle. Systems theory can be applied to the understanding of how families stabilize around new interaction patterns after an illness event or after the acute phase of treatment and how they interact with health professionals. Family development theory likewise provides a necessary view of how the family's position in its life cycle interacts with the health issues. For example, spinal cord injuries are most apt to occur to young adults in families who are in the launching phase of the family life cycle; these families get "stuck" on the launching pad, and this has implications for all family members. Family constructivist theory can contribute an understanding of how a family's "paradigm" for viewing itself in relation to the social environment influences how it manages a chronic illness and how it interacts with health professionals (Reiss & De-Nour, 1989).

The fourth theory that applies well to the adaptation phase is McCubbin and Patterson's family stress and coping theory. This theory goes beyond Hill's more acute crisis-oriented model to focus on families' adaptation following a crisis or disrupting event. Important considerations in this model are the pileup of other stressful life events that occurs while the family is adjusting to a serious illness, the family's new resources during the adjustment period, the family's perceptions of the new situation, the family's level of functional and dysfunctional coping, and the family's overall adaptation. Family stress and coping theory seems especially useful for understanding the multiple factors over time in a family's experience with chronic illness.

SUMMARY AND CONCLUSION

This chapter has offered a framework for understanding how family theories can be applied to family health experiences that are faced daily by primary care health professionals. My approach has been general and suggestive rather than detailed and critical. I have introduced a conceptual vehicle to organize the vast literature on families and health, in order to reduce the task of applying family theories to every illness or health behavior. I then proposed which family theories potentially can shed the most light on which aspects of the family's experience with health and illness. The model and discussion presented here are intended as a beginning map to guide family health researchers in their selection of family theories.

FIVE

Family Theory in Family Medicine

IAN R. McWHINNEY
JOAN M. PATTERSON

Within the field of family science, several theories have evolved over the years, each of which has some relevance for clinical practice, research, and training in family medicine. However, there is not, as yet, a comprehensive theory of the family in family medicine. If we are to draw on family theory in relation to the health care system, it is important to know what kind of health system we have in mind. Even within the primary care specialties, a theory that may be sufficient for pediatrics or internal medicine may be inadequate for family medicine. The available theories linking families with health and disease—discussed by Doherty in Chapter 4 with regard to primary health care and by Steinglass in Chapter 3 with regard to medical illness—have not been developed with primary care in mind and particularly not with family medicine in mind.

Why is this important? We would argue that if family medicine is to continue to emerge strongly as a discipline, it needs to develop its own theory of the family based on clinical research. The development of a scientific base is enhanced, strengthened, and accelerated by being theoretically driven as opposed to being atheoretical. Thomas Hobbes has been quoted as saying that the purpose of theory is to tie facts into bundles. We do not have a theory of the family in family medicine because we have so few facts, and we have so few facts because there have been so few empirical studies. We need an integrative theory of family medicine that incorporates critical constructs from family science with critical attributes of family medical practice.

Family medicine is distinct within primary medical care in that one physician provides care to males and females in all age groups, and is, therefore, available as a physician for the whole family group, whatever its composition. This affords the unique opportunity to know not only the history and functioning of the individuals in that social system, but also the patterns of relationships linking these members to each other, the history of those interaction patterns, and how the system responds to normative and nonnormative changes. Knowledge of a patient's social context is critical when a physician is concerned about health promotion, diagnosis and treatment of disease, and management of chronic conditions. Family medicine has greater potential than other specialties to embody the major attributes of primary medical care defined by the National Academy of Sciences Task Force (Estes, 1977): accessibility, comprehensiveness, coordination, continuity, and accountability.

We have identified several critical attributes of *family medicine* that we believe should be accounted for in an integrative theory of the family in family medicine:

(1) In family medicine, there is a *history* to the relationship between a family and its members and the family physician(s) that evolves over time. The social-historical context in which this relationship evolves also has relevance for clinical practice. This raises several questions in need of further scientific inquiry:

   (a) How is this relationship formed and how does it develop over time?

   (b) Under what circumstances and how does this relationship get transferred from one generation to the next?

   (c) Are there types of physician-family relationships?

   (d) How do the ages, genders, and personalities of the physician and the family members affect the maintenance or undermining of this relationship?

   (e) What impact does social change have on this evolving relationship?

(2) A family physician (potentially) cares for all the members of the family unit and (potentially) cares for the unit itself. What implications does this have for enhancing or undermining health behaviors?

   (a) How does caring for the whole family unit affect clinical decision making about the individual patient?

   (b) How does the family physician's relationship with one family member affect his or her relationships with other family members?

    (c) What is the relationship between the functioning of the family system and the health of individual members, and which should be the locus of intervention and under what circumstances?

    (d) What is the significance of individual illness or family illness clusters as cues to family problems?

    (e) Can any given physician effectively treat all the individuals in the family and the family system as well?

(3) Given that the physician has a history with the family and (potentially) a relationship with all its members and the unit, the physician becomes a part of the system(s) he or she is treating to a much greater extent than is the case with a medical specialist or even a primary care physician who treats only one age group.

    (a) How does this greater exposure to any given family shape physician behavior?

    (b) Do family physicians and their patients hold views and beliefs, especially about illness and disease, that are more similar than would be the case between other physicians and their patients?

    (c) Does this greater exposure to a given family enhance or undermine the family's health behaviors? Under what conditions?

HISTORICAL FACTORS INFLUENCING THE FAMILY-PHYSICIAN RELATIONSHIP

In family development theory (Mattessich & Hill, 1987), in which individual and family change over time is emphasized, several constructs are relevant to a theory of family medicine. The *family life cycle* is divided into stages characterized by major family events, particularly the addition (e.g., birth) and exiting of members (e.g., death). Each stage of the family life cycle is characterized by *developmental tasks,* which are normative expectations for how the family is to fulfill its functions for its members and society. In many instances, these normative expectations are associated with particular health-seeking behaviors (e.g., seeking prenatal care during pregnancy). The *normative transitions* between stages are periods of added stress for families as they acquire new *role behaviors.* Since primary prevention is one of the major foci of primary care, family physicians particularly could be instrumental in developing and testing strategies to help families anticipate and prepare for these transitions (called anticipatory socialization).

Each family has a *role complex,* which is the combination of all the roles of all the family members. Each role has a *reciprocal role* either within (e.g., father-son) or outside the family (e.g., doctor-patient). When any family member changes a role, the whole family system is affected to some extent because of the linkages among roles. Since the family physician (potentially) sees the whole family, he or she is uniquely positioned to do some important prevention work to facilitate these reciprocal role changes. Similarly, the nature of the physician-patient relationship and changes in it over time have an impact on the family's role complex and patterns of functioning (called *interaction structures* in family development theory).

Steinglass, in Chapter 3, emphasizes the developmental perspective by calling attention to *systemic maturation* of the family as a unit. He points out that some stressor events, such as chronic illness, can skew the family's organization toward the person with the illness at the expense of the development of the rest of the family unit. If this kind of developmental distortion is prolonged, it can exact a price with regard to the health and well-being of the family unit and its other members. Illuminating ways in which a physician may unintentionally collude with this distortion or, conversely, help the family to avoid it would be another way for family medicine to contribute important understanding to the process of adapting to chronic illness.

In family development theory, attention is called to historical time. Edward Shorter emphasizes in Chapter 2 how changes in family structure in contemporary culture are affecting primary care. Two of these changes are especially important: the increase in single-parent families and the increase in social isolation. We agree that these developments or social changes are having a major impact on primary care. Any change—whether social change, normative family life-cycle change, or some other type—creates stress for those affected. When this stress is intense and prolonged, and when prior supportive resources are less available, changes in the immune system may render a person more susceptible to physical illness. Research in the field of psychoneuro-immunology (Borysenko, 1984) has extended our understanding of the biological pathways for these disorders.

We are skeptical about Shorter's position on the increase in somatiform disorder. The whole concept of somatization seems somewhat loose and imprecise. The DSM-III, it is true, gives a definition of somatization disorder that is quite rigorous (American Psychiatric Association, 1980). It would, for example, be impossible to categorize postinfective fatigue or irritable bowel syndrome as somatization disorder using these criteria. On the other hand, the DSM-III also has a category called "atypical somatiform disorder," which allows physicians to so label patients who have symptoms without physical findings. This category is based on the dubious assumption that patients without physical findings do not have physical disorders. It is doubtful whether somatization disorder as rigorously defined in the DSM-III has increased in prevalence. It was a common and difficult problem in the 1950s (when McWhinney entered practice). It figured prominently in Balint's book, *The Doctor, His Patient and the Illness* (1964). Balint referred to this disorder as "the fat envelope [chart] syndrome." It is worth noting that these bulging charts are produced by physicians, not patients. It is we, not the patients, who write the voluminous reports, letters, and operation notes. Perhaps somatization disorder is more a disease of the health care system than a disease of patients. As for so-called atypical somatiform disorder, there is no evidence that irritable bowel syndrome and postinfective fatigue are primarily psychiatric disorders.

For many stressed individuals, a family physician is an important temporary refuge in times of trouble (Gorlick & Promfret, 1988). Perhaps, in contemporary times, an individual's relationship with a family physician is more stable than his or her other interpersonal relationships. It would be an interesting empirical exercise to determine if a family physician is more likely to be a source of support for patients than other physicians because continuity of care and treating the whole family lead to greater trust and confidence. In any case, the family physician may well have the opportunity to influence a person's adaptation to normative or catastrophic life experience, especially during crisis. This is one of the best times to effect behavior change, including health behavior change, because people in crisis are often amenable to efforts of others to help them relieve their discomfort. Physicians need to be cautious about fostering dependency in their patients, however. In the ongoing relationship with patients and their families, there is a risk of support becoming dependency. While this "refuge role" is an important one contributing to a certain stability for persons in our society, prolonged support from a physician to the exclusion of support from natural networks should also be investigated for its long-term effect on adaptation.

The reader might note that in the above section, several constructs from stress theory were discussed—distress, crisis, adaptation, support, and so on. This is another theoretical framework, for which there are family versions (Patterson, 1988), that could inform the scientific study and practice of family medicine. In family stress theory, the emphasis is on family effort to achieve a balance between family *demands* (stressor events and ongoing role and relationship strains) and *capabilities* (coping behaviors and resources) for managing these demands. This balance is mediated by the subjective *meanings* attributed to both demands and capabilities. The outcome is a level of *adjustment* or *adaptation* of the family and its members. Because relatively similar stress concepts are used to explain the stress of organic systems, individual systems, and social systems such as the family, stress theory is particularly relevant for testing the biopsychosocial model (Engel, 1977), given our increased understanding that stress can be transferred from social to psychological to biological systems. Family stress theory is also useful for studying and working with families who are dealing with chronic stress situations, such as chronic illness or even chronic unemployment. Chronicity implies a past, present, and future and, again, given the historical context of the family physician-patient relationship, these constructs might be incorporated into an integrative theory for family medicine.

FAMILY PHYSICIANS' CARE FOR THE WHOLE FAMILY

Family systems theory is the family theory most often applied to family practice by family therapists working in medical settings. The family system consists of the members it comprises *and* the patterns of relationships linking these members to each other (called the principle of nonsummativity—the system is more than the sum of its parts). These patterns serve to maintain a relatively stable system by prescribing and limiting members' behavior. However, at times this homeostatic balance is challenged when normative or nonnormative events call for a change in the patterns of interaction. This need for flexibility and reorganization of the system is called morphogenesis. Achieving a balance between change and stability (in these functioning patterns) is a central dialectic for families, with the extremes of this dimension usually viewed as dysfunctional. The other central dialectic for families is the balance between the closeness and apartness of members— that is, the tension between being an individual and functioning autonomously versus being connected and functioning as a unit or group. Again, the extremes are viewed as dysfunctional. These two dialectics are reflected in most of the systems models of family functioning (Walsh, 1982).

Another underlying assumption of systems theory is circular causality; that is, a change in one member causes a change in other members and in the group, which in turn affects the first individual in a circular chain of influence. Steinglass emphasizes this perspective by observing that the health or functioning of the family system affects the health or illness of individual members; he refers to the large body of literature that views the family (a) as a protective and buffering resource to individual health and, conversely, (b) as a factor in the etiology or exacerbation of illness. Campbell (1986), too, in his excellent review of family and health research, points out the importance of this social epidemiology model for family medicine. Presumably, a family physician treating the whole family has greater opportunity to have knowledge of and promote the protective factors, as well as to have greater knowledge of dysfunctional family patterns that may exacerbate illness. In both cases, the ability to assess and utilize this kind of family information could enhance a physician's effectiveness. However, we have collected very few systematic data about which kinds of health promotion or medical problems call for a family approach, at which stages of the life cycle, involving which family members, or even involving which members of a clinical team.

We do not really know how family physicians work with families. Some family theorists have assumed that they work in the same way as family therapists, and there actually have been attempts to impose these methods on family practice without any consideration of the wide differences in context between these fields. The results have not been stellar, and, regrettably, some investigators have blamed family physicians for it (Bishop et al., 1984; McLean & Miles, 1975). Clearly, we need more careful studies that document the nature of patient-physician-family relationships. The concept of the therapeutic triangle, introduced by Doherty and Baird (1983), calls attention to the notion that the physician does not have a relationship with just the patient. Family medicine, more than any other medical specialty, takes advantage of this reality and is fertile ground for systematic study of these interlocking relationships.

Noncompliance is another important issue that has received considerable attention in medical practice for which better understanding of the interlocking relationships among patients, families, and physicians could be helpful. One of us (Patterson) has observed that the nature of physicians' relationships with noncompliant patients often mirrors that of control battles these patients have with family members. How often does a physician unwittingly collude with an angry spouse who is trying to get his or her partner to quit smoking, lose weight, or exercise more?

Family practice is also an optimal context for studying the question of family illness clusters, because records are kept of all illnesses in all members of the family. Almost 30 years ago, Kellner (1963) called this to our attention; however, we have done little or no empirical work to increase our understanding of this phenomenon. Some recent texts on the family and health do not even list Kellner among the references.

PHYSICIANS ARE
PART OF THE SYSTEM THEY TREAT

Developments in family systems theory in the last decade are particularly relevant to the observation that physicians are part of the system they treat. As Steinglass points out in Chapter 3, the assumption in family systems theory has tended to be that health care systems and providers are relatively fixed entities—independent variables. In family medicine, this is a flawed perspective. The family physician has to be included as part of the system he or she treats. In second-order cybernetics of the "new" family systems theory (Hoffman, 1990), attention is called to the "observing system." In other words, the physician does not stand outside the patient or family as a static source of information, giving them diagnoses and treatment plans and admonishing them for "noncompliance." Rather, the physician is part of a dynamic system. The physician's behavior is continuously shaped by the patients and families he or she sees—by the information they present, by the observations made, by knowledge of them from the past (or even presumed knowledge by generalizing from other patients), by the responses the patient and family make to what the physician says or does, and so on. In many ways, this is an extension of symbolic interaction theory (pointed out by Doherty in Chapter 4) wherein our behavior is continuously shaped by what we impute to others and what we think they are imputing to us. So it would be very naive to think that the physician is unchanging and static in this process. We continuously shape each other's behavior.

Also relevant to this notion that the physician is part of the system he or she treats are social constructivist theories (Gergen, 1985), such as Reiss's (1981) family paradigm theory, which emphasize that the beliefs and meanings individuals have are socially construed and shared. Reiss describes a family paradigm as the beliefs families have about their internal relationships and about their relationship to the world outside the family. There are three dimensions of a family's paradigm: (a) *configuration,* the sense of mastery felt by the family relative to its belief in a patterned, lawful environment; (b) *coordination,* the family's view of itself as a highly connected group as opposed to more isolated individuals; and (c) *closure,* the family's tendency to be closed to new experience and dominated by tradition. A family's paradigm is likely to shape the way its members relate to health care providers and may well influence the "fit" between doctors and families. Conversely, as Reiss has pointed out, major stressors, particularly crisis-producing events, shape family paradigms; hence acute or chronic illness and the family's experience with the physician and the medical system may well change family members' ways of thinking and acting.

Beliefs about health, illness, and even providers of health care are developed through social interaction and are shaped and evolve over time. Thus a new patient brings to a physician a set of beliefs about health and illness that have been shaped by his or her immediate social context, and the experience with the physician may well further shape these beliefs—particularly if the initial "fit" between the patient's and the doctor's belief systems is good enough for the patient to return to this doctor. Bloch (1989) has written about the coevolution of illness events and family events, as well as the coevolution of the relationships among patient, family, and physician. In the case of family practice, where there is a history to the physician's relationship with a family, the notion of coevolution is particularly relevant. Family medicine is an optimal context for further study of the relationships among levels of systems—the disease in the cells and organ system(s) of the person, who lives in a family system and who seeks medical help from a health care system. These multiple relationships occur in several domains—cognitive, behavioral, and emotional. It seems to us that one of the most important contributions family practice can make to medical science is to articulate this coevolutionary process.

We do not know how family physicians and families influence each other over time because, as far as we know, nobody has done the kind of research that could answer this question. Thorne and Robinson (1989) have conducted a study that might well serve as a model for the kind of research that is needed in family medicine. They examined the evolving relationships between providers of health care and 77 chronically ill patients or close relatives of chronically ill patients. Qualitative data from repeated interviews over a 3-year period were used to develop the theory, which was then tested in further interviews (the grounded theory approach) (Glaser & Strauss, 1967). They report that the relationships evolved through three stages: naive trust, disenchantment, and guarded alliance. Four relationship types—hero worship, resignation, consumerism, and team playing—formed the context in which shattered trust was reconstructed in the stage of guarded alliance. Most informants engaged in more than one of these relationship types over time, and different relationship types were developed with different providers of care. The reconstructed trust was highest when the informants had developed both trust in a health care provider and confidence in themselves.

We provide this example not for its findings, interesting as they are, but for its methods. Studies that will help us develop a theory of the family in family medicine will require similar methods; such studies will need to be qualitative in nature and should cover periods long enough to capture the evolving relationship between families and family physicians. Data should be collected from family physicians as well as from families. While it is a complex task to tie all of the facts into bundles, the work will provide us with exactly what family physicians need to know. We may often be deceiving ourselves about the relationships we have with our patients and their families.

In summary, as Steinglass, Doherty, and Shorter have pointed out, there is no one family theory that is totally relevant for family medicine. Rather, we might draw from several family theoretical orientations, keeping in mind the uniqueness of family medicine as a discipline and health care system, in developing an integrative theory of the family in family medicine.

PART II

Methodology

SIX

Research on Family Health Care: A Methodological Overview

MAURINE H. VENTERS

Social scientists have long recognized that the family is the most important social group within which illness occurs and is resolved (Litman, 1974; Richardson, 1945). More specifically, the family defines and validates whether or not an individual is sick, then determines the utilization pattern of health care services. Finally, the family is a major influence on compliance with suggested treatment regimes and the recovery process. Thus the family is the basic unit of care (Litman, 1974). Clinicians have confirmed this observation empirically and have further observed that family-oriented care is more likely than individual-oriented care to promote effective primary health care outcomes (Geyman, 1977, 1978; Schmidt, 1978).

Researchers, however, are more cautious in supporting this hypothesis, due to certain methodological difficulties in using the family as the unit of analysis in relation to family care. While a few studies show that family care exists, and other studies identify a limited number of determinants of family care, there is lack of agreement concerning the most appropriate indicator to measure family care. These limitations have presented difficulties in identifying the full range of benefits of family-oriented care over individual-oriented care.

It is the purpose of this review to use interdisciplinary studies to discuss methodological issues related to indicators used to measure family care, as well as attempts to measure the prevalence, source, determinants, and benefits of family care. This information will then be used to suggest future research directions in light of the potential to improve clinical decision making and primary health care policy formulation.

WHAT IS FAMILY CARE?

While definitions of primary health care are numerous and not always consistent (Kane, 1977), most definitions assume that some level of family involvement in care is one dimension of primary care (Fry, 1973; Kane, 1977; Reynolds, 1975; White, 1967). Primary care has been defined in various ways, including according to characteristics of the services provided, such as first contact and general versus specialized (Aiken, Lewis, Craig, et al., 1979; American Academy of Family Physicians, 1975; American Medical Association, 1966; Association of American Medical Colleges, 1968; Silver & McAtee, 1975; Thacker, Salber, Osborne, et al., 1972; Weiner & Starfield, 1983); according to characteristics of the clinical practice, such as comprehensive, accessible, family centered, coordinated, and continuous (Alpert & Charney, 1973; Parker, Walsh, & Coon, 1976; Starfield, 1979; Weiner & Starfield, 1983); and according to physicians' perceptions of their practice population, that is, the percentage of the practice population for whom the physician maintains primary responsibility for care (Armondino & Walker, 1977; Weiner & Starfield, 1983).

One of the most complete approaches to measuring primary care was used by Holmes, Kane, Ford, and Fowler (1978), who measured specific tasks accomplished by the physician in performing the care. This physician performance-based measure used four operational indicators: continuity of care (percentage of all individual patient visits to the primary care physician), coordinated care (percentage of referrals who return to the primary care physician), comprehensive care (percentages of visits that yield nonprimary care information), and family care (information obtained about family history, number of visits by other family members to primary care physician). Findings showed that primary care physicians perform continuity of care and coordinated care at high levels. Comprehensive care is performed at a low level, due to limiting focus of the visit on the primary care complaint. Family-centered care is performed at a moderate level, due to minimal numbers of visits to the primary care physician by other family members.

Definitions of family health care are also numerous. *Family-centered care* has been defined as treatment of intact family units (Bauman & Grace, 1974; Williamson, McCormick, & Taylor, 1983), as perceived care delivered to all members by the same physician (Fujikawa, Bass, & Schneiderman, 1979; McKenna & Wacker, 1976), as observed and perceived use of the same physician as the female head of household (Murata & Kane, 1976), and as level of communication with the family about the primary care treatment of one member (Doherty & Baird, 1986). *Family-focused care* has been defined as treatment of individuals within the context of their families (Bauman & Grace, 1974; Geyman, 1977; Mannker, 1976; Merkel, 1983).

These various definitions have created confusion among primary care physicians in attempting to clarify the role of the family as the unit of care and difficulties among researchers in comparing findings across family care studies (Bauman & Grace, 1974; Carmichael, 1976; Curry, 1974; Geyman, 1977). More valid, reliable, and standardized indicators of family care are needed in order to move ahead and accurately measure the prevalence, determinants, and benefits of family care. A limited number of initial efforts have begun in this direction. These efforts are discussed in the following sections.

DISTRIBUTION OF FAMILY CARE

What Is the Extent of Family Care?

Family medicine, as a discipline, emphasizes the importance of exploring health, illness, and care within the context of relationships among family members and between the family and the community (Gordon, 1978; Ransom & Vandervoort, 1973). Thus a major guiding concept of family medicine is family care. This is the belief that individual care can best be accomplished through an awareness of and the concurrent care of other members of the individual's family (Bauman & Grace, 1974; Curry, 1974; Curry & Grant, 1973; Geyman, 1977; Grace, 1977; Williams & Leaman, 1973). This family focus has been accompanied by an increase in family-oriented medical technology and education. In the clinical setting, for example, there are increasing attempts to assess family functioning in relation to health care outcomes

(Smilkstein, 1978), to initiate family charting systems (Arbogast, Scralton, & Krick, 1978; Grace, Neal, Wellock, et al., 1977), and to utilize family summary cards (Grace et al., 1977). In the medical education setting there are increasing amounts of family-related materials and information available to teach family systems theory concepts and family therapy approaches in relation to health care outcomes (see, e.g., Cauthen, Turnbull, Lawler, & Friedman, 1979; Christie-Seely, 1981; Doherty & Baird, 1986; Elliott & Herndon, 1981; Guttman & Sigal, 1978). The actual extent of family care, however, may not be as common as would be suggested by the increase in family-focused activities (Merkel, 1983).

The few studies that have actually documented the extent of family care among voluntary patients suggests that this form of care exists but is not a dominant type of health care. McKenna and Wacker (1976) show, for example, that 20% of adult couples from a university population report sharing the same physician for matched husbands and wives. Fujikawa et al. (1979) show that 28% of families from a private family practice population report sharing the same physician for all members. Murata and Kane (1976) use more objective data to show that 45% of families enrolled in a health insurance study reported sharing the same physician for all members. The extent of actual use, however, was more conservative. Only 17% of families actually used the same primary care physician for the majority of visits by all members.

Thus limited available evidence suggests that while family care exists, it may not be the care of choice selected by the majority of the population. Studies based on objective physician-based performance data are needed to measure the actual use of family care for free-living populations of families.

Who Uses Family Care?

Studies show that use of family care varies by certain patient characteristics, including couple age (older couples are most likely to share the same physician), family life-cycle stage (families with young children are least likely to share the same physician), family educational level (families with less educated adults are most likely to share the same physician), and family size (families with many children are least likely to share the same physician) (Bartholomew & Schneiderman, 1982; Murata & Kane, 1976). Family care, however, is not significantly related to the availability of family physicians, family income, insurance coverage, population size (Murata & Kane, 1976), distance from the clinic, patient attitudes about physician characteristics, or patient attitudes about family care (Bartholomew & Schneiderman, 1982).

Studies also show that use of family care varies by certain health care system characteristics (Cowen & Sbarbaro, 1972), including reimbursement policies of funding agencies (i.e., reimbursement for specialized services discourages use), type of physician training (i.e., disease-oriented trained physicians discourage use), and access to care (i.e., easy access encourages use). Cowen and Sbarbaro (1972) show that 45% of the study population of 100,000 medically indigent patients who had easy access to family-centered care actually used this care on an ongoing basis. (*Family centered* was defined as physician awareness of the existence and health status of other family members.) Perhaps most families fail to perceive the benefits of family care even when it is readily available.

FUTURE RESEARCH DIRECTIONS: WHAT ARE THE BENEFITS OF FAMILY CARE?

Family practitioners assume that "awareness of the family produces better medical outcomes" (Christie-Seely & Guttman, 1984). Unfortunately, there is limited evidence derived from rigorously designed and executed studies to support this assumption. Future studies could provide valuable findings by using a longitudinal, case-control research design to compare actual use of family-oriented over individual-oriented care. Indicators for "better medical outcomes" must be more clearly identified in measurable terms in order to produce valuable findings that benefit clinical practice and health care policy formulation.

One fruitful hypothesis for future testing is suggested by concepts from family systems theory and evidence from related studies. Compared with individual-oriented care, family-oriented care (awareness of the family environment by the physician) permits a more complete prevention, diagnosis, treatment, and rehabilitation plan.

Family-Oriented Prevention

Although prevention of risk for disease and prevention of disease are important functions of family practice, most prevention activities are limited to immunizations and periodic health exams (Christie-Seely, 1984a); many times strategies to promote healthier life-styles are overlooked. Concepts suggested by family systems theory (Broderick & Smith, 1979; Hill, 1971) direct attention to certain dimensions of the family environment that influence the development of risk, disease, and behavior change. These behavioral concepts arise from viewing the family as a social system whose members continuously interact in seeking to maintain boundaries, working toward goals, and maintaining a functional equilibrium between stability and growth. Awareness by the physician of these aspects of the family environment permits a more accurate assessment of the etiology of risk behaviors (smoking, sedentary life-style, inappropriate diet) and the potential for change. Extensive evidence exists, for example, that cardiovascular risk is learned and reinforced in the family environment (Venters, 1986). Because family physicians are involved with family members over long periods of time, they are in an ideal position to detect unhealthy family lifestyles that contribute to the development of risk for cardiovascular disease as well as other conditions. Because family physicians are involved with all family members, they are in an ideal position to promote change toward healthier family life-styles.

Future studies could provide valuable knowledge upon which to base health promotion activities by focusing on the following questions: Do isolated families (those with closed family boundaries) limit contact with physicians and other sources of health promotion information? If so, are these families at greater risk for disease? Which family goals and interaction dimensions promote healthy life-styles, and which contribute to the development of risk? The answers to these questions could then be used to create health education materials that would assist busy clinicians in promoting the health of their clinic populations.

Family Environment, Diagnosis, and Treatment

Clinical observation suggests that awareness of the family system minimizes missed, incorrect, and incomplete diagnoses and promotes a more complete treatment plan (Christie-Seely & Guttman, 1984). This is especially true for conditions associated with family dysfunction, such as chronic stress, headache, depression, anxiety, fatigue, insomnia, hypertension, and vague complaints. A limited number of studies show that the family environment is associated with illness outcomes. Meyer and Haggerty (1962), for example, used a group of families with three or more children to show that level of family stress is positively related to level of individual risk for streptococcal infections. Medalie et al. (1973) used age-adjusted data provided by 10,000 adult men to show that among those who reported the most severe family problems, there was a threefold increase in the incidence of angina pectoris over those who reported the least severe family problems. In these situations awareness of the family environment is essential to establish an appropriate treatment plan, which may include some degree of family therapy.

Future research could assist physicians in establishing an effective treatment plan exploring the following questions directed at identifying family determinants of utilization: To what extent does stress, and other indicators of family dysfunction, result in inappropriate utilization of health care services? Do families change in a predictable manner over the family life cycle in terms of utilization of health care services?

Future research could assist those who formulate health care policy by exploring the following questions: Do certain characteristics of the health care system (i.e., reimbursement policies, HMO versus fee for service) have positive or negative impacts on utilization of family health care? If so, what are these characteristics?

Family Environment and Rehabilitation

Clinical experience has shown that awareness of the family environment assists physicians in predicting the extent of compliance with treatment/rehabilitation plans. A limited number of studies support this observation by showing that family attitudes toward medical care, family relationship problems, and family disorganization are significantly associated with extent of compliance with a suggested treatment/rehabilitation plan (Alpert, 1964; Diamond, Weiss, & Grynbaum, 1968; Oakes, Ward, Gray, Klouber, & Moody, 1970; Schwartz, Wang, Zeitz, & Goss, 1962). Litman (1966), for example, shows that positive family reinforcement promotes positive response to a rehabilitation plan for patients with a severe orthopedic condition.

Future studies could assist clinicians in predicting level of compliance to treatment of different conditions by identifying specific family skills, family structures, and family interaction patterns needed to manage different conditions. Family compliance with a demanding home treatment regime for a chronic and severe condition, such as childhood cystic fibrosis (Venters, 1981), for example, would be expected to demand different family skills from those used in compliance to a less severe acute condition, such as asthma.

CONCLUSION

The role of the family unit in health care needs further clarification. Does this imply treatment of intact family units, or care of individuals within the context of their family environments, or merely individual care with some degree of physician awareness of the family? As shown by the evidence in this review, all approaches have been used. Each approach may provide valuable contributions to a better understanding of the relationship between family involvement and delivery of effective health care. Most studies, however, fail to clarify the approach used in relation to the problem investigated. Existing studies also fail to clarify indicators of family care in measurable terms. Two exceptions are studies by Murata and Kane (1976) and Holmes et al. (1978), which could serve as a basis upon which to build future studies of the prevalence, determinants, and benefits of family care.

Research is needed that uses a combination of subjective sources of data (i.e., patient and physician reports) and objective sources of data (i.e., medical records, utilization data). Researchers should measure not only perceived utilization, which is now recorded in most existing studies, but also actual utilization, which has rarely been recorded.

In addition, future research should establish accurate measures of family characteristics—family life-cycle stage, family size, family structure, family function, and ability of a family to exercise free choice among physicians—and should then control for these potentially confounding family variables when comparing the uses and benefits of family-oriented care with those of individual-oriented care.

Finally, future research should be directed toward answering the following questions: Which families and which medical conditions benefit from family care? Which medical conditions are made worse by family care? Can, or should, family care be made available to large populations? Is family care practical, on a cost-benefit basis, for the current health care delivery environment?

While present studies show that family care exists, future studies need to use more rigorous measurement and research design tools to identify more clearly the determinants, benefits, and limitations of family care.

SEVEN

An Ethnographic Approach to Family Research in Primary Care

HOWARD F. STEIN

This chapter introduces the ethnographic method as a tool of understanding family-based health care decision making (Agar, 1980, 1986; Geertz, 1973; La Barre, 1978; Spiro, 1982a; Stein, 1982b, 1983b). Meant to complement the biomedical clinical method, the ethnographic method has much in common with the patient-centered, phenomenological approach described by McWhinney (1986). It is based on ongoing ethnographic research and clinical teaching/supervision experience since the early 1970s. I address two interrelated methodological issues inherent in the hypothesis that the inclusion of the family unit in the delivery of health care will produce better health care: (a) Can we take for granted that we share common meanings and assumptions when we use the word *family*? (b) How do contemporary medical institutions include the family unit in the delivery of health care? Thus, how is *the family* defined, bounded, and treated in such "inclusion," and by whom? Whatever the family is as an entity, it is also an idea, a concept, and an attribution. Clinical ideologies strongly influence clinical research on families, and likewise determine the type of health care defined as "better."

MULTIPLE MEANINGS OF AND ASSUMPTIONS ABOUT *FAMILY*

To understand why meaning-oriented methodology is useful to the study of health behavior, consider the concepts of "family unit" and

61

"household unit" widespread in quantitative research. Cultural assumptions we commonly bring to such studies influence what and how we measure (Berger & Luckmann, 1966; Murdock, 1949, 1967; Shapiro, 1989a, 1989b). The family as a "unit" has been idealized as an antidote to individualism and social isolation. This reified image is itself a cultural creation (Stein, 1983a, 1984). I have seen family physicians and family therapists label Hispanic or Italian families as pathologically "enmeshed" when in fact these families' culturally shared style of closeness differs from that of the Anglo or acculturated practitioners (Keefe, 1984). Like anthropological theories that treat "culture" as a living form apart from the people who create and sustain it (de Mause, 1982; Devereux, 1980; La Barre, 1972), many family research models and strategies describe families as if they were "entities" (Sander, 1979; Stein, 1986). Yet "unrelated" (by kin ties) people living in an adjacent apartment or nearby home may be more directly involved in an individual's health-related decision making and care than members of that person's immediate household.

A few examples might help us to apply externally derived units of study with caution. Isolated single-nuclear Western European-American family farmsteads and ranches that dot the North American Great Plains from Texas to Saskatchewan and Ontario dramatically contrast with traditional Iroquois communal dwellings called longhouses, in which several related nuclear families all resided. Among the original Israeli kibbutzim (collective farm settlements), founded in revolt against the traditional East-Central European patriarchal extended family, husbands and wives lived together. Their children, however, did not live with, nor were they primarily raised by them. Children instead lived in age-graded group dwellings and were supervised by women employed by the collective. In many societies, pubescent children leave the parental home and join men's or women's secret lodges to learn the society's (and their gender's) lore and to prepare for adult role and status. Many military and religious orders in modern society employ this residence pattern. Here, definitions of *family* and *household unit* vary throughout the individual/family/cultural life cycle.

From my ethnographic research among Slovak-, Rusyn-, and other Slavic-American families in the former "Steel Valley" of Western Pennsylvania, I often observed multigeneration extended families living in the same home or in adjacent or several nearby "neighborhood" houses. In terms of family functioning, a household unit in this instance often encompassed several distinct buildings, as did the family members' own notions as to what was subsumed under a family unit.

Family studies investigators and family physicians must be able to move freely among and to encompass multiple meanings and uses of the term *family.* Here I briefly outline several of these. First, there is the *evolutionary, biological, precultural basis for the family* (Bidney, 1947; La Barre, 1951, 1968; Spiro, 1979). La Barre (1951) writes:

> Our species, Homo sapiens, is the unique animal which has a fully familial kind of sociality. In fact, I believe that it is uniquely the *biological* nature of human nature to be familial in its structure. The universality of the human family is based upon unchangeable *biological* grounds, not upon shifting cultural or moral grounds. This is not to say that locally we cannot have considerable differences in the *form of marriage*—polygyny, polyandry, and the like—but these local phrasings of the *form* of marriage never can and never do impugn the basic biological *norm* which the *family* constitutes. (p. 54)

As Spiro (1982b) has shown, precisely because of the universal nuclear family norm—deeply and widely embedded as this family structure often is in extended families and clans—the Oedipus complex, discovered by Freud, is universal. This directs us to a second meaning of family: the *internal family,* product of growing up in a biological family, but as amplified and elaborated by fantasy and defense processes to militate against anxiety. This "inner family," which we all possess as a result of symbolization and the capacity for language, constitutes a *representational system* that in turn is expressed in family and wider social interaction (Sander, 1979).

A third meaning of family is more behavioral and cognitive than phenomenological. Studies in family *interaction* and family *structure* (Minuchin, 1974) research identify formal and informal rules, roles, adaptive strategies, subunits, and so forth. Researchers in family studies, social history, and anthropology (kinship studies) tend to use this conceptual and methodological approach to families. A fourth meaning of family—one that can be gleaned from individual self-report, participant observation in an individual's many contexts, and observation of social interaction—is that of the *personal network.* Here, "Family *is* what family means to me." People might include pets, neighbors, godparents, friends, coworkers, and more in their family constructs, which might change over time, influenced by stages of the life cycle and by the considerable mobility of North American society. Nonkin may play decisive roles in health care, prevention, and risk.

There is, fifth, the *ideological family,* a culturewide image and fantasy about what an ideal family ought to be, based on nostalgia (Stein, 1974, 1983a, 1984, 1987b). An example might be the romanticized image of the patriarchal Victorian family, one where roles were clear. This ideology is an insidious filter in much family research, teaching, and therapy.

WHOSE FRAMEWORK?
ISSUES IN THE "INCLUSION" OF FAMILY

The issue of units of study brings me to the difference between insiders' (e.g., those being studied or treated) and outsiders' (e.g., those conducting research or formulating social policy) viewpoints. Attention should be paid to differences between what is *expressed* by patients, family members, and health researchers and professionals and what values, conflicts, meanings, and the like can be *deduced* from their behavior, affect, and word usage (Richards, 1956). Recognition should be given to the distinction between people's explicit, espoused, ideal values and their operant or inferred ones (Spiegel, 1971).

Devoting nuanced attention to one's patients, informants, or subjects is easier said than done, however, for some methodologies are accorded greater prestige and truth value than others. The framework of the scientist-outsider commonly takes precedence over that of the patient-family-community-insider. Certain kinds of facts or data qualify as clinical truth, and certain ways of arriving at it (methods) are accorded higher status. Preferred ways of knowing, categories of knowing, influence what is admitted into the canon of knowledge itself. A number of dichotomies are rife throughout North American science, not only its biomedicine, such as hard/soft, quantitative/qualitative, objective/subjective, explanatory/descriptive, numbers/narrative, measurable/intuitive, empirical/deductive, controlled/anecdotal, scientific/impressionistic, organic/mental. These are all well-known *cultural* dichotomies and *hierarchies of knowledge.* Within medicine, the former member of each pair is "good" and the latter is at best suspect and at worst "bad" science and medicine.

Ultimately, the official clinical ideology called biomedicine is also a cultural or "folk" model, even though we accord it a high and distinct status by calling it "professional," in contrast with "lay." We are all natives—insiders to some groups and outsiders to others—even as we aspire also to be scientists and transcend the tribal. Our proudest scientific, medical frames of reference remain interpretations.

Culturally sensitive techniques consist of eliciting the constructions, meanings, experiences, perceptions, and rules of the "natives" (those being studied). In medical studies this viewpoint is that of patients', family members', and community members' ideas that they bring to health and illness definition, experience, and behavior. By contrast, familiar "nonnative" or professionals' approaches include standardized epidemiological or sociological questionnaires, problem-oriented medical records, and "SOAP" classification of clinical data. These consist of constructions and inferences that reflect the interests and assumptions of physicians and social scientists. Investigators' categories are often unwittingly imposed on their studies and investigated "in" the data. Researchers may erroneously regard the professional viewpoint as automatically objective and that of the patient, family, or culture being studied as inherently subjective. Researchers' subjectively based categories can often render the world of patients and their families opaque (Agar, 1980, 1986; Brody, 1987; Devereux, 1967; Guba, 1981; Henry, 1963, 1967, 1973; Kleinman & Good, 1985; Spradley, 1979).

As researchers, our personal and cultural blind spots may prevent us from asking better questions and eliciting crucial data. To be scientific, our methods must help us to face, understand, and resolve those anxieties the subject awakens. Our methods must include insight into both the part we play and the subject. The insider/outsider, or observed/observer, distinction draws our attention to unstated assumptions and meanings that both researchers-practitioners-teachers and patients-families-communities-cultures bring to health and sickness behavior. Beyond the fact of their mere difference, these frameworks can potentially correct and learn from one another, as well as reflect different types of knowledge (Browner, Ortiz de Montellano, & Rubel, 1988; Spiro, 1982a, 1986). From the scientific viewpoint, patients' or families' illness constructions may well be wrong. An insider viewpoint, however, helps the researcher or practitioner to elicit patients' and families' stories, to try to work within them, to try to negotiate common ground, and to recognize limitations upon clinical ambition.

Discussing primary care theory and research, Kleinman (1983) advocates the ethnographic method to elicit meanings associated with illness and treatment:

> Qualitative description, taken together with various quantitative measures, can create a standardized research method for assessing validity. It is especially valuable in studying social and cultural significance, e.g., illness beliefs, interaction norms, social gain, ethnic help seeking, and treatment

responses, and it is the appropriate method to describe the work of doctoring. . . . If the ethnography of meaning is not legitimated in primary care research, even though it is legitimated in anthropology, sociology, and social psychology, then meaning will not receive a scientifically appropriate assessment in primary care. (p. 543)

The battle line between "qualitative" and "quantitative" research is spurious. The issue is not whether to "narrate and interpret" or to "count and sort," but whether our perspective introduces distortion from the outside and, because we call it science, we cannot recognize our own error. The dichotomy misses the genuine distinction between good and poor methodology as based on whether the subjects' feelings, experiences, and constructions are acknowledged or discounted. Good description and interpretation foster the construction of good theory—and more contextualized clinical intervention.

Quarterlies such as *Culture, Medicine and Psychiatry, Family Systems Medicine, Medical Anthropology, Ethos,* and *Medical Anthropology Quarterly* regularly publish qualitative health-related studies. Similarly, Sage Publications, in Newbury Park, California, has published numerous titles in its Qualitative Research Methods series and also publishes a new journal, *Qualitative Health Research* (Agar, 1986; Kirk & Miller, 1986). There also exists a thriving Qualitative Family Research Network.

WHAT IS ETHNOGRAPHY?

Ethnography consists of the attempt to comprehend a person's, family's, and group's lifeways (Stein & Apprey, 1985, 1987). Ethnographers work with individuals and groups to observe, participate with, and interview them in their various contexts (home, lay network, occupational, religious, and so on). The ethnographic method requires a long-term interest and commitment and is naturalistic, sensitive to context, open-ended, and serendipitous. Family medicine might welcome the ethnographic approach to studying doctor-patient relationships, the social organization of a clinic, or family health decisions and practices.

In a recent summary of ethnographic techniques, Stuart Plattner (1989) identifies the following as key components of qualitative research: (a) "the ability to talk to people in their own language," (b) direct observation methods and the ability to distinguish patterns, (c) interviewing skills and techniques to explore the organization of knowledge, and (d) "data recording and retrieval" (p. 32). Although asking questions is part of ethnographers' repertoire (especially on a narrow topic such as a ritual or specific health behavior), active listening and facilitating the informant to tell his or her story and the actual observation of the story in action are even more vital. One is reminded of Michael Balint's aphorism, as true in ethnography as in psychotherapy or biomedicine, that if you ask a question, all you will get is an answer.

The method cannot be culturally standardized nor can it be learned instantly. Many fieldworkers conduct interviews and participant observation in the field for many months before key patterns and linkages begin to emerge. Still, the anthropological literature is as rife with controversy over interpretation as the literatures of natural science, cosmology, and medical science are rife with disputes (Heider, 1988). No methodology is immune to ideological distortion.

At its best, family medicine intuitively uses an ethnographic approach to understanding sickness, healing, and prevention. Family medicine ideals of continuity of care (of knowing people and their families over time) and comprehensiveness of care (the often elusive whole person, whole problem, and system) share a theoretical, philosophical, and methodological core with anthropology. The relationship of ethnographer and informant has as its parallel the relationships between the physician and the patient, family, colleague, and staff member. Each relationship is the foundation of the work performed. I need hardly remind this readership that the great physicians and clinical researchers of history all were naturalists: Bernardino Ramazzini, William Harvey, John Snow, Rudolf Virchow, Louis Pasteur, Alexander Fleming, Robert Koch, and others.

In family studies, this approach often enables us to uncover the story that confers upon an illness episode its timing and timeliness, its meaning, its organization and direction, if not its outcome. In modern North American biomedicine, without the family or contextual story, we have only organismic fragments that, when taken alone, trivialize rather than encompass the lives in which they occur. The ethnographic method helps the researcher/clinician to discover and trace out patterns, textures, recurrent sequences, symbols, meanings, and feelings that other eliciting methods often fail to notice. It is, moreover, meaning oriented with respect to both (a) patients' and families' illness behavior and (b) researchers'/clinicians' underlying assumptions.

The ethnographic study of patients' and their families' health-related decision making utilizes introspective (self-report) and interactive research strategies. The former consists of eliciting patients' and family members' perceptions of, reconstructions of, and feelings about illness episodes. The latter consists of researchers' observations of the family's negotiation and management of such episodes (e.g., in the clinic, hospital, home, or hospice).

The observer is always a part of what is observed. The observer's cultural biases and unconscious thoughts influence data collection and analysis (Devereux, 1967; La Barre, 1978; Stein, 1985; Stein & Apprey, 1985, 1987). Among the methodological complications of observer bias are (a) perceiving data in terms of one's specialty interests and clinical ideologies, (b) seeing/hearing what is absent and not seeing/hearing what is present, (c) distorting data by overemphasis or underestimation of their significance, and (d) confirming preconceptions and rationalizing exceptions to methodological or theoretical paradigms. Observers' use of methodology primarily to diminish anxiety impedes scientific advance (Devereux, 1967; La Barre, 1978; Stein, 1985). Often the observer who is not looking for something can perceive data in a novel way. In observing, one never knows beforehand what to look for and can therefore discover what others may have overlooked (Heath, 1976, 1980).

An influential school within medical anthropology attempts to determine the "explanatory model" constructed by patients and how it interacts in clinical relationships with the biomedical explanatory model constructed by health care professionals (Chrisman & Maretzki, 1982; Eisenberg & Kleinman, 1981; Good, 1977; Kleinman, 1980). In a study that involved seven patients over 10 months in a variety of contexts, Trostle, Hauser, and Susser (1983) explored the management of epilepsy from the patient's point of view. Numerous other researchers have documented the extent to which the popular sector (Kleinman, 1980), consisting of an individual's family circle and friends, influences how a symptom is defined, what steps (if any) are taken, and whether, when, and with whom outside help is sought (Chrisman, 1977; Litman, 1974; Stein, 1982a; Zola, 1972). Within the family medicine literature, authors such as Like and Steiner (1986), Eckert and Galazka (1986), Stein and Pontious (1985), Snider and Stein (1987), and Kuzel (1986) discuss the ethnographic, naturalistic, and hermeneutic (meaning-oriented) approach to patients', families', communities', and cultures' health belief and action models.

USES OF ETHNOGRAPHY AS A METHODOLOGY
IN FUTURE FAMILY HEALTH RESEARCH

I recommend three overlapping foci for future ethnographic research in primary care: (a) a focus that begins with the individual *patient* and traces out his or her familial and wider personal network, which influences health beliefs and behavior; (b) a focus that is not directly patient care oriented but rather more descriptive and process oriented—such as home-based interviews with people with hypertension or epilepsy, naturalistic studies of home and neighborhood, occupational and community environments—to develop a baseline picture of people's lived-in worlds from which professional health strategies and policies could be developed; and (c) a focus on the emotional, cognitive, developmental, and wider psychosocial (e.g., political and economic) aspects of the researcher's and practitioner's assumptive world. As ethnographer, one constantly shifts attention between understanding the observed and understanding oneself (Davidson, 1986; R. C. Smith, 1984; Smith & Stein, 1987; Stamm, 1987).

Ideally, at least, a family practitioner begins with the patient's family—a family the patient declares. Over time, a deeper understanding of the family picture emerges, correcting the physician's initial image. This is accomplished less by knowing beforehand precisely what questions to ask than it is by letting the relationship, the focus, and the timing shape what is pursued.

Often diverging from researchers' and practitioners' preference is the fact that most patients in North American society go to the doctor "one at a time," many of them steadfast individualists. Patients may be puzzled when a physician requests a family session or recommends family therapy. Professionals' ideologies about treating "the whole family unit" or "the whole person" often collide with practice realities in which patients far more easily accept diagnoses of something malfunctioning in their bodies than of something awry with themselves, their families, or their lives. North American medical education and practice are largely built around the internal medicine metaphor of the skin-bounded assortment of organ systems, an orientation that many patients share with their physicians.

Some patients and their families seek in medical care a quasi-automotive "fix-it shop" to distance themselves from painful emotional and family issues (Zborowski, 1969). Their "explanatory model" (Kleinman, 1980) often coincides with that of more mechanistically oriented practitioners.

Patients and family members may reject physicians' systems-oriented effort to include the family in actual treatment. Astute family physicians working with them will primarily (or at least initially) include the family through conceptualization only, making "family-level interventions" through the patient or through the subsystem that appears for health care.

Intimate personal knowledge of one's practice community is the foundation of an ethnographic approach to clinical work. Family physician-based ethnographic research might begin with an open-ended approach to understanding individual patients, eliciting and working within their "explanatory models" (Kleinman, 1980; Kuzel, 1986; Like & Steiner, 1986; Snider & Stein, 1987). For family physicians who choose not to make home visits themselves, home health care nurses, physicians' associates, social workers, and similar allied health personnel might learn ethnographic techniques of gathering contextual data at a patient's home, neighborhood, and/or workplace, and place summaries of these in the medical chart.

The ethnographic framework would be a useful addition to more conventional and culturally standardized studies and medical interventions in the family life cycle, for instance, with respect to questions of (a) risk assessment and reduction, (b) increased family vulnerability to illness, (c) family diagnosis or health appraisal, (d) a family's acute response to illness, and (e) family adaptation to chronic illness. The ethnographic approach helps researcher and practitioner alike to understand these issues from within the experience of the family.

Thus: How do families assess and define *risk*? What family functions or meanings might be served by behavior patterns that physicians identify as biomedically high risk (e.g., alcoholism, obesity, eating high-cholesterol foods, driving motor vehicles without seat belts, teenage sexuality without contraceptives, cigarette smoking, ignoring symptoms such as elevated blood pressure or high blood glucose)? To what illnesses do families perceive themselves to be especially vulnerable— or, conversely, immune? What does that vulnerability (or immunity) mean to family members? How does a family system (interacting with other social systems) diagnose itself and appraise its members' symptoms? How does a family's acute response to illness differ from responses that health care providers prefer or expect from families? What, to a family, is an acute medical situation, in contrast with how a physician defines acuteness? With respect to chronic illness, what is regarded as adaptive behavior from the family's viewpoint, in comparison with the conception of adaptiveness from a biomedical framework? How do a family's responses to direct questions differ from those lived answers, so to speak, that one might observe on the family's home ground, in the neighborhood, the workplace, and the like? The astute observer and open-ended interviewer commonly gleans "answers" to such questions without ever having to pose them.

Finally, the cultural climate in North American society affects how family considerations and "the family unit" are to be included in health care. How family issues are embraced by the health care system will determine whether health care improves. A corporate, bureaucratic, business-oriented model of efficiency has come to define *better* in ways that vitiate all we have learned in the century since the inception of the anthropological, Freudian, and systems revolutions (Freud, 1910/1957; Kormos, 1984; Ritzer & Walczak, 1986; Stein, 1987a; Stephens, 1984). *How* family issues and "the family" are defined, bounded, treated, and billed in such inclusion directs our ethnographic attention away from the "object" of clinical investigation and treatment and toward societies of physicians, social scientists, insurance companies, and government agencies who do the defining and setting of policy. Clinical ideologies, and the bureaucracies and power positions they serve, strongly influence family research. They determine the type of health care defined as "better."

Freud (1910/1957) wrote that "no psychoanalyst goes further than his own complexes and internal resistances permit" (p. 145), a point that holds for any clinician or researcher and for group resistances (such as narrow research paradigms) as well. In an age characterized, in the United States at least, by minimalism, diminution of the sense of relatedness and compassion toward others, survivalism, militarism, nationalism, nuclearism, corporatism, and social Darwinism, it is difficult to be optimistic about the future of "continuity" and "comprehensiveness," values that characterize naturalistic research and family medicine's official self-image (Kormos, 1984; Ritzer & Walczak, 1986). This professional and social climate scorns intimacy and depth in clinical relationships and research alike. The danger is that primary care researchers and practitioners will replicate this cultural, corporate, "bottom line" paradigm in family research strategies and in health care. The result would be the reduction of "the family" to yet another quasi-organ system on the assembly line that "produces" a product line of cure, prevention, and wellness. The holistic ethnographic standard thus has a vital critical, as well as descriptive and interpretive, function in medicine's future (Morley, 1988).

In sum, a valid discourse on family research in primary care must include not only an open-minded approach to such concepts as family and household, and to the identification of units of study, but also an inquisitive attitude toward the very society—and its members' categories—in which the study is being conducted. The subject of such research becomes simultaneously the family (in its various guises), we who study the family, the health care institutions that include the family, and the wider society that subsumes and interacts with all of these.

EIGHT

New Directions in the Methodology of Family-Centered Health Care Research

DONALD C. RANSOM

The ideas of *better health care* and *more effective results* lend themselves easily to interchangeable use. Ideally, these terms should amount to the same thing, but increasingly they do not. Good health care (a myth—we are really talking about good medical care) and effective results are value-laden concepts. Both medical politics and economics play roles in deciding what these terms should mean. Thus *effective results* cannot be assumed to mean the same thing in Canada that it means in the United States, particularly in relation to primary care.

Family-centered care can be inconvenient and unwieldy for practitioners and third-party payors. It broadens their focus and responsibility to include others who are invested in the patient. It forces a provider's practice to be more visible. It requires communication with the patient's intimates, in series and simultaneously in conjoint meetings, and this can lead to complicated and troublesome situations. It puts pressure on the doctor to deal face to face with what is important to both patient and family members. Yet it may increase patient satisfaction and lead to better cooperation and better health in the long run.

But who is interested in the long run? When I have suggested to health maintenance organization insurers in California that it makes good sense to invest in a broadly conceived family-centered approach to care because it will pay off in the long run, I have been informed that,

AUTHOR'S NOTE: The research reported in this chapter has been supported by NIMH Grant Number 38468.

for the third party, there is no long run. The average length of enrollment for subscribers is so brief (about 3 years) that it makes no economic sense to spend time and money now investing in an individual or a family who will be gone before any dividend can be collected. Californians play musical chairs, if not with their jobs, then with the health plans those jobs offer. They switch to one of several choices that looks promising during open enrollment each year, or they are told what new plan is the only one the company now has to offer. In Canada, people are covered through a federal universal health care system that supports each province in the creation of provincial insurance plans that are available at either no charge or a minimal charge to individuals of that province. Individuals can supplement these plans with other plans offered by either their employers or private insurance companies. In the long run, everyone stands to gain from discovering what good health care is and then investing in it. This matter has no direct bearing on the issues of good research design and methodological rigor, but it has much to do with the incentives for asking certain kinds of questions and allocating funds to study them.

In exploring some new directions for research in this chapter, I want to address several issues that follow from joining the special nature of family practice or family-centered primary care with the special demands of studying "the family." First, I sketch out a framework for thinking about research on families and health, illness, and care, and then introduce 11 ways in which families influence the health of their members. Second, I take up some current issues regarding the conceptual status of the term *family,* the logic of family measurement, and the warrant of family research findings. Third, I raise the question of "variable"— contrasted with "case" (person and family)—centered research design and analysis. I close the chapter with a caveat about the felt need to "prove" that family-centered health care is more effective than an "individual" approach.

FAMILY MEDICINE
AND THE FAMILY DIMENSION

In 1970, I reviewed the relevant literature and identified four overlapping categories that outline the focus and content of the family dimension of family practice (Ransom, 1981). At that time it was important to define family medicine as a field of inquiry and to establish a frame of reference that would both bound its concerns and distinguish its efforts from narrowly intraindividual biological approaches on the one side and broader community and public health approaches on the other. It seemed clear that a "middle range" of variables invited opportunities to study familial and other primary social environments in relation to health, illness, and care. This middle-range view was not partial to any given family form, but instead called attention to "family" as a proxy for primary human relatedness, the relevant contexts of the patient's life, and emphasized the meaningfulness of symptoms, intervention, and all behavior related to health, illness, and care. Because meaning is always a social construction, this necessarily meant studying those contexts of meaning that applied to questions of interest to the provision of primary and personal care. In 1981, I presented this category system as follows:

(1) family roles in the etiology, predisposition, mediation, and maintenance of illness
(2) effects on the family and its members of illness and the treatment of illness
(3) family-health services provider relations
(4) families as their own health-restoring and health-promoting agencies

FAMILY MEDICINE MEANS
NEW OUTCOMES AND NEW VARIABLES

In a subsequent paper, I argued that

the reason family physicians are interested in the family is because expanding the conceptual field within which health and pathology are understood, coupled with enlarging the focus of interventions to include the immediate social environment, leads to more effective and humane care of the person. (Ransom, 1983, p. 101)

The perspective being proposed was not meant to limit the physician's imagination only to "treating the individual in the context of the family." That approach does not go far enough, either in practice or in research, because, although it includes the family as a relevant environment, all that constitutes that environment is "flattened out" on a single logical plane and simply added to a set of variables that either helps or hinders the physician's efforts to work with the patient. The conventional underlying biomedical model is expanded but left unchallenged, resulting in a phenomenal tinkering but no categorical shift.

I was joining the voices that were encouraging family physicians to break loose from a restraining image conveyed by their more strictly biomedically minded teachers. In the conventional model the family is visualized as a field of forces impinging upon the patient and the physician, but family relations are not viewed as constituting in any essential way both the patient's condition and the caregiving process (neither are doctor-patient relations, for that matter). In contrast, the significance of a family-centered approach, and the challenge for future research to take up, is that the structure and process of persons being and behaving together as "family" constitute in some measure the minds and bodies of the members. Those relations are inscribed "in" and lived "through" the persons we see in the office every day.

In formal terms:

> Although neither can be reduced to the other, in the world of human interaction an ontological unity exists between the state (or process) of a family and the states (or processes) of its members. That is to say, what the individual is doing, along with any processes that can be identified with or used to describe that individual (psychological or physical) and what the relevant family is doing, along with any processes that can be ascribed to the family, are occurring simultaneously as an unbroken unity of action or process in the world. In this sense, the patient's condition and the physician's ability to heal are seen as immanent in the relationships constructed by the principal persons involved. (Ransom, 1987, p. 384)

In other words, a 60-year-old mother's recurring hospitalizations because she cannot breathe, and her three grown sons' respective obesity and ulcer, lawbreaking, and depression and chronic unemployment are all reticulated by a common family history and a mutually constructed reality that organizes a pattern of finely tuned role relationships. One could never know this with assurance without knowing each one and without seeing them together, especially in their home.

Caring for individuals "in the context of their families" is no small feat. Researching family relations and health and care is an even greater challenge. I am not suggesting simply adding a few social variables to an extended biopsychosocial model. What is involved ultimately is documenting how persons and primary groups create the health-relevant conditions for each other's existence, and how family physicians can understand and make use of this process.

When we think about family process this way and then think about the aims of family practice—to provide comprehensive and continuing care to persons, to work with those persons to prevent disease and disorder and maintain health, to deal effectively with whatever people go to doctors for—we can easily see that research in family medicine involves new outcomes and new variables. Of course, we should be studying the natural history of disease and the treatment of common problems. But when we think of the family as a unit of care in this broader sense, together with the ambitious aims and responsibilities of modern family practice, we catch a glimpse of why we cannot confine ourselves to studying only the sorts of variables and outcomes that are of interest to our subspecialty colleagues. Neither should we adopt models of studying practice that assume that all doctors and all patients are interchangeable, or that show no interest in the effects of intervention with one person on another.

An example of what this means is the following. I recently saw a list of 23 criteria for auditing charts to evaluate the quality of care of diabetes. Nowhere on that list was there any mention of whether patients felt better over a period of time or felt more in control or confident in managing their illness. Nor was any attention given to whether the illness was affecting their lives or causing problems for anyone else, or whether any other person was helping or hindering the process of controlling the diabetes. This was an illness without a person and a patient without a family or other significant relationships. The patient was being viewed implicitly as a container of a disease that is not connected to anything or anybody. This is both a fiction and an impoverished set of criteria for "good" care. Further, it is a limiting set of variables for interesting research.

It is this sort of example that leads me to suggest that the "individual-oriented primary care" versus "family-centered primary care" distinction may be misplaced. The greater contrast is between disease- or procedure-focused and person-focused approaches, instead of between individual and family approaches. If *individual* means person, then taking the person seriously and fully necessarily means including significant other people and relationships in that person's life. Who makes the difference, how, and in what way are good questions for researchers to study.

If we consider the variety of ways in which families make a difference in the health of their members, the implications for family-centered primary care and the identification of new variables and the approaches to management those variables suggest can be addressed. Below, I describe 11 ways in which family processes, relations, and membership influence individual health status. These categories are overlapping but different enough to suggest distinguishable research questions and strategies.

(1) Resources and support. Families can provide material resources and instrumental support for their members. These include both the capacity and the proclivity of the family to provide food, clothing, shelter, money, and access to medical care and community resources.

(2) Health-related habits. Through modeling, teaching, encouraging, and reinforcing, family members form health-related habits and practices. Families play a principal role in shaping personal life-style, which, in turn, shapes health. Doherty and Campbell (1988) place primary emphasis on the family's influence on smoking, alcohol use, diet, exercise, periodic screening, and adherence to safe driving and seat belt use—six major causes of premature death according to the U.S. surgeon general (Califano, 1979).

(3) Values and beliefs. Families transmit and reinforce values and beliefs that shape health and health practices. The family is a filter and conveyer of cultural and ethnic beliefs. Over time, families also construct their own "characterological styles" (Steinglass, Bennett, Wolin, & Reiss, 1987) or "paradigms" (Reiss, 1981).

(4) Communication. Families create structures that organize and constrain both intrafamilial and extrafamilial communication. This includes rules that prescribe family member behavior. Pratt's (1976) theory of the "energized" family is rooted in this dimension, as is, for example, most work on the circumplex model and health (Olson, McCubbin, et al., 1983).

(5) Information filtering. By identifying and translating information from within (the family) and from without (the wider natural and social environment), family members define each other's experiences and appraise particular illness episodes (i.e., potential disequilibrating events). Family interaction also performs the essential function of assimilating and accommodating potential informational incongruities, from all sources (Moss, 1973).

(6) Belonging and purpose. Families provide a sense of belonging and having a meaningful place; families also provide roles that involve mutual obligation and dependence. Family life creates opportunities for

members to exercise and sustain personal commitment, to engage in meaningful activities with purpose, and to affirm their innermost opinions, values, and beliefs (Totman, 1979).

(7) The family as haven. Families provide a sense of being nurtured, loved, valued, esteemed, and cared for. Feelings of security and protection generated within the family can enhance health and contribute to resisting disease, even in the face of other known environmental and biological risk factors (Medalie & Goldbourt, 1976; Sagan, 1987).

(8) Family mood and emotion. The family environment contains members' emotional lives and regulates family members' moods and emotions. In particular, anxiety and potential fight-or-flight responses are modulated by family interaction.

(9) The internal environment. By creating and sustaining an internal environment that is stress reducing and/or stress enhancing, family relations are on balance potentially harmonious, peaceful, and supportive or abusive, exploitive, tense, and full of conflict and worry, in the extremes.

(10) Self-sacrifice and cooperation. Families by nature create conditions in which one (some) member(s) can be forced to accommodate another (others). Everyone is familiar with the way a variety of health-related problems are created through codependent behavior and transformed when someone breaks away from that codependency. I refer here to any change in health status that will significantly affect others if the relationship is to be maintained.

(11) Symptoms and illness as symbols. Sometimes families induce members to enact roles in which symptoms and illness are symbolic and purposeful in maintaining family relationships. The playing out of family politics and intrapsychic dynamics within the family environment shapes members' physical, emotional, mental, and social development. Jackson's (1965) early work on family homeostasis, Laing's (1967) concept of "transpersonal defense" and his use of the process of "mystification" (Laing, 1965), the exploration of "enmeshment" by Minuchin and his colleagues (see, e.g., Minuchin, Rosman, & Baker, 1978), and Kerr & Bowen's (1988) use of the concepts of "triangles" and the "family projection process" are all examples of work that has contributed to research on this complex source of family influence on health.

NEW APPROACHES TO EVALUATING OUTCOME

These processes suggest two approaches to investigating the outcome of management: those in which intervention with one member or subgroup of members is assessed in terms of its affect on another, and those in which work with one member, or a subgroup of the family, can be assessed in terms of a measured change in the status or process of the immediate family as a system. An example of the former is Hoebel's (1977) success in modifying cardiac risk-related behaviors of husbands by working only with their wives. A related piece of work is the finding that husbands' adherence to a regimen of coronary risk-reduction medication is in some ways better predicted by their wives' attitudes toward the prevention protocol than by their own (Doherty, Schrott, Metcalf, & Iasiello-Vailas, 1983). Another example of the first kind is assessing the impact on other family members of intense intervention with the immediate patient. Medalie's (1978) cryptic tale of the "hidden patient," in which his singular focus on a postcoronary husband allowed him to miss a trajectory toward suicide in the patient's wife, is an often-cited example. A cardiologist might not think of this sort of occurrence as within the scope of his or her medical responsibility or research agenda, but a family physician should.

An example of the second approach is work by Schroder, Casadaban, and Davis (1988) with the parents of children with cystic fibrosis. The aim of this study was to increase the communication and problem-solving skills of parents and thus improve the care they could provide for their child, as well as to increase the likelihood that they could deal effectively with each other, thereby reducing individual stress and marital morbidity. Although most studies will continue to focus on the health status of individual members of families, it is also useful to look at aggregate family statistics as well as family group functioning, as this study does. Another such example might demonstrate that efforts to work with families to deal successfully with managing a chronic illness in one member might lead to reduced utilization for the entire household over the course of the next year or to a change in the pattern of visits to the doctor. Similarly, the effects of such a focus could be ascertained in terms of how differently and how well the family functions as a group in the face of the next crisis. Such process data are complex and much more difficult to measure than data about one person; however, much of the work of primary care is best done out in the shadows, away from the brighter light cast down beneath the lamppost.

CHALLENGES OF
FAMILY-CENTERED RESEARCH

This section takes up the conceptual status of the term *family* together with related problems of family measurement, complex subjects that are central to new developments in family and health research. I will briefly introduce two general areas that require continuing work if future studies are to realize the hope of moving beyond generalities to describing more differentiated and specific findings of the kind clinicians can use. The first area is the logic of family measurement. The second is the multidomained and multifaceted nature of the family construct, a condition that calls for increased multivariate assessment. Additional details can be found in four recent papers in which these themes are developed: Fisher, Kokes, Ransom, Phillips, and Rudd (1985), Fisher, Terry, and Ransom (1990), Ransom (1986b), and Ransom, Fisher, Phillips, Kokes, and Weiss (1990).

We all know intuitively what a family is, but what is a family, or what stands for the family, for purposes of research? In research terminology, the family is a construct. As such, it can be defined according to the researcher's aims, but it can never be directly measured. Family research using numbers depends upon constructing reliable and valid indices to represent an idea of a family, which can then be subjected to further analysis.

The great difficulty for research is that the family construct is both multidimensional and multileveled. Families are composed of persons of different genders and generations who are similar and different from each other in potentially interesting ways. Each person occupies a different role in the family and has a unique memory of family history. The individuality of each person's part in the family composition is important and so are patterns of family interaction. The challenge for measurement is that the family is not a homogeneous "thing" that can be described in an undifferentiated fashion or a group whose members can be assumed to be affected by events similarly.

The variety of meanings of the term *family,* the multidimensional and multileveled nature of those meanings, and the extraordinary range of assessment and measurement techniques available to tap them have combined to create a pervasive condition of confused and sometimes confounded investigation and reporting. (A good collection that explores these issues is *Family Variables: Conceptualization, Measurement, and Use,* edited by Draper & Marcos, 1990.) Further, as the popularity of family systems theory has increased, researchers have felt the need to construct measures and report results in terms that reflect the family as a whole. Some of these measures, unfortunately, have added to instead of reduced the confusion.

The most common threat to the validity of conclusions drawn in family research is the implicit and often unexamined assumption of identity among the concepts or units of interest, the units of analysis, and the unit actually being measured. For too long too many family researchers have labored under the illusion that what they are studying is what they are interested in, when, unfortunately, their data are not designed to answer their questions. This problem has been referred to as "an error of the third kind," or a "Type III error" (Mitroff & Featheringham, 1974; Raiffa, 1968).

One approach to handling this problem is found in a heuristic classification scheme that identifies a set of links connecting the types of family data that are obtainable, the specific measurement methods that can be employed, and the kinds of statements and conclusions that the data can logically support (Ransom et al., 1990). The scheme identifies three distinct ways in which the construct family can be described and measured:

(1) *Families can be described according to member composition or a unit characteristic.* This simply means families can be categorized or ordered according to some group attribute, such as family size or income, or whether or not a family contains a member with a chronic illness.

(2) *Families can be described according to family member descriptions or ratings of expressed ideas and feelings about family life and other family members.* This captures a central dictum of symbolic interactionism, well put by Harley Shands (1971): "At the point of sophisticated acculturation we find . . . a central paradox: the human being lives in a system which in an important sense lives only in him" (p. 68).

(3) *Families can be assessed in terms of a functioning unit, qua unit, that involves descriptions or ratings of family interaction or accounts of the joint products of family interaction.* This type of family data represent a range of traditions from unobtrusive naturalistic observation to structured family interaction tasks performed in the laboratory under highly controlled conditions. The distinguishing feature of such data is that they are obtained when the relevant group is convened and thus can speak either to the group processes themselves or to the effects of group processes on the individual participants. I suggest that data of this type provide the best grounds for direct statements about "family interaction" or "family functioning."

One simple observation illustrates why it is important to think clearly about these issues when planning future studies. Self-report questionnaires are best used when they provide data about individual attitudes and opinions. What people think and feel about their families is important to know in family and health research. However, how much sense does it make to ask three individuals in a family to offer their perceptions or rate their feelings about something and then add these scores together, divide by three and produce a measure that represents the family as a group? After going through the trouble of selecting items, scaling dimensions, and performing all the psychometric work necessary to produce a reliable and valid questionnaire, why bypass the level of personal responses (the data) in order to compute a spurious average phenomenology of the family? The abandonment of individual scores in favor of a contrived and logically questionable family measure leaves the most interesting and potentially valuable information out of the analysis. Future work would be better served if such information (individual scores) were preserved, patterned, and analyzed to reveal the rich varieties of family composition that we know exist. In the last several years, family researchers have shown an increasing awareness of this issue, and the use of a mean score to represent the family unit in studies based on self-report is declining.

In a different vein, for the same reason it is unwise and unnecessary to characterize a family by means of only one member's appraisal, it is also a gamble to assume that a given family process (or a particular kind of family-centered medical intervention) affects all members in the same way. Differences by gender, generation, birth order, and role in the family system all need to be considered in thinking about variations in family influence.

A good example from the family literature is a study by Bell and Bell (1982) of the effects of family climate on female adolescent maturity. When a subset of girls who scored high on psychological and social measures of maturity were compared with a contrasting group who scored low, from a sample of 99 families participating in the study, low-scoring girls came from families in which scores on scapegoating and cross-generational coalitions were high. It would be tempting to conclude that the types of families that produce girls with low ego development had been identified and described. Yet this would not be true, because a subsequent analysis found the siblings of these low-maturity girls to have relative high maturity scores. These siblings were also less likely to have been involved in cross-generational coalitions.

This suggests that precisely which child and what role relationships within the family make the difference and, in the study of relative adolescent maturity, generalizations about what kinds of families produce what kinds of adolescents would not hold up.

A major challenge for research is the multileveled and multidomained nature of the family construct. Having just discussed the need to be clearer about which level of the construct is being assessed and what sort of data this represents, I will now turn to the problem of choosing aspects of the family to study that are useful in health-related research. For quantitative studies, a crucial question is always what variables to employ.

The assessment of families in most studies in the family and health literature has been restricted in both scope and depth (Fisher et al., 1990). There are some noteworthy exceptions, but, in general, studies have proceeded as though a group of families was assembled only to have blankets thrown over them to conceal the richness and variety of their internal structure and process and their variety of opinions and points of view. Then peepholes would be cut—most often one, but sometimes two—and through these apertures all information representing each family would be gained. This information then stands for the family in whatever analysis is done. In the peephole approach, family members are rarely seen working together or talking with one another. Further, when self-report is the only method of data collection, as it typically is, individual differences among members are usually not recorded. Even when they are, the breadth of the differences assessed is generally limited.

There are serious construct measurement (sampling) problems inherent in these conventions. Consider for a moment that what an investigator finds interesting about families spans several domains, such as beliefs, habits, communication, and organization, and that each of these in turn has several facets describing each domain, such as the clarity, quantity, and distribution of communication when the parents talk to one another. How does the investigator know the family has been adequately measured with the data collected (construct sampling), and, further, what are the grounds for thinking that the aspects chosen shed more light on the research question than other features that describe a family? The common presence of this problem explains in part why correlations between family measures and health are usually low and difficult to interpret, and why studies are so difficult to replicate. Because there is no single best general indicator of family functioning or family member attitude, it is important instead to identify patterns among various family facets, and which facets and which patterns depend upon the particular health questions being asked. The point concerning future work, however, is that one cannot find such patterns through the peephole approach.

AN ILLUSTRATION FROM THE CALIFORNIA FAMILY HEALTH PROJECT

In 1982, the California Family Health Project was convened to begin working on these and other issues in family and health research in a systematic way. A study was designed to address both the logic and the scope of family measurement. With Lawrence Fisher as principal investigator, we obtained an award from the National Institute of Mental Health to study the influence of family functioning on health outcome. This population-based study sampled 225 families in the San Joaquin Valley of California. To be included each family had to have at least two adults and an index adolescent between 13 and 18 years old living in the family home. About 12 hours' worth of information was obtained from each family, including individual questionnaires from everyone in the household; a couple interaction task focused on talking about intimacy, conflict, and loss; and a family problem-solving task requiring family members to work together as they played a beanbag tossing game. The couple and family interaction tasks were videotaped and later coded on many dimensions. In addition, each member completed the RAND Health Assessment Questionnaire (Ware et al., 1984), the Rosenberg Self-Esteem Scale (Rosenberg, 1965), and a brief scale of current work and school activities developed for this study (Fisher, Ransom, Terry, Lipkin, & Weiss, 1992).

The data collection was designed to sample four domains identified from past work as relevant to understanding the family's influence on member health: family structure/organization, family world view, family problem solving, and the expression and management of emotion within the family. Figure 8.1 presents a multidimensional scaling solution of one domain, family structure/organization, for the parents in the study (Fisher, Ransom, Terry, & Burge, in press). The solutions by gender were very similar and thus were combined for the figure.

Multidimensional scaling uses proximities among any kind of objects (questionnaire scale scores, in this instance) as input. The chief output

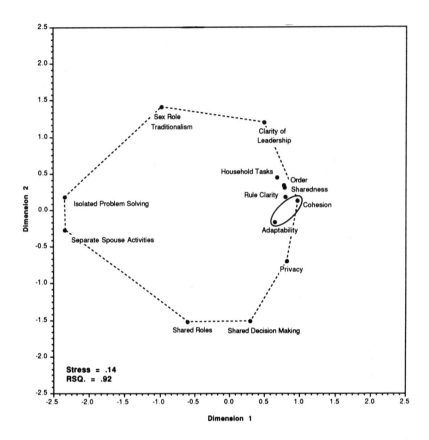

Figure 8.1. MDS Configuration for Family Structure/Organization: California Family Health Project Husbands and Wives

is a set of coordinates that provides the basis for a spatial representation consisting of a geometric configuration of points. MDS plots variables in n-dimensional space, such that the closer in rank the correlation between two variables, the closer they are depicted in graphic representation (Kruskal & Wish, 1978). The result is a picture that is not restricted to portraying linear relationships. The display presented in Figure 8.1 depicts the mutual distance, or similarity, of the 13 structure/organization scales used in our study, in two-dimensional space.

The scales represented here are Adaptability, Cohesion, Rule Clarity, Sharedness, Order, Organization of Household Tasks, Clarity of Leadership, Sex Role Traditionalism, Isolated Problem Solving, Separate Spouse Activities, Shared Roles, Shared Decision Making, and Personal Privacy. If structure/organization is thought of as a domain, each of the scales in the graphic measures some facet of that domain, and their mutual relationship, the shape, portrays information about both the empirical structure of the domain and how well it was sampled by the scales employed.

In the language of Louis Guttman, the shape of family structure/organization approximates a "circumplex" (Canter, 1985; Shye, 1978). In a circumplex, values in the cells of the correlation matrix are highest along the diagonals and opposite corners, lowest in the mid-region, and high between adjacent items. A circle without big gaps means that all regions of the domain are well represented and that the sampling process is adequate. Guttman's interpretation of circumplex relations is that qualitatively different variables in a given domain have an order among themselves, but without a conceptual beginning or end point.

Figure 8.1 illustrates the scope of assessment problem discussed above. The Family Adaptability and Cohesion Evaluation Scales, better known by the acronym FACES (Olson, Russell, & Sprenkle, 1983; Olson, Sprenkle, & Russell, 1979), is a standardized questionnaire aimed at finding out how persons think and feel about certain aspects of their families. Through its three editions, FACES has become the most widely used assessment device in the family and health literature. Its items compose two scales, Family Adaptability and Family Cohesion. Family Adaptability aims to measure the extent to which a family system is flexible and able to change, and Family Cohesion assesses the degree to which family members report being separated or connected to their family. The bipolar Cohesion scale, when transformed into two unipolar ends to form an Enmeshment scale and a Disengagement scale, has worked well in illness studies. The Adaptability scale also has been useful, depending upon what illness or recovery dimension is involved. The joining of Adaptability and Cohesion into a single bivariate score that classifies a family in terms of the circumplex model has generally been less successful than using the scales separately. We included FACES II in our study along with seven scales from the California Family Life Scales, developed for our study, and four additional scales selected from other work (Fisher et al., in press).

As can be seen in Figure 8.1, Adaptability and Cohesion appear at about 3 o'clock and 3:30 on the circumplex ring. They are quite close to each other, their product-moment correlation being .70. They associate well with our health measures, on balance, higher than the other scales used in the structure/organization set. The point for this discussion, however, is that, in relation to the domain of family structure/organization, the two scales sample only a small region. Furthermore, this particular domain is only one of four in our study and only one of several others that could have been chosen. This example illustrates how the exclusive reliance on the FACES instrument affords only a peephole of the kind referred to above. This is not a criticism of the instrument, but simply a caveat, graphically illustrated.

Low budgets and practical necessities often curtail aims to assess families extensively. It is not reasonable to expect that every office-based study will conduct a major multidimensional and multileveled assessment of the families involved. My aim in taking up this discussion is simply to mobilize opinion toward pursuing two objectives. The first is to increase the level of support for family research centers so that more time and energy can be invested in large-scale studies designed to identify and measure family domains of relevance to health and health care. The second is to increase the general level of awareness of the methodological issues involved, so that we will no longer see studies based on one questionnaire given to one family member that draw conclusions about "family functioning" and health.

THE SHIFT FROM VARIABLES TO SUBJECTS

If family and health investigators are to produce research that is more vivid and useful to clinicians in the future, they will need to shift from the near-exclusive convention of doing "variable-centered" research to also doing "family-" and "person-centered" studies. Most clinicians are unaware that there is a "variable-centered" versus "case-centered" issue in research design and analysis. They generally assume that all research conclusions apply to the subjects on whom the data were originally collected rather than to the sample as a whole—a kind of imaginary subject—on which the analysis is performed. The statistical analysis, in the great majority of studies, is performed on group means and on the correlation matrix of the variables measured for the set of subjects, in which the variables are the units of analysis, not the cases (i.e., persons or families). This distinction does not amount to much practically when only one "independent" variable is measured. For example, if you ask 100 subjects the question, How satisfied are you with your family life? the responses can be scaled from 0 to 5 and the data can be analyzed as a continuous variable in relation to, say, the number of visits to the doctor in the last year. The conclusions about "high" and "low" satisfaction and frequency of physician visits based on the group means can be thought of in terms of the individuals without a breach in logic. People at one end of the continuum can be thought of as satisfied, and those at the other end, dissatisfied. The switch from thinking in terms of variables to thinking in terms of subjects is automatic because it is the score on one variable that locates the subject. Conclusions couched in language such as "People who express dissatisfaction with their families are more likely to visit their family doctors" have meaning to the clinician.

But in multivariate research designs, which are now rapidly surpassing univariate studies, the situation is different and potentially problematic. Imagine a large sample of subjects measured on three additional continuous family variables that might influence physician visits instead of just the one, and that all four contribute significantly to a multiple regression analysis. Imagine further that the four variables together form a predictive equation that accounts for a quarter of the variance in visits to the doctor ($R^2 = .50$). It is natural to think, as in the single-variable example above, that persons who are dissatisfied with their families, as well as who score high on b and c and low on d, have higher utilization rates. But the regression equation does not model the individuals as discrete units in the analysis; it works on the variables across all subjects taken as a group. The intuitive translation from the variables to the subjects is inappropriate. In fact, it is possible, though unlikely, that no single subject in the entire sample can be described meaningfully in terms of the regression model.

To be confident in speaking in terms of individuals, or families, the units entered in the analysis must be individuals or families. This is not the case in multiple regression and path analysis, in which equations provide the best prediction or model for the sample as a whole. The regression approach to modeling may be optimal for use by the public health officer or the national policymaker, but clinicians see patients one by one and in many situations benefit more from conclusions that can be described in terms of actual patients, instead of in terms of sample or population tendencies (i.e., variables). This immediately suggests a need to enrich our research options, adding to the variable-centered tradition by searching for ways to create case-centered approaches for primary care research, types of cases that could be referred to as "kinds of people" or "kinds of families," a reference that fits the clinician's frame of mind.

There are at least five approaches to constructing typologies that hold promise for the family and health investigator. Each supplies families rather than variables as units for statistical analysis.

(1) Observe family interaction and classify the interacting unit according to a set of predefined criteria. A good example is Ainsworth's (1982; Ainsworth, Blehar, Waters, & Wall, 1978) attachment classification system, in which samples of interaction were used to designate mother-infant attachment systems: Group A, "anxious/avoidant"; Group B, "secure"; and Group C, "anxious/ambivalent." Another good example is Steinglass et al.'s (1987) work with alcoholic families. Exploring the notion of "family temperament," these researchers were able to classify families according to whether they were "high" or "low" in terms of "energy level," had "less" or "more" permeable boundaries in terms of "preferred interactional distance," and were "inflexible" or "flexible" in terms of their "behavioral range," based on coded observations of family interaction in the home. Various combinations of these three dimensions produce qualitatively vastly different family temperaments. Families could further be distinguished according to "family identity" or "shared system of belief." Drawing on Reiss's (1981) concept of the "family paradigm," Steinglass et al. show that families with similar temperaments can be quite different when family identity is introduced as a conditional dimension. Several family "types," classifiable through observing behavior in the home in terms of these two principal sets of "regulatory structures," can be shown to differ dramatically in the difference drinking makes, and how drinking is handled over time. These differences, in turn, have implications for both primary care and alcoholism treatment programs.

(2) Choose a point on a continuous variable and draw a distinction by which families can be classified. This is usually not recommended with continuous variables and makes no sense in univariate studies because information and power are lost in the conversion from continuous to categorical scores. But when several continuous variables are used in a contingency table, drawing cutoff levels for each one can form a classification scheme in which conditional relationships among scores provide the basis for identifying families. Olson's circumplex model is based on the cross-tabulation of two variables, adaptability and cohesion, although in three editions of FACES, the questionnaire on which the model has been tested, the scales seem to work better for health

outcomes when they are broken out separately (e.g., Ramsey, Abell, & Baker, 1986; Reeb, Graham, Zyzanski, & Kitson, 1987). A better example from the family and health literature is David Reiss's (1981) classification of "family paradigms" based on the pattern of family behavior during the card sort procedure. Three scaled dimensions, "configuration," "coordination," and "closure," when divided into "high"- and "low"-scoring families, can be structured into a contingency table that produces eight possible types for subsequent analysis. Three of the eight logical possibilities emerge empirically and form the basis for model testing: "environment-sensitive," "interpersonal distance-sensitive," and "consensus-sensitive" types of families. The value of systems such as this and that of Steinglass et al. (1987), mentioned above, is that they capture varieties of family beliefs and dispositions to behave that can differentiate among families according to pattern and style, rather than simply rate variables that apply to families on a dimension that usually reduces to an index of "good" or "bad" features. Although difficult to demonstrate, such an approach allows for the possibility that different family types are associated with different outcomes for different problems or illnesses. Reiss is one of the few researchers so far able to identify such contingent relations (see Reiss & Klein, 1987).

(3) Perform a cluster analysis on the cases of the variable correlation matrix in order to reduce the number of family members or families in the sample to a smaller set with similar profiles. Cluster analysis programs use a range of algorithms that group people or families into homogeneous classes on the basis of their similarities (Lorr, 1983). The cluster solution produces empirical types that can be entered into subsequent analysis and confirmed or modified in future studies, if they prove useful. As Filsinger (1990) has recently pointed out, the logic of typological thinking is underappreciated, and cluster analysis is underutilized in family studies. In discussing taxonometric methods in health psychology, Filsinger and Karoly (1985) note: "The typological approach stresses that what is important for the functioning of the organism is the unique combination of characteristics which the organism possesses; . . . it is the typological approach which preserves the unity of the organism" (p. 378). The same thing can be said of families, only the complexity of classification is even greater, considering the kinds of issues raised in the middle section of this chapter.

All of the major mainframe statistical packages offer clustering routines, and there are also good programs available for both IBM-compatible and Macintosh desktop computers.

(4) Perform a Q- rather than an R-factor analysis of the data matrix, thereby operating on the subjects instead of the variables (McKeown & Thomas, 1988). When the data matrix is transposed, the cases of observation become the columns while the "measures" of those cases become the rows. An analysis can then be performed that produces a reduced set of factored subjects instead of the more familiar reduced set of factored variables. The logic of this technique is based on the premise that all observations in Q technique are related to a common underlying unit of measurement, namely, "self-significance" (Stephenson, 1953) (or, for our purposes, family significance). The common metric is the degree of salience or applicability to the case of any item or descriptor in the array of variables employed. The resulting factors can be considered as heuristic types and entered into subsequent analyses that preserve the cases (persons or families) as units in the analytic process.

This is a useful exploratory technique that can be applied to many multivariate data sets to complement or provide a contrast for the R analyses undertaken. Simply perform a Q principal components analysis on a data set, and if the solution is a good one and the profiles of subjects loading on common components make sense, see if the groupings are associated with other variables under investigation in ways that are interesting and offer insights unavailable in conventional variable-centered analyses.

(5) Develop a Q sample of stimulus statements that cover an area of research interest, conduct Q sorts on a set of persons or families, group those subjects according to similar profiles, and enter the set of prospective "types" as units in subsequent analyses. The Q-sort technique, proposed by Stephenson (1953) and elaborated by Block (1961), provides a means to transform a diverse array of qualitative information into a standard quantitative format. It begins by compiling a deck of cards, each containing a statement or descriptor that captures some facet of the domain to be studied. The specific content of the items is tailored to the purposes of the research at hand. Thus a deck can be compiled to describe family qualities or health behavior of interest to the clinician, in which the family is the referent; or a set of items can be compiled that describes important aspects of the interaction between the doctor and the patient, in which the doctor-patient relationship is the referent. Unlike using questionnaires or rating scales, in which each item is rated from 1 to 5 by the subject or the researcher, the Q-sort technique requires a forced distribution in which each statement or descriptor is

placed into a series of piles ranging from most to least salient for each subject in question.

Q decks can be built on logical/conceptual grounds by designing items that cover all areas of a priori interest to the investigator, so that a given number of items applies to each facet of a mapped conceptual domain, or they can be built more empirically by simply attempting to cover a known area with an adequate set of items. A good example of the latter approach from the family and health literature is Dakof and Mendelsohn's (1989) investigation of patterns of adaptation to Parkinson's disease. A brief discussion of this work provides a good illustration of the suggestion that we should be engaging in more studies that combine qualitative and quantitative methods.

Dakof and Mendelsohn's study began with three in-depth interviews held in the home of each of 44 Parkinson's patients; sample members ranged in age from 50 to 80. The first interview was held jointly with both members of the couple, the second was held with the patient alone, and the third was held with the spouse alone. A content analysis was then performed on audiotape recordings of 20 randomly selected cases. Q-deck items were then written to cover the range of content and condense the narrative accounts into pithy descriptors. Additional items drawn from a Q sort developed for use with cancer patients (Mendelsohn, 1979; Mendelsohn, de la Tour, Coudin, & Raveau, 1984), and items suggested by previous research on stress, coping, and chronic illness (e.g., Antonovsky, 1979; Kobasa, 1979; Lazarus & Folkman, 1984; Taylor, 1983; Turk, 1979) were then added to the item pool. After appropriate statistical analysis, a 95-item Q-sort deck was retained. Examples of items include the following: for affective reactions to the disease, "Is angry and embittered"; for personal relationships, "Social contact with friends and family is a source of enjoyment"; and for social role functioning, "Maintains family responsibilities effectively." After listening to the three tape-recorded interviews, two independent judges sorted the items into nine categories from "most characteristic" to "least characteristic" of the patient in question, with the following required distribution: 5, 7, 11, 15, 19, 15, 11, 7, 5. Each item for each person then received a score between 1 (least characteristic) and 9 (most characteristic). In this approach the judge must make comparisons between items rather than between subjects; that is, the Q sort is an "ipsative" rather than a "normative" method (Mendelsohn, 1979). Thus the configuration of descriptive items becomes central and the particular organization of attributes forms patterns that describe the uniqueness of persons or couples or whatever unit is in focus.

The next step was to correlate each patient's composite Q sort with the composite Q sort of every other patient. (It is important to remember that these Q correlations measure the degree of association between the array of item scores of persons, whereas correlations typically are used to determine the degree of relationship between variables.) The resulting matrix of between-patient correlations was then subjected to principal components analysis, which was used as a guide for the formation of clusters. Four clusters or groups or "types" of patients were identified: "sanguine and engaged," "depressed and worried," "depressed and misunderstood," and "passive and resigned." These cluster assignments were then employed as units for subsequent analysis. As the reader can imagine, these categories represent very different kinds of people, and the results showed considerable variation in the ways in which the Parkinson patients and their spouses adapted to their illness. Because the discussion of results is centered on patients and not variables, this sort of study is vivid and is couched in terms that are accessible and potentially useful to the clinician.

To sum up, the virtue of the Q sort is that it produces a unique description of each subject, but the use of a standard descriptive language permits systematic comparisons between subjects. Through the use of conventional correlational techniques, the degree of similarity in the overall pattern of description between any two subjects can be estimated. It is also possible to treat each item as a variable in its own right and to ascertain the relationship of item scores to other variables of interest (Mendelsohn, 1979). Thus, for person- or family-centered research, the Q-sort technique provides a means through which the pattern of qualities and behaviors that make up each patient can be represented while, at the same time, generalizations can be established.

This ability to capture quality and pattern provides the rationale for the use of Q methodology and puts a new twist on the qualitative versus quantitative methods debate. What I am advocating here complements Stein's (1990) suggestion that "good 'emic' description and interpretation foster the construction of good 'etic' theory" (self report, see p. 68) (p. 12). It also complements Blake's (1989) suggestion that we need qualitative descriptions to identify context and meaning to better understand both prototypical cases predicted by quantitative methods and outliers that defy variable models. I am suggesting that a hybrid approach worth pursuing is to perform qualitative analysis with quantitative methods. My point is simply that conventional quantitative approaches may help us to predict the value of one variable by knowing the scores on other variables, but what is lost is the focus on the whole set of indices that capture the conditional and contingent relationships of descriptors that characterize the uniqueness of a given case, whether that case is a person, a couple, a family, or any other social unit (Filsinger, 1990). It is the wholeness of the unit under investigation that carries the unique identity for which it is known and that is essential for understanding its functioning (Pearse & Crocker, 1943).

IS FAMILY-CENTERED CARE MORE EFFECTIVE?

Family medicine has perhaps unnecessarily undertaken the responsibility of proving that its methods and approach to patients are more effective than what is conventionally called the "individual" approach (see, for example, Schmidt, 1987). This position implicitly assumes that the individual approach has already been spelled out and proved effective, an assumption that may not be warranted. Many standard approaches to patient care have not been routinely subjected to systematic comparison, nor are they always supported by research evidence. They prevail because they have become conventional ways of behaving within an established group. Of course, a context-oriented primary care should study its practices systematically and make every effort to produce research of the highest quality. But there is no need or good reason to wait until a "family-centered" approach has been proved "more effective" than an "individual" approach.

I am wary of this "needing to prove to proceed" position for three reasons. First is the problem of commensurate "outcomes" introduced earlier. What desirable outcomes over what period of time are actually being sought? A second issue is the more immediate question of preferred styles of intervening and doctoring. Talking with family members to influence the care of a patient is not like prescribing an untried drug. If a family physician decides a patient has hypertension and wants to prescribe a change in diet and exercise along with taking pills, should he or she really hesitate to meet with the person in the family who does most of the grocery shopping and food preparation, or resist bringing in the entire household to review what hypertension is, why it must be treated, and how the suggestions being made are supposed to help, simply because there is no proof that this approach is effective? I think not (Ransom, 1987).

My third concern over the "wait for proof" point of view is that the payoff rationally expected from such a position is based on a mistaken notion of how everyday science normally progresses (Kuhn, 1970). I doubt that even if research "proves" convening the family is useful for many kinds of problems, the typical internist or cardiologist will change his or her style of practice. Perhaps a new generation of family physicians will, but not primarily because of the research evidence. It will be because of a socially constructed change in the sense of professional identity that includes seeing families as part of everyday practice.

For the same reasons that I think we should not adopt a "wait and see" attitude, I also think we should not be intimidated by those who say that only prospective research is worthwhile or that clinical studies without control groups are useless. Such designs are desirable, but they are necessary only for certain kinds of studies that are often expensive and difficult to conduct. Again, we should be rigorous and strive to collect trustworthy data, but at this stage of development, creativity and exploration are as necessary to the successful future of family-centered health research as are tight controls and statistical analyses that strive primarily for significant p values and secondarily for new insights and understanding. Likewise, we need good "sawdust" research as much as we need well-funded studies whose designs are set down well ahead of collecting the data (for a good example of "sawdust" research, see the study by Huygen, van den Hoogen, van Eijk, & Smits, 1989).

CONCLUSION

In this chapter, I have reviewed some implications that the special nature of primary care and family study holds for the design of future research and have made suggestions for some directions that research might take. The ambitious scope of practice combined with the multi-leveled and multifaceted nature of families creates investigative challenges that we have only begun to address. As our efforts mature beyond frameworks supplied by those who have taught us, we might be able to shift our analytic focus from variables to persons and families and provide answers to questions in terms that are useful to the world of everyday practice.

NINE

Comments on Methods:
The Family in Primary Care

WALTER W. ROSSER

The three preceding chapters on methodology question the role of the family systems concept in family medicine research and outline methodological problems involved in the study of the impact of illness on the health of individuals and families. The methodological problems of researching the role of the family in health care are highlighted by the different approaches taken by the authors.

Maurine Venters raises questions about the lack of appropriate definitions of *family, family involvement,* and *family care*. The approach to analysis she discusses could be described in two ways: as the single-cause, single-effect model of analyzing the family or as the social epidemiological approach to analysis. These approaches have been discussed by Tom Campbell as describing the family as an "ethologic factor" in health and illness, to be rigorously defined, measured across populations, and manipulated by physicians (Doherty & Campbell, 1988). This approach to research is the most rigorous and the most productive in demonstrating a clear association between social support and decreased mortality (Broadhead et al., 1983).

Venters's chapter outlines problems with the current definitions of the family as a unit of care. Her review of studies of families reveals that the few studies that have been conducted used different definitions of *family* and have detected that only between 20% and 45% of persons

AUTHOR'S NOTE: I would like to acknowledge the assistance of Dr. Lorne Becker in the preparation of this chapter.

attending family practices receive care as a family unit. From this review it is clear that more standardized, valid, and reliable measures of family care are needed to make progress in measuring the extent of family care if the approach is to describe the family as an ethologic factor in health and illness.

Venters expresses the view that until these definitions are improved, important questions that need answering will go unanswered. For instance, Is family care beneficial or detrimental to health? Can preventive programs be more effective if introduced with a family systems orientation? Are rehabilitation programs more effective when the family environment is considered? Although these questions are important, Donald Ransom would argue that they are too broad to be answerable.

In Chapter 8, Ransom argues that the unit of analysis should be the subject. "Family" interventions may vary from clinical problem to clinical problem, and thus there may be no global answer for the question, Is family-centered care beneficial? The answer may come from different, specific family interventions for different problems, such as intervention with the other smokers in the family for an individual smoker who wishes to stop, rather than the more general approach. Ransom's approach to analysis of family interventions is in sharp contrast to Venters's socioepidemiological analysis.

Ransom and Stein both argue for a family systems approach moving from the more linear cause-and-effect approach. Ransom supports a shift from looking at multiple subjects using a limited number of variables to looking at variables using multidimensional scaling techniques showing the interrelationships among variables. This allows identification of individuals with a specific constellation of variables that could be described as a syndrome. Although this is more appealing to physicians, since they can identify patients with similar constellations (syndromes), the research output using this approach has been somewhat disappointing.

Ransom peels off the layers of methodological complexity involved in research on the impact of a family on an individual. He is pessimistic about the reductionist direction of the medical model, and states the need for much more qualitative input into the methodology that we use. He argues this point:

> But when we think of the family as a unit of care in this broader sense, together with the ambitious aims and responsibilities of modern family practice, we catch a glimpse of why we cannot confine ourselves to studying

only the sorts of variables and outcomes that are of interest to our sub-specialty colleagues. Neither should we adopt models of studying practice that assume that all doctors and all patients are interchangeable or that are not interested in the effects of intervention with one person on another.

He further illustrates the layers of complexity of methodological issues when he says:

> It is this sort of example that leads me to suggest that the "individual-ori-ented primary care" versus "family-centered primary care" distinction may be misplaced. The greater contrast is between disease- or procedure-fo-cused and person-focused approaches, instead of between individual and family approaches. If *individual* means person, then taking the person seriously and fully necessarily means including significant other people and relationships in that person's life.

Who, how, and what difference the procedure focus versus a person focus makes are good questions for researchers to pursue. Ransom's list of 11 reasons supporting the study of family impact on individuals provides convincing support for his view. His arguments about the difficulties in analysis and methodology not only apply to assessing family systems but are mirrored by the complexity of fully studying many of the important questions in family practice. I would argue that the distinction between family systems approach and family medicine research is yet another artificial barrier, as the two are concurrent.

Ransom provides persuasive support that the unit of analysis in studies of family systems should not be variables, which are traditionally used as the unit of analysis in both qualitative and quantitative methodology, but subjects. He says we cannot assume that we have developed the appropriate methodology to study the individual in family practice and thus are ready to develop new methods for family systems analysis. One might suggest that methodology development need not be sequential but should develop in parallel, and new methods required are not exclusive but an integral part of a new research paradigm.

In Chapter 7, Howard Stein provides us with a brilliant argument for the use of qualitative approaches in the research that is required to answer questions about family systems. He states:

> Our methods must include insight into both the part we play and the subject. The insider/outsider, or observed/observer, distinction draws our attention to unstated assumptions and meanings that both researchers-practitioners-

teachers and patients-families-communities-cultures bring to health and sickness behavior.

The fact that every interaction involves two perspectives on a problem begs the issue of bringing the views closer together, allowing each of the involved parties to learn from the other.

From the scientific viewpoint, solo patient viewpoints of their own family functioning may well be wrong. However, an insider viewpoint helps the researcher or practitioner to enlist patient and family stories, to recognize their limitations, and to be able to negotiate broader family input for better understanding of problems. Stein provides a very eloquent argument for the incorporation of the principles of family systems research using ethnographic methodology, not only into research, but also into our daily practice.

A major problem is the medical model and the reductionist organ-centered approach to medical diagnosis and management and the resistance to a patient-centered biopsychosocial approach. Stein shares Ransom's pessimism about the future because of the current resistance to incorporating ethnographic concepts into either our daily practice or our research efforts. However, Ian McWhinney (1986) proposes that we are in the midst of a paradigm shift that is evolving through the 1990s, shifting from a medical to a biopsychosocial model. Implicit in such a shift will be the integrated use of quantitative research methodology with qualitative strategies. On an optimistic note, one might ask, How can we not include qualitative approaches when attempting to answer practical questions in family medicine research? We might further question how we mindlessly embrace the randomized control trial as our purest research methodology with the knowledge that the method was originally developed to determine which different strains of wheat seeds would grow best under constant conditions. This is not to argue against the use of the randomized controlled trial, but to argue for its cautious use answering questions based on a deep understanding of human behavior.

Since the very name of our discipline is based on the assumption that provision of health care to a family as a unit is more effective than care to individuals, Green, Eriksen, and Schor (1990) ask the question, "How can a discipline with the word family in its name exclude the family systems approach from its research agenda?" (p. 108). During the last few years there has been much rhetoric about prevention and health promotion through improved life-styles. It is difficult to imagine how programs promoting life-style changes such as lowering dietary fat content or smoking cessation can be administered to isolated individuals independent of their "family" environments. Yet, lacking the appropriate measurement tools, most, if not all, problems are assessed using the individual as the unit and do not include measurement of the impact of or on "the family," however defined. Raising these questions, which we should not ignore if our discipline is to remain credible, pressures us to consider which of the three approaches should be favored: the social epidemiological approach, the family systems approach, or the ethnographic approach.

The social epidemiological approach is soundest in output but is not as easily converted to clinical practice as the family systems approach of Donald Ransom, which has yet to yield convincing results. The ethnographic approach should probably be incorporated into the family physician's daily work.

Those of us who have attempted to answer questions relevant to prevention or management of common problems in family medicine know that ignoring or excluding consideration of the family influence on illness behavior as measured by qualitative methods risks a major pitfall. Although a question may be superficially appropriate and the quantitative methodological design of the study fundable, not considering qualitative methods during question development may result in an answer that will come up short. The answer will lack the depth of understanding of human behavior that a practitioner who has followed patients for 15 or 20 years can rapidly detect. The researcher will realize that the question may have been technically answered, but the shallowness of the methodology and the lack of consideration of the family and contextual variables in which the illness or preventive procedure occurs provide an unsatisfactory answer.

A colleague recently described an excellent example of this phenomenon. He developed an intensive program to provide support to recently widowed men. The individuals were subjected to a battery of valid and reliable psychological tests and then randomly allocated to control and intervention groups. Assessment for their psychological well-being occurred again after the intervention using the same psychological tests, and there was no difference in test results between the intervention and control groups. In desperation, he tried a "focus group" approach to reassess both groups and found that quite dramatic differences were readily detectable. The use of such unconventional methods made it difficult for him to get the study published (Tudiver, Hilditch, & Permaul, 1991). Experienced family physician researchers have become so cognizant of this situation that it has been a frequent topic at research meetings during the last 2 years, and a book on the need for qualitative and quantitative approaches as a foundation for family medicine research has been produced (Norton, Stewart, Tudiver, Bass, & Dunn, 1991).

This story supports the collective contention of Venters, Ransom, and Stein that much needs to be done. We should be grateful to these three authors for critiquing three methodological approaches to studying the family. The ethnographic, family systems, and socioepidemiological approaches will all contribute to the improvement of available methodology for studying the impact of interventions on family health. What we now require are new measurement instruments that are created from the strength of established methods rather than as an amalgam of what we now know.

Beyond being more innovative and creative in developing new measurement instruments from a broad base of anthropology, sociology, or psychology, we also need to incorporate into the psyches of all family physicians the ethnographic approach to gaining an understanding of patients, their values and meaning attached to health. The patient's context clearly has an effect on his or her health and well-being. Those of us with educational responsibilities have a duty to make these principles an integral part of our postgraduate training programs, as well as to convince our practicing colleagues of the importance of these principles in understanding how we can be of maximum benefit to the patients we care for in our practices.

It is clear that striving for a new method of studying the family system has the potential reward of significantly deepening our understanding of how physician innovations affect individuals and their significant others. The product of research developments should be improved health for the entire population.

PART III

Education

TEN

Different Portraits of Medical Practice: Model Conflict in Training Physicians to "Think Family"

DIANA McLAIN SMITH

The possibility of integrating a family perspective into the practice of medicine has captured the interest of many in the medical profession. Particularly in the area of family medicine, researchers are showing that by "thinking family," physicians can improve their evaluation and treatment of presenting complaints (Rogers & Durkin, 1984; Sawa, Henderson, Pablo, & Falk, 1985), develop a better understanding of how family factors are related to the etiology and maintenance of illness (Crouch & McCauley, 1985; Guttman & Steinert, 1987), provide early detection of psychosocial problems (Bishop, Epstein, et al., 1984; Lesser, 1981; Sawa et al., 1985), and more effectively prevent and treat illness (Rogers & Durkin, 1984; Sawa, 1988; Sawa et al., 1985).

No physician would deny the value of these outcomes. The ability to prevent, accurately diagnose, and effectively treat patients' illnesses is the very essence of the medical profession as it is now conceived. Yet few physicians take a family perspective in their practices. In fact, most researchers find that physicians do not involve themselves in family matters even when patients might desire it (Hansen, Bobula, Meyer, Kushner, & Pridham, 1987), that they do not elicit much information about family factors (Crouch & McCauley, 1985), and that they tend to overlook psychosocial problems that can have strong effects on the health of patients and their families, such as excessive alcohol use or incapacitating illness (Rogers & Durkin, 1984). So, despite its promise, the idea of "thinking family" has not yet taken hold.

This gap between potential promise and current reality has spawned a number of well-regarded training programs in family work (e.g., Bishop, Byles, & Horn, 1984; Bishop, Epstein, et al., 1984; Epstein & Bishop, 1981; Guttman & Steinert, 1987; Lesser, 1981; Sawa, 1988; Sawa & Goldenberg, 1988; Sawa et al., 1985; Weston, 1987). Recently, research on these programs has revealed an intriguing puzzle: Once back at the office, physicians used what was taught in ways that "differed markedly" from the models and techniques "prescribed" by the trainers (Bishop, Epstein, et al., 1984, p. 384; Guttman & Steinart, 1987; Lesser, 1981; McLean & Miles, 1975; Weston, 1987).

This chapter takes a look at this puzzle in light of (a) the pedagogical principles that underlie most professional training programs, (b) what happens when these principles are used to train physicians to practice medicine from a family perspective, and (c) some additional principles to consider—principles that are designed to deepen and further learning about and from different models of medical practice.

PRINCIPLES, PUZZLES, AND POSSIBILITIES

It is not easy to figure out what it means to "take a family perspective." Some think it means recognizing psychosocial problems and referring families elsewhere. Others see it as a way of managing only those illnesses that affect the entire family. And still others define it as a way of working with families to ameliorate family dysfunctions related to medical problems.[1] But while definitions might vary, almost everyone agrees that at a minimum, it requires thinking and acting in ways that enable physicians to elicit, recognize, and understand how family factors affect the health and illness of their patients.

Some Pedagogical Principles

With this view in mind, a variety of family practitioners have set out to train physicians to take a family perspective. Since the pioneering McMaster work, most of these programs have subscribed to a similar set of pedagogical principles that might be summarized as follows:

(1) Provide family models and interventions that are time efficient, effective with families, and clinically relevant, that is, behavior and problem focused (Crouch & McCauley, 1985; Epstein & Bishop, 1981; Guttman & Steinert, 1987; Lesser, 1981; Sawa, 1988; Sawa & Goldenberg, 1988).

(2) Get institutional support for the training and its use in practice (Bishop, Byles, & Horn, 1984; Guttman & Steinert, 1987).

(3) Make the goals and objectives of the training clear and define each step in the training process in an achievable and logical sequence (Bishop, Byles, & Horn, 1984; Cleghorn & Levin, 1973; Guttman & Steinert, 1987).

(4) Design the training so that it is skill oriented and takes into account the progressive stages of skills acquisition, moving from conceptual understanding to intervention with less to more difficult families (Bishop, Byles, & Horn, 1984; Cleghorn & Levin, 1973; Guttman & Steinert, 1987; Lesser, 1981; Weston, 1987).

(5) Provide both theory and the opportunity to discuss the theory (Bishop, Byles, & Horn, 1984; Guttman & Steinert, 1987; Sawa & Goldenberg, 1988).

(6) Model the new thinking and skills and provide opportunities for learners to practice the new model in a variety of situations, from role plays to actual family cases (Bishop, Byles, & Horn, 1984; Guttman & Steinert, 1987; Lesser, 1981; Sawa & Goldenberg, 1988).

(7) Provide trainees with detailed feedback from both the trainers and their peers (Bishop, Byles, & Horn, 1984; Guttman & Steinert, 1987; Lesser, 1981; Sawa & Goldenberg, 1988).

(8) Create group processes that facilitate the learning of the new skills (Bishop, Byles, & Horn, 1984; Lesser, 1981; Sawa & Goldenberg, 1988).

The pedagogical theory behind these principles goes something like this: If a program provides an ecologically valid model that is skill based and clearly articulated, and if learners can discuss and read about the model in theory, see it modeled by an expert, and rehearse its skills in progressive stages in a peer-group context, then the learners should acquire the new skills for use in their own practice.[2] This theory is consistent with the most recent research on learning and instruction (see Glaser, 1990, for an excellent overview). To synthesize briefly, this research construes learning as a social and cognitive process (Greeno, 1989) through which learners acquire the domain-specific knowledge, cognitive structures, and problem-solving skills that permit the competent performance of some task in a particular task environment (Glaser, 1990). To foster what they call "skill acquisition," almost all of these programs emphasize the need for modeling, practice, and a group setting that fosters "joint negotiation for understanding" (Glaser, 1990, p. 32). Within this view, the ultimate sign of success is competence that continues independent of the instructor—an outcome contingent on the transfer of responsibility from instructor to student for achieving the task's goal (see Belmont, 1989). At this point, the theory proposes, learners can maintain and appropriately generalize new knowledge without "hints, explanations, and demonstrations" from the teacher. And so it is at this point that we can say a student has learned (Belmont, 1989, p. 145).

The McMaster training model illustrates well the principles embedded in this approach to learning. Within this model, trainers teach a problem-centered and behavior-focused model that speaks to and builds on physicians' current activities and competencies (Epstein, Bishop, & Baldwin, 1982; Lesser, 1981). They clearly articulate their goals and a logical sequence for achieving them (Bishop, Byles, & Horn, 1984). They take a skill-oriented approach, distinguishing three sets of skills and a logical stage sequence for learning them (i.e., perceptual, conceptual, and executive skills). They model the skills to be learned and provide opportunities for practicing them under different circumstances (Bishop, Byles, & Horn, 1984; Bishop, Epstein, et al., 1984). They make sure that learners get detailed feedback (Bishop, Byles, & Horn, 1984). And finally, they try to use group processes to support and facilitate the learning of the new skills (Bishop, Byles, & Horn, 1984).

Some Puzzling Surprises

With a sound theoretical base and many opportunities to convert "know what" into "know how," the McMaster model has succeeded in many ways well documented in the literature (see Bishop, Byles, & Horn, 1984; Guttman & Steinert, 1987; Sawa & Goldenberg, 1988; Sawa et al., 1985). At the same time, trainers have also come across a number of intriguing surprises. For instance, McLean and Miles (1975) discovered that physicians trained in family work found it difficult to structure and control their contact with couples (cited in Bishop, Epstein, et al., 1984). Similarly, Lesser (1981) found that their physicians had difficulty in confronting patients, in giving up control over the patient-doctor agenda, and in speaking in descriptive language that was relatively concrete and minimally value laden. A few years later, Bishop, Epstein, et al. (1984) observed that their physicians used "the skills they had learned . . . [but] not in a systematic and documented way." Instead, they "applied informal treatment intervention in an irregular fashion." And finally, Guttman and Steinert (1987) discovered that their residents discarded family interviewing techniques except when faced with interpersonal problems.

These surprises soon sparked an interest in the puzzle: What makes it difficult for physicians to learn and use the models and techniques as prescribed by the trainers? So far, most researchers offer three explanations, which I refer to below as contextual, methodological, and paradigmatic.[3]

Some Pieces to the Puzzle

The contextual explanation understands the learning problem as one of poor fit between model and context. In this view, learning is diluted by contextual factors that make transfer of the family model problematic. Those who take this view suggest that either the context or the model should be changed to achieve a better fit. For example, they advise trainers and physicians to seek better institutional support (Bishop, Byles, & Horn, 1984; Guttman & Steinert, 1987); they tell trainers to redesign their models to fit practice constraints, such as time pressures and caseload size (Hochheiser & Chapados, 1985); they suggest ways to change patient expectancies by using techniques that signal a different doctor-patient relationship (Hansen et al., 1987; Rogers & Durkin, 1984; Steinert & Rosenberg, 1987); and they recommend that doctors reduce their caseloads to make more time for family-related activities (Bishop & Epstein, 1985).

The methodological explanation comes at the same puzzle from a different angle. From this perspective, physicians do not use the prescribed models because they are idealized models based on the "reconstructed methods of reasoning" used by exemplary practitioners in family work (P. E. Johnson, 1983; Rogers & Cohn, 1987). This method relies on exemplars' plausible, but often inaccurate, accounts of what they think they do across a range of cases. As a result, we end up with models that articulate relatively general and abstract rules that, while elegant, are quite disconnected from how they actually think and act in particular cases (P. E. Johnson, 1983). So no wonder physicians deviate from the models taught during the training. The exemplars do too! (see Rogers, chap. 11, this volume, for an excellent account of this problem).

The paradigmatic explanation takes yet a different cut at the puzzle. From this perspective, the problem is one of conflicting paradigms. In learning to "think family," physicians bump up against, and meet internal resistance from, the dominant biomedical paradigm already learned and internalized. Researchers who see the puzzle this way speak of it in strikingly similar terms. Without exception, they say that learning requires "a quantum leap," "paradigmatic shift," or "a major and significant shift in thinking" between "radically different frames of reference" (Bishop & Epstein, 1985; Guttman & Steinert, 1987; Hochheiser & Chapados, 1985; Lesser, 1981; Sawa, 1988; Weston, 1987).

In the next section, I focus on this last piece of the puzzle. In particular, I look at how we learn in the face of radically different paradigms or frames of reference. I have chosen this focus because the contextual and methodological pieces to the puzzle are so well addressed elsewhere.

NAVIGATING THE SHIFT

When speaking of paradigm shifts, researchers allude to what I call the *biomedical* and *systems* paradigms (see Sawa, 1988). We might think of these paradigms as representing the constellation of models held by the different members of a particular community of practice. Models within these communities might vary, but they will all hold a family resemblance to one another. That is, they will all share a distinctive way of construing a practice based on an interrelated set of assumptions about how to understand and solve practice problems and how to frame one's role, task, context, and relationships to others (D. M. Smith, 1989). Consequently, community members will take as "given" the same assumptions and standards and will rarely disagree over fundamentals (for an account of scientific communities, see Kuhn, 1962, p. 11).

Trainers who see different paradigms at work in the world of medicine are now proposing ways to navigate the shift between the biomedical and systems paradigms. In doing so, most offer a kind of fit-and-build theory designed to span the two paradigms. As Sawa (1988) recommends: "[Trainers] must find a common ground in order to transmit language, skills, and concepts that fit in the work of [physicians]. . . . [And physicians] must build on the skills they already possess and enlarge their knowledge and their view of their own profession" (p. 92).

The theory embedded in this approach goes something like this: If a training program and its models are designed to fit and build upon physicians' current ways of thinking and doing, then the new knowledge will be more familiar and more likely to take as intended.[4] In this section, I consider some limits to this theory and propose an additional approach in light of the biomedical and systems paradigms.

Paradigm Spanning

The fit-and-build theory of learning is based on the assumption that learning to move from one paradigm to another is primarily a continuous process. We might reasonably expect this assumption to hold when learning involves the incremental acquisition of skills, techniques, concepts, and facts that do not raise questions, doubts, or disagreements over fundamentals (see Kuhn, 1962). But we might expect it not to hold when basic assumptions and values fall under contention. When this happens, instructor and participant are apt to clash over whose model should prevail, and even enthusiastic participants will find that what they wish to learn at times contradicts what they now value, know, and do. In these moments, learning will become a conflictual and discontinuous process, characterized by quantum leaps as well as successive increments.

This means that unless systemic models do away with the very assumptions that distinguish them, they are likely to conflict with those within the biomedical paradigm. As I will illustrate below, these models hold fundamentally different assumptions about matters of health and illness and about how to frame a physician's role, task, and patients. These assumptions in turn transform the social and cognitive context in which "same" diagnostic and treatment activities occur, making the fit-and-build theory problematic.

A Tale of Two Practices

The biomedical and systems paradigms paint very different portraits of a medical practice. Models within the biomedical paradigm frame the physician's role as that of a technically competent expert (Sawa, 1988) who controls the agenda of the patient-doctor encounter (Lesser, 1981) in order to restore health (Sawa, 1988). They conceptualize disease separately from persons in their family contexts, and they conceive of the body as separate from the mind. They rely on cognitive structures characterized by relatively simple, linear causal chains that focus primarily on biological factors. They offer disease-based knowledge, and they ask physicians to pay attention to physical complaints when generating hypotheses. Finally, they construe intervention as a primarily technical activity aimed at eliciting information about, and treating, an individual's physical symptoms. Those who subscribe to this paradigm have developed an ideology of practice that celebrates the wonders of technology and justifies the role of a distant expert (see Schon, 1983, p. 300).

The biomedical paradigm, studied at medical school and reinforced by institutions, is readily recognized by physicians, patients, and the culture at large. For this reason, it is the dominant paradigm within the world of medicine. In contrast, the systems paradigm is not widely recognized or accepted by physicians, institutions, or the culture. Models within this paradigm frame the physician's role as that of an interpersonally and technically competent practitioner who shares control with a responsible patient—a patient who is viewed in his or her family context—regarded as a partner in the joint task of restoring and maintaining the health of family members. Systemic models conceptualize matters of health and illness in a family context, and they conceive of the mind and body as interrelated. The cognitive structure of these models includes relatively complex causal relationships that connect an interrelated web of psychological, social, and physical complaints. They see intervention as a psychosocial and technical endeavor aimed at eliciting information about, and helping to maintain, the health of the individual in his or her family system. Those who work within this paradigm have developed an ideology of practice that celebrates the notion of the patient-as-the-family and that equates "good family life with good health" (Marinker, quoted in Weston, 1987, p. 8).

As these accounts suggest, the two paradigms differ markedly on the fundamentals (see Table 10.1). In practice, systems models will tell a physician to share control with a patient in order to get at and address what is construed as the nested set of psychosociobiological factors affecting the patient's health, whereas biomedical models will tell a physician to control the encounter in order to carry out the primarily technical task of diagnosing and treating what is considered a specific somatic complaint.

The plot thickens. When trainers prescribe models that hold values, goals, and assumptions that are significantly different from those held by participants, they will inevitably spark what I call *model conflict*. Sometimes this conflict is expressed externally, as people lock horns over how a problem should be set and solved. At other times the conflict might take the form of an internal dilemma, as a participant discovers

TABLE 10.1 Different Portraits of Medical Practice

	Biomedical Models	*Systemic Models*
Framing assumptions		
Own role	technically competent expert; distant, in control	interpersonally and technically competent practitioner; shared control
Patient's role	passive recipient	responsible agent
Patient	individual outside social context	individual in context, or family-as-patient
Role relations	differential status; relationship of deference	equal status; relationship of partners
Task	to restore minimal level of health	to restore and maintain health
Cognitive frameworks		
Matters of health and illness	considered separate from the individual and context; mind and body separate	considered in relation to the "whole" person in context; mind and body interrelated
Causal structures	relatively simple, linear causal chains that focus on biological factors	relatively more complex causal webs that focus on psychosocial-biological factors
Domain-specific knowledge	disease-based knowledge that generates hypotheses related to physical complaints	disease and family-based knowledge that generates hypotheses related to psychosocial and physical complaints
Intervention aims		
Diagnosis	elicitation of information about physical symptoms	elicitation of information about psychosocial and physical factors and inquire into family matters
Treatment	to make technical interventions to restore minimal level of health	to make psychosocial interventions (or referrals) as well as technical ones— aimed at maintaining and restoring the health of individuals in their families

that the "hardest task . . . is to unlearn old habits" (see Weston, 1987, p. 2). At still other times, both kinds of conflict might erupt as an ambivalent practitioner challenges someone who represents a novel and contradictory way of doing things.

These moments of conflict are full of potential learning. In such moments, it becomes possible to learn significantly new ways of seeing and doing things that might otherwise go unnoticed, because we are so caught up in our own ways of seeing and doing things. But few trainers see or harness this creative potential; instead, they consider conflict problematic. They label as "difficult" participants who express the doubts, anxieties, and challenges that conflict triggers. They call actions that depart from the prescribed model "inconsistent" and "illogical," or "noncompliant" and "resistant" (see, respectively, McLean & Miles, 1975; Bishop, Epstein, et al., 1984). And they look for ways of overcoming, reducing, or bypassing these responses so they do not "slow down" the learning process.[5]

It is not surprising that trainers take this view. While potentially fruitful, model conflict ignites intense, anxiety-producing feuds. Heated disagreements can break out over what facts are important and how they should be named, understood, or handled. Is a complaint of chronic stomach pain suggestive of a possible ulcer, severe family stress, or both? In answering this question, one physician quickly argues that both possibilities should be pursued. In his view, it is necessary to get at the psychosocial as well as the biological aspects of a problem in order to form a complete diagnosis. But another physician takes a different view. In his mind, what counts is diagnosing and treating a possible ulcer before it causes serious damage. He does not believe it is necessary to take "precious" time to explore these "extraneous" factors. And so, before long, they start quarreling over what is important in diagnosing and treating the "same" problem.

When these physicians later turn to the question of what worked, the controversy intensifies. Both agree on the "facts" of the case. The ulcer was accurately diagnosed and treated, and the symptoms were relieved without attending to the possibility of family stress. But while one physician sees this as the solution, the other sees it as the problem. To him, the problem is not solved until the psychogenic source of the ulcer is also identified and addressed. But the first physician puts those activities outside the purview of his role. So once again they find themselves stuck, each unable to see the situation as the other does.

Some Difficulties

As this example illustrates, it is not easy to learn in the face of model conflict. The question of what is wrong and how best to fix it is a matter of values and assumptions as well as fact, and these matters are not easily explored or settled. What is worse, when people do take up these questions, they tend either to downplay basic differences or to marshal facts in support of their view. These findings are remarkably robust. Whether the training involves lawyers (D. M. Smith, 1987b, 1989), managers (D. M. Smith, 1988), educators (D. M. Smith, 1986a), journalists (D. M. Smith, 1986c), or therapists and consultants (Argyris, Putnam, & Smith, 1985; D. M. Smith, 1986c), learning tends to break down in predictable ways when fundamentals are at stake.

So what makes it so difficult to learn from fundamental differences? One difficulty is the nature of learning itself. All learning occurs in the context of a learner's existing beliefs, values, understandings, and theories—no matter how implicit these might be (Greeno, 1989). Professionals bring with them highly organized, complex, and often tacit forms of knowledge (Glaser, 1990) that over time become connected to their conceptions of themselves as skilled practitioners (Argyris et al., 1985; D. M. Smith, 1992). Second, this knowledge has embedded in it its own values, goals, ideologies, and assumptions, to which adults become deeply committed (Argyris et al., 1985).

For this reason, no one in his or her right mind is likely to be unambivalent about "unlearning" what has taken a lifetime to learn: how to practice a profession in ways commonly regarded and rewarded as competent. Instead, individuals will struggle to make their current ways of seeing and doing things work as well as or better than the proposed alternative. They will try to incorporate techniques without altering underlying assumptions or role relations. And they will challenge the alternative model in all sorts of ways to see whether it is worth the investment of time and energy to learn it (Argyris et al., 1985). And if, after all this, they do decide to take the leap of faith change requires, they will still face many moments of feeling "deskilled" (Bishop, Byles, & Horn, 1984, p. 33). As Bishop and Epstein (1985) reflect on their own experience as trainers: "When there is professional identity confusion, training can be complicated or slowed as trainees wrestle with whether or not the knowledge and skills to be learned are part of, relevant to, or acceptable in their chosen profession" (p. 484).

A second difficulty compounds the first. In my research on professional training, I am finding that people bring into the training an implicit model for learning. This model leads participant and trainer alike to talk in abstract, value-laden terms that are rarely, if ever, submitted to rigorous reflection. For instance, the individuals I observed did not systematically illustrate their different assertions about what does and does not work so that others could independently evaluate for themselves. And when they did illustrate through role plays or video-tapes, they did so to demonstrate or practice an approach, not to explore potential limits or liabilities in it. They rarely inquired into alternative ways of seeing the data, and they almost never encouraged others to identify data that might contradict the illustrated approach. Moreover, when people did offer "feedback" to those practicing or demonstrating an approach, they acted as if they assumed their the feedback was correct and that the task was to get the role player to accept it. The possibility that the feedback might miss something did not appear to occur to them. So when a role player raised doubts or pointed to data that the feedback missed ("But I did say X!"), the observer saw this as defensive and saw the defensiveness as problematic. As a result, neither the role player nor the observer learned much that was significantly new (Argyris et al., 1985; D. M. Smith, 1986a, 1986b, 1987b, 1988, 1989).

None of these individuals set out to stymie the learning in these training programs. Rather, they acted as if they were unaware that their views and practices were in part a function of their models. Korzybski (1933) would say that they were confusing the map with the territory. I would add that even when they did see different maps, they assumed that their own maps fit the territory best. Therefore, they did not see the need to explore their feedback publicly or to use their role plays as experiments that might produce surprises—surprises that could lead them to reconsider either their views or their models.

My own research findings are consistent with those reported by Lesser (1981) in his research on the training of residents. Lesser's residents had trouble speaking in descriptive language that was relatively concrete and minimally evaluative. Both sets of findings suggest that participants enter training with a model of learning that holds assumptions, values, and rules of inquiry that hamper learning when fundamentals are in question. This model holds such assumptions as "It is wrong to be wrong," "All defen-siveness is counterproductive," "The map is the territory," and "My map is the best map." It contains self-confirming rules such as "Speak in abstract categories," "Get the other to accept my feedback," "Ask leading questions," and "Demonstrate my approach without inquiring into alterna-tive views or seeking contradictory data." Finally, it values unilateral control and the avoidance of failure and mistakes (see Argyris & Schon's model I theory-in-use, 1974; also see Argyris et al., 1985, pp. 276-319; Brown & Levinson's research on politeness strategies, 1978; Nisbett & Ross's research on inferential strategies, 1980).

TABLE 10.2 Instrumental Learning

Learning Activity	Rules of Inquiry
Inquiring	Ask for accounts, perceptions, and evaluations without asking for the concrete data and thinking that led to them.
	Ask questions that lead others to your view (lawyering or easing in).
Observing	Make observations based on implicit reasoning.
	Do not actively encourage different reactions, data, or explanations.
Inventing options	Pose options (frequently without illustrating them in action).
	Keep the thinking behind the option implicit.
	Elicit abstract perceptions and evaluations of the option.
	Do not actively encourage alternative options.
Mapping options	Make attributions about an option's intentions and consequences without making your (causal) thinking explicit.
	Make these attributions so abstract that it is difficult to connect them to concrete data, making them hard to use or reject.
Critically reflecting	Keep criteria implicit and do not reflect publicly on the thinking and values behind them.
	Unilaterally impose or relinquish your own criteria without reflecting publicly on the implications of doing so.

Copyright 1989, Diana McLain Smith, Action Design Associates, Newton, MA.

When professionals grapple with routine problems, this instrumental approach to learning is sufficient, because goals are usually given or shared, and the means for achieving those goals are relatively easily definable. But when people contest goals, and when the means to contested goals are multiple, ambiguous, and complex, this model breaks down, because its self-confirming features prevent us from using conflict to explore possible limits, gaps, and/or mistakes in the different views (Table 10.2).

Most training programs both recognize and strive to bypass the impact of these two difficulties. For example, trainers affirm the current skills of participants while asking them to change them. They set and enforce ground rules to prevent potential disruptions and distractions caused by participants' reactions. They design ways to circumvent "getting personal" or "evaluative" by suggesting that trainers not ask "What didn't work?" but rather "What should the person do differently?" (see Smith & Putnam, 1989). In this way, trainers hope to avoid or reduce the defensiveness that gets sparked when participants are challenged unilaterally.

While these structures and strategies do reduce the negative impact of the two difficulties just described, they also run the risk of reducing group members' capacity to deepen their learning through engaging conflict. For this reason, in the next section I propose some additional principles designed to approach these difficulties differently.

GENERATIVE LEARNING

Consider this possibility: The physicians who "deviated" from prescribed models were conducting their own impromptu experiments. They may not have thought of it this way, but once back at the office, they started adapting and testing out the new model, and through an iterative process of trial and error, they began to integrate aspects of it into their own evolving models of practice (see Weston, 1987). The trouble with these experiments is that neither trainer nor participant thought of them as such, and so neither thought to collect data that might allow us to reflect rigorously on the "results" and to consider their implications for developing more effective models of family medicine.

But it is possible to make this kind of experimentation a part of the learning process itself. Whenever people raise doubts, pose challenges, or express anxieties, they provide a window onto their own models of practice and where they conflict with the prescribed model. So long as both trainer and participant remain open to inquiry, it is possible to use these reactions to design experiments that yield significant new insights into practice differences. Sometimes these insights will lead professionals to reconsider and further develop their models. When this happens, they will face what Kelly (1955) calls an "elaborative choice." They must decide whether to define more precisely and complexly the knowledge within their models or to redefine the model's fundamentals in order to develop and enact radically new ways of understanding, experiencing, and acting. As Kelly puts the choice:

> Here is where inner turmoil so frequently manifests itself. Which shall a man choose, security or adventure? Shall he choose that which leads to immediate certainty or shall he choose that which may eventually give him a wider understanding? (p. 65)

Each choice requires a particular kind of inquiry and learning. When we are interested in developing better means for solving problems in light of given goals, ends, and values, then instrumental inquiry is sufficient for settling the problem and developing our knowledge. But when we go after fundamentals, it is necessary to engage in what I call *generative inquiry*. This type of inquiry involves a dialectical process in which model conflict—both internal and external—is used to fuel a creative reconsideration of a model's assumptions, goals, and values. The process is dialectical in the sense that it involves a conversation between conflicting assumptions and values; it is creative in that it generates significantly new models through the transformation of the conflicting assumptions and values under contention. We can say that generative learning has occurred when new models are discovered and enacted in the world (see Argyris & Schon's concept of double-loop learning, 1974; Watzlawick, Weakland, & Fisch's concept of second-order change, 1974).

In this section, I identify some interrelated principles for guiding generative learning. These principles include engaging model conflict, getting to know what we know, and negotiating a context for the joint negotiation of understanding.

Engaging Model Conflict

As already argued, disagreements over how to set and solve a problem or how to frame a role and task hold the potential for producing significant learning. Pursuing basic disagreements opens up the possibility of discovering new ways of seeing, thinking, and doing that might lead people to reexamine and redesign their practice models. For this reason, engaging conflict is a core principle of generative learning.

Implementing this principle requires a two-pronged effort aimed at both surfacing conflict and designing ways to explore it rigorously. To surface conflict, trainers repeatedly encourage participants to confront different perspectives and approaches by asking questions such as, "What might prevent you from seeing or doing it this way?" or "Does anyone have a different view of the problem or a different approach to the case?" These kinds of questions bring model conflict to the surface as participants describe their own views and approaches to the problem as well as their expectations about what other approaches might yield.

With these data, trainers can then design different kinds of experiments to explore conflicting views. Sometimes, they might demonstrate how they would enact a strategy from the proposed model while encouraging participants to identify results they consider problematic. For example, participants might say that a proposed strategy is "too cumbersome" with patients or "too time-consuming" to be useful in the "real world" of practice. These reactions might lead the trainers either to redesign their strategy or to illustrate how they would enact the strategy so that it addresses the concerns raised by the participants. At other times, the trainers might confront the thinking that leads participants to see the results as they do, pointing out inner contradictions in their views or asking them to illustrate the concerns or an alternative way of addressing them. For example, they might ask participants to role-play, to recount experiences, or to bring in concrete data from their work that can illustrate their concerns and/or how they might deal with them.

Looking at practice differences this way makes it possible to experiment in the true sense of the word—in the sense of remaining open to the possibility that one's expectations might not pan out. This then makes it possible to use conflicting views and models to discover their limits and to design new models in the learning context itself. The basic idea is to generate data on what different models actually yield, so the group can publicly reflect on them in light of shared data, different perspectives, and overarching criteria, such as the early detection of illness and the effective and efficient treatment of a complaint. Because these reflections are necessarily bound by the different models' current ways of seeing and doing things, they are sure to raise new doubts and new experiments (Argyris et al., 1985).[6]

Getting to Know What We Know

With experience comes both awareness and unawareness. As experienced professionals, we have spent years in professional schools, we have spent still more years going to conferences and seminars, and we have read all the current texts and professional journals. We know the different dialects spoken by the different members of our community, and we can use these dialects to express what we know. As we develop this kind of knowledge—what I call *expressed knowledge*—we gain greater awareness.

But other knowledge lies at the periphery of awareness. Through the everyday business of doing our work, we come to know more and more about how to practice, and become less and less able to say how we know it. We recognize a pattern in some problem and we immediately know what to do, but, if asked, we cannot say how we know it. In these moments, we come up against the "paradox of expertise" (P. E. Johnson, 1983, p. 79). We have come to know what we know so well that we lose awareness of what we know, and we lose awareness that we have lost awareness. As with any skill, the knowing is in the action (Schon, 1983, 1987), and this knowledge cannot be readily expressed. Instead, it is displayed in our actions. For this reason, I call this kind of knowledge *displayed knowledge.*

Both expressed and displayed knowledge combine and interpenetrate to make up our models of practice. Over time, these models become so ingrained in how we think and act that we do not pay attention to them. Instead, they form the intuitive background understandings that make obvious what we see and do in the different practice situations we face. When these models are then shared by the culture at large and reinforced by its institutions, they become a part of the taken-for-granted aspects of professional life that rarely get questioned (see Garfinkel, 1967). Because we must see our models in order to critique and develop them, an important principle of generative learning is to offer ways of mapping the knowledge embedded in our models of practice.

Because our models consist of both expressed and displayed knowledge, we must draw on a range of methods that will permit us to access and represent both kinds of knowledge. When reflecting on expressed knowledge, trainers can use what P. E. Johnson (1983) calls "reconstructed" methods of reasoning. These methods are used to find out how a practitioner thinks about her approach to some problem-solving activity, for instance, diagnosis. With these methods, we ask what the practitioner intends, what strategies and plans she follows, and what thinking informs both. Her accounts then give us a window onto the knowledge she uses to represent and express what she knows, to plan prospectively, and to explain retrospectively what she does and the results she gets.

It is more difficult to access and represent displayed knowledge. Reconstructed methods are no longer adequate, because they depend on practitioners' accounts of what they think they do, not on what they actually do. The difficulty is that displayed knowledge is what Polanyi (1967) refers to as "tacit" knowledge. To capture tacit knowledge, we must first access the thoughts and actions practitioners actually use and display in particular cases. To do so, we can observe practitioners at work and ask them to describe the on-the-spot thoughts and feelings that run through their minds as they grapple with some practice problem. P. E. Johnson (1983, p. 82) refers to these as "authentic" methods, because the internal processes elicited can be connectable to actual behavior.

In our work, we combine reconstructed methods, authentic methods, and observations of actual practice in order to represent (map) the knowledge used by the professionals (Argyris et al., 1985, pp. 236-247; D. M. Smith, 1987a). To see how this might be done, let's look at an example that involved a family counselor in one of our seminars. The counselor subscribed to a client-centered counseling approach, understanding this (in part) to mean that "the client knows best what he needs and my job is to help him come to his own decision; counselors should not make judgments or evaluations, since this disempowers the client; and it is important to be genuine and empathic." This approach, learned at a counseling program and reinforced every day at work, had become so deeply embedded in the counselor's expressed knowledge that she spoke its language with eloquence and expressed an abiding commitment to its values and assumptions.

During our seminar, the counselor brought in a case that provided direct data on a recent session with the father of a young boy in trouble at school. Perplexed by their interaction, she brought in the case so that she might understand more clearly what happened in the session. As she recounted it, the father had been referred to her by his family doctor to discuss the possibility of counseling for the boy. As the session began, the father made a number of requests that his son be evaluated to see whether counseling was indicated for him. The counselor, whose expressed view considered evaluation inappropriate, initially resisted these pleas by making a series of moves designed to deflect them, saying things such as, "You're not quite sure this is a problem for a therapist," while thinking, "He wants me to evaluate his son and that's not appropriate." For the next half hour, the two went back and forth within an interlocking script of plea and deflect until the counselor became more persistent and the father more frustrated.

The family counselor was troubled by the encounter. She had expected the father and son to be seen together, but instead the father showed up alone, and the counselor felt caught in a bind. On the one hand, the father was the client, and so her expressed view told her that he should know best. But on the other hand, he was making requests for an evaluation that this same expressed theory considered problematic, so she could not genuinely follow them. She then managed her dilemma by making a series of private evaluations about the client's needs and gently prodding him to come around to her view by asking a series of leading questions. By the end, she discarded the expressed assumption "The client knows best" in favor of the displayed assumption: "The

TABLE 10.3   Mapping a Family Counseling Encounter

Contextual Cue	Rules	Consequences
When asked to provide an evaluation	Ignore client's question.	Client defensiveness
	Act as though I am not ignoring it.	Reduced learning for both client and counselor
	Reflect back the client's statement.	Continued blindness and blaming of the client
When asked again	Ask client what he or she wants.	Escalated client frustration
	Attribute privately that he or she should know; ignore that the client has expressed what he or she wants.	little learning
When asked again	Unilaterally advocate an opposing view.	Client becomes angry and gives up
	Do not make reasoning explicit.	Little learning
	Do not invite inquiry.	Continued blindness

client knows best except when I know better, and I know best when I know better."

These inner contradictions came to light during a group discussion of the case. The counselor became so intrigued that she then went off and constructed a map of the encounter. In her map, she identified the rules she displayed in action, the contextual cues that triggered them, and the consequences of these rules for outcomes she considered critical by her own expressed criteria (see Table 10.3). This map, based on an individual case, ended up being quite generalizable to other practice episodes in which she had also felt caught, leading her to reflect on the underlying assumptions and values in her counseling model. In so doing, she questioned her expressed view that she should avoid evaluations altogether, and she began to speculate that it is most important to make those evaluations open to discussion and revision. She also came to see how many of her actions displayed a tacit frame of conflict as a zero-sum game and a bipolar frame of control in which control is either taken or relinquished, but never shared.

By providing methods, exercises, concepts, and analytic frameworks for reflecting on actual encounters, a training program can help participants map their models as they evolve them over time (D. M. Smith,

1987a). It is through this kind of reflection that practitioners can begin to see patterns of practice that will illuminate the inner contradictions and limits that characterize their own models. When this happens, practitioners frequently begin to design action experiments aimed at developing their models. For example, once this family counselor discovered the unintended consequences of how she thought and acted, she embarked on a series of experiments in which she reframed her task and redesigned the propositions that had entrapped her in her own inner contradictions.

Self-Reinforcing Loops

Sometimes, this kind of experimentation leads practitioners to adopt new techniques or actions without questioning or redesigning fundamentals. At other times, it uncovers deeply embedded assumptions and values that make it difficult to adopt new and desired actions. When this happens, a process of transformation unfolds as practitioners reconsider the taken-for-granted assumptions and values that, until then, had gone unnoticed and unquestioned.

If we now consider Weston's (1987) account of his own training experience, we can see how this kind of generative experimentation might be used to explore different models of family medicine. Using his own experience as an indicator, he conjectures: "It may be that the family doctors in the [Bishop, Epstein, et al., 1984] study incorporated the new information into their own model of family practice rather than using a different family therapy model for certain patients" (p. 5). If we could foster, map, and rigorously reflect on these adaptations, we might be more able to explore how physicians evolve their models over time, how they transform their models in light of new insights, and how their evolving models affect outcomes both paradigms hold dear, such as the early detection of illness and the effective and efficient treatment of a complaint. In this way, we might use our training efforts to invent and develop more efficacious models of practice.

Negotiating a Social Context
for Joint Negotiation of Understanding

As already illustrated, participants enter the training process with well-developed models of practice to which their professional identities are tied and their allegiance given. They also bring with them instrumental models of learning that are well suited for learning about techniques and strategies, but ill suited for inquiring into fundamentals. The combination of these two difficulties makes it hard for participants to engage model conflict from an experimental, reflective stance capable of generating significantly new alternatives.

Indeed, most participants frequently find themselves caught in a painful learning dilemma. On the one hand, they may wish to learn about their own and others' models, so they can develop and improve their effectiveness; on the other, they may wish to protect themselves from the pain and vulnerability that conflict and learning can incur. When participants get so caught in this dilemma that they see no way out, they will begin to defend themselves in ways that prevent learning. Some will unilaterally cut off any exploration of their thinking. Others will withdraw and refrain from challenging or inquiring into others' views. And still others will make global assertions about what is wrong with other models while refusing to explore the basis of their assertions or to illustrate an alternative (see Argyris et al., 1985, pp. 276-318).

To make matters more complicated, trainers who engage in generative learning will act quite differently from participants (see Table 10.4). Their model of learning will ask that they illustrate their views, that they publicly explore competing assertions, that they encourage people to develop different ideas, and that they design experiments that allow competing views to be examined rigorously in light of concrete data. Because these rules contradict those followed by participants, the trainers and participants are likely to clash (see Table 10.2).[7]

This means that trainers will face their own conundrum: How can they create a context characterized by "generative norms" without unilaterally imposing their rules on participants, thereby violating the very norms they are striving to enact? To navigate this dilemma, trainers must first negotiate the learning norms by which they will negotiate their conflicting views and models of practice.

For this reason, negotiating the learning context is another principle of generative learning, and it can be enacted by (a) publicly exploring different rules of inquiry in light of concrete data and a shared interest in effectiveness, and (b) engaging the assumptions that underlie instrumental and generative models of learning.

In publicly exploring different rules of inquiry, trainers create opportunities for group members to reflect on the way they learn in light of what they actually do and their shared interest in improving their professional effectiveness. So, for instance, if participants make unilateral assertions or conceal their thinking, trainers might show how such

TABLE 10.4 Generative Learning

Learning Activity	Rules of Inquiry
Inquiring	Ask for accounts, perceptions, and evaluations and the concrete data and thinking that led to them.
	Actively elicit counterexamples and alternative views.
Observing	Make observations based on explicit reasoning while encouraging different views or counterexamples.
	Regard observations as probes that elicit new information that might alter your view.
Inventing options	Pose options, frequently illustrating them in action.
	Regard options as experiments, reflecting publicly on the thinking behind them and the results they yield.
	Encourage others to identify an option's limits or unintended consequences, asking them to illustrate.
	Encourage others to invent and try out alternative options.
Mapping options	Regard attributions about an option's intentions and consequences as hypotheses to be publicly explored.
	Connect causal attributions about intentions and consequences to concrete data and explicit reasoning.
	Invite others to pose alternative interpretations or to identify data or gaps in reasoning that might disconfirm the attribution.
Critically reflecting	Make criteria explicit and reflect publicly on the thinking and values behind them.
	Submit your own and others' criteria to public critique in light of different values, interests, and data.

rules are self-confirming, because they make it difficult to discover mistakes—which is a necessary condition for effectiveness. Because all practitioners value effectiveness, this possibility makes them take notice of how they learn. If the trainers can then show through both logic and action how generative rules might betters serve effectiveness, then most participants will soon strive to approximate them (Argyris et al., 1985).

Once the participants themselves are committed to generative norms, trainers can scaffold their efforts at enacting them. In so doing, they help participants reach the new norms when their own efforts fall short. In such moments, trainers might ask participants to illustrate abstract claims, to make explicit the values and reasoning behind evaluative comments, or to elicit alternative views or data that might contradict their views. So long as participants see these moves as supporting rather than undermining their own efforts, they will tend to welcome them.

With this kind of scaffolding, most participants get to the point where they can meet the generative norms with little difficulty. The problem is that they remain dependent on the trainers for doing so. If they are ever going to sustain this learning on their own, they must internalize the model's underlying values and assumptions independent of the trainers. Often, training programs do not allow enough time for this kind of learning to occur. But when time is available, trainers will need to do more than just scaffold. They will need to engage the conflicting values and assumptions that underlie the two models of learning.

Of course, this makes the learning process even more complex, because it means engaging fundamental differences between models of learning as well as practice. Those willing to take on the added complexity can start by first chronicling how participants learn—that is, by observing what they do and inquiring into their on-the-spot thinking and feeling. From these data, trainers can start to form hypotheses about what assumptions might be informing the way participants are thinking, feeling, and acting as they learn. If participants confirm the hypotheses, the trainers can then build by predicting how these assumptions might affect participants' deeply felt and expressed aspirations to learn about their practice and how to improve it. If these predictions can then be connected to observable events in the seminar, they will usually strike participants as compelling accounts of moments when their own learning stood still, leading them to take notice of the assumptions and values that guide how they learn. This notice can then be used to foster an internal critique that explores how the assumptions participants display in action interact with those they express, leading them to reexamine and at times to redesign their models of learning in the interest of effectiveness (for a description of this process, see Argyris et al., 1985, pp. 394-449; also see Schon, 1987).

IMPLICATIONS: TRAINING DOCTORS
TO TAKE A FAMILY PERSPECTIVE

No matter how the field of medicine decides to define a family perspective, moments of conflict are apt to arise. Systemic assumptions—even when embedded in "user-friendly" models—will sometimes collide with the assumptions learned within the biomedical paradigm. The question is how we choose to see and use these moments. If we assume that conflict will derail the learning process, we will probably design a learning context in which we never get the chance to discover otherwise.

But if we see the possibility of using conflict to deepen and extend everyone's learning, then we might design a learning context in which conflict fuels rather than undermines the learning process.

In this section, I briefly outline some of the most important and controversial implications of generative learning for the design of training, so that they can be considered critically in the context of training physicians.

Increments of Time

Whenever we learn a new skill—such as how to play tennis or the piano—we expect to devote increments of time over an extended period. When professionals try to learn skills that are not only novel but contradictory, spending increments of time over extended periods is even more necessary. But most training programs take professionals out of their own contexts, put them into intensive, several-day training sessions, and then send them on their way with only the briefest of follow-up, if any at all. No one I know has learned to play a good game of tennis this way, so I don't understand why we expect people to develop professional skills this way.

A different design might include shorter chunks of time spread out over a longer period, with independent learning experiments to be carried out at work between training days. With this design, participants could incorporate and adapt the ideas in the course of their work and bring the results of these attempts back into the learning context, where they could be examined for what they might tell us about effective medical practice (more on this below).

Training in Context

Professionals often experience a large gap between the world of training and the world of practice. To oversimplify the distinction for discussion purposes, the world of training provides explicit models, and it supports relatively low-risk experimentation with training cases carried out under "slow" time. The world of practice provides only fuzzy practice norms and standards, and it requires professionals to practice with high-risk, "live" cases in real time. The advantage of the training world is that it fosters experimentation and reflection, and makes it possible to compare different approaches to the "same" case. The limitation of this world is that it is not obvious how to generalize what is learned there to real-world practice. Cases, and the contexts in which they are situated, are unique and highly variable, making generalization problematic. Too often professionals recount times when the real world prevented them from doing what they were encouraged to do in training, or when they used the "right" strategy in the "wrong" instance, leading it to backfire.

At present, too much training is divorced from professionals' actual contexts. Even training that relies on live cases still does so under relatively controlled circumstances in a context that is supportive of the experimentation. But what happens when physicians return to colleagues and bureaucracies that do not support their efforts? And what happens when their patients do not expect them to ask all these personal questions about family life? How do physicians transfer what they have learned to these cases within these contexts?

To date, many researchers suggest that we revise family models to fit the context. But how will we ever change the world and move beyond current limitations if our only response to a mismatch is the acceptance of the status quo? In contrast, other researchers too quickly discount the pressures that physicians face, suggesting they reduce caseloads without saying how they can do so within contexts that require them to keep caseloads heavy.

Another possibility is to design training so that a conversation can take place between the world of training and the world of practice. If training is delivered in smaller increments over longer periods, professionals can then try out ideas in their work and bring actual cases back into the training for purposes of reflection and experimentation. This back and forth between training and practice will permit professionals to develop their models more reflectively, and it will help them build up their own stock of exemplars for practicing medicine from a family perspective in real time. At the same time, trainers and researchers should also learn, as they see what happens to their models once they encounter the world of practice as seen through the eyes of other physicians' models.

User Demanding?

In this chapter I have offered a perspective on professional training that suggests we put conflict in the center of a reflective training process. I recognize that this perspective contradicts the model of training that is now in good currency, and I recognize that it puts more demands on trainers, participants, and institutions. For this reason, it might be accused of being "user demanding" for the trainer. And from my point of view, it is. But it may be that the demands posed by generative learning better fit the demands posed by learning when that learning turns on fundamentals. In any case, that is a proposition that should spark some conflict!

Notes

1. For a discussion of different levels of involvement, see Doherty and Baird (1986); for examples of different ways of defining what it means to take a family perspective, see Hochheiser and Chapados (1985), Weston (1987), Bishop and Epstein (1985), Sawa (1988), Guttman and Steinert (1987).

2. My research on professional training suggests that this training model is in good currency across professions—whether the training involves lawyers, managers, or consultants and therapists (D. M. Smith, 1986a, 1987a, 1987b, 1988, 1989).

3. Although these explanations can be separated for analytic purposes, they are closely intertwined. Contextual factors shape—and are shaped by—physicians' models of practice, especially the ways those models tell them to think about health and illness, the physician's role and tasks, and patients. Moreover, the methods we use to represent what we know will affect how well those models take context into account. If we use reconstructed methods alone, we will create models that are quite distant from actual practice and the reality physicians face.

4. The portraits drawn here are for discussion purposes. They represent discrete, ideal types. In reality, a practice will have fuzzier boundaries than those drawn here. By making the distinctions so stark, I hope to draw attention to the assumptive bases of the two paradigms, not provide a rich description of an actual practice.

5. Most training programs designed to help professionals develop new skills adhere to this very same principle. Whether aimed at managers, lawyers, consultants, or doctors, the training is designed as if it assumes a basic continuity between the models participants bring into the training and the models being taught. This is so even when the trainers speak of the models as fundamentally different and as requiring a paradigmatic shift.

6. This process is much more complicated than the space of this chapter allows me to describe. When participants try out an approach, they will evaluate the results from the perspectives of their own models. So they might like what they get, even if others do not. This makes the question of what worked a difficult one. In part, the difficulty can be resolved by recourse to an internal critique. Professionals will hold multiple values and criteria, so we can look at how well an outcome satisfied the different criteria, assuming that it is not satisfactory to meet one criterion while violating all the others. A second avenue is an external critique in which we appeal to shared values and criteria that go beyond a particular model. The early detection of illness might be one such criterion. The idea here is to examine outcomes in light of data and criteria considered legitimate by the actor him- or herself.

7. In reality, instrumental and generative models of learning are not the discrete categories this description implies. In actual cases, the boundaries will again be fuzzier, as individuals draw on aspects of each model, making the differences more continuous than discrete. Nevertheless, when observing a group of learners, it is possible to say that individuals fall more toward one end of a continuum than the other (see Smith, 1987b).

ELEVEN

Exemplars of Family-Oriented Care: How Do We Know What They Do?

JOHN C. ROGERS

For nearly two decades, family medicine has been attempting to bring "family-oriented health care" out of the realm of idealistic rhetoric and into the concrete world of clinical practice. This process has been tedious as scholars attempt to describe just what family-oriented health care is, and researchers attempt to determine whether in fact it exists and is effective. As the scholars and researchers have gone about their work, the educators have responded to the need to teach something about family to the growing number of residents. It is clear that the teaching has gone far beyond any research base to support it, and it often appears that the family scholarship is simple trying to catch up to the clinical instruction. It also appears, however, that the teaching even goes beyond current clinical care in that what is taught may only rarely resemble actual clinical practice in the community.

This lack of coherence becomes apparent when one reviews the textbooks written by recognized exemplars of family- or systems-oriented health care: Doherty and Baird (1983), Sawa (1985), Christie-Seely (1984b), Henao and Grose (1985), Crouch and Roberts (1987), and McDaniel, Campbell, and Seaburn (1990). In each of their works, these exemplars build a case for the need for a family or systems perspective, review the research linking family factors to illness and health behaviors, describe the theoretical model they embrace, propose a clinical care framework of assessment and intervention, and provide generous case examples, often including transcripts of doctor-patient conversations.

These scholars have described a number of styles of family-oriented health care that presumably reflect their teaching and patient care.

The thesis of this chapter, however, is that, despite the best of intentions, the works do not accurately reflect these exemplars' typical modes of family-oriented teaching or clinical practice. The models are not totally inaccurate; they are idealized descriptions. The incongruence between the scholarly works and actual teaching and clinical processes is due to inherent limitations and biases in the methods by which the works were developed.

Alternative methods of knowing about clinical practices can overcome these biases, thereby providing more realistic descriptions of how exemplars do family-oriented care. In this chapter, I briefly summarize the exemplars' works, review empirical evidence that the proposed models do not always work in family practice, introduce theoretical arguments against the methods used to develop the models, and describe alternative techniques of producing professional knowledge that could be used to develop different models of exemplary family-oriented care.

EXEMPLARS' MODELS

Family Medicine

Family Therapy and Family Medicine: Toward the Primary Care of Families (Doherty & Baird, 1983). Doherty and Baird briefly review the support for their tenet that the family is a primary social context for health care. They then state that "the hallmark of a family-oriented physician will be that he or she will make the option of assembling the family a routine part of the therapeutic contract for a number of serious or chronic problems—traditional biomedical problems as well as explicitly psychosocial problems" (pp. 18-19). They adapt Minuchin's model of family dynamics, with its four basic notions (transactional patterns, adaptation, family subsystems, and boundaries), for the assessment of family dysfunction in family practice. The assessment framework derived from this model includes four basic questions: What are the sources of stress on this family? How adaptable or how rigid is the family ? How cohesive is the family? What is the family's repeating interaction related to the problem? Based on this assessment framework, Doherty and Baird "propose that in the context of family medicine, family counseling has four distinct functions or purposes: education, prevention, support and challenge" (p. 89). They go on to describe 14 basic counseling techniques.

Family Dynamics for Physicians: Guidelines to Assessment and Treatment (Sawa, 1985). This textbook authored by Russell Sawa presents a family assessment framework that includes brief screening devices for individuals as well as a whole-family assessment described as the Primary Care Family Assessment. This family assessment framework consists of four dimensions: connectedness, family developmental stage, internal family function, and physical and emotional health. The framework is based primarily on the McMaster model of family functioning, with some structural concepts taken from Minuchin and other features, such as three dimensions (structure, function, and development), the genogram, and the family life cycle, adapted from Karl Tomm's tripartite model. As with the other texts discussed here, the specific skills necessary for assessment and counseling are delineated. Transcripts of family interviews, with marginal notations about physician counseling skills, are again used to illustrate the application of the proposed framework.

Working With the Family in Primary Care: A Systems Approach to Health and Illness (Christie-Seely, 1984b). This textbook edited by Janet Christie-Seely, as well as those edited by Sergio Henao and Nellie Grose (1985) and Michael Crouch and Leonard Roberts (1987), is less systematic in the description of the theoretical model, assessment framework, and intervention strategy for the particular approach, due to the multiauthored nature of the text. Nevertheless, an overall model does emerge. For example, Christie-Seely's edited volume includes a review of the premises associated with a family or systems orientation, a discussion of the characteristics of the "healthy" family, a presentation of a model of the family's response to crisis, and a review of the role of the family in illness and medical outcomes. The proposed family assessment tool is based upon eight indicators of family functional health that are grouped into four categories: identity processes, coping with change, information processing, and role structuring. The tool is also based in part upon the McMaster model of family functioning. Some additional factors were added to produce the components described by the acronym PRACTICE: presenting *P*roblem or reason for interview, *R*oles and structure, *A*ffect, *C*ommunication, *T*ime in the family life cycle, *I*llness in the family past and present, *C*oping with stress, and *E*cology and culture. In addition to the assessment tool, the skills required by primary care clinicians to work with families are described in detail. Clinical cases illustrate application of the PRAC-TICE assessment tool, as well as several of the management skills.

Principles of Family Systems in Family Medicine (Henao & Grose, 1985). This text edited by Sergio Henao and Nellie Grose is structured like many of the other works, with parts addressing the philosophical and theoretical basis of a family systems approach, the systemic evolution of the family, and clinical application of a family systems approach. After introducing the "systemic properties of the family," the book represents as its theoretical foundations structural family therapy (Minuchin), the strategic approach (Weakland & Fisch), and the intergenerational point of view (Bowen theory). The clinical application chapters do not follow a uniform assessment and intervention model, but present evaluation and treatment strategies tailored to particular problems. Family group meetings are central to the described interventions.

The Family in Medical Practice: A Family Systems Primer (Crouch & Roberts, 1987). In this book, several family systems theories are compared and characteristics of family systems are highlighted. Drawing on the McMaster model, the circumplex model, Doherty and Baird's work, and Minuchin's model, the volume proposes an informal screening assessment consisting of four areas to explore:

(1) Exactly what happens regarding the symptoms and the family?
(2) What are the sources of distress for this patient? For this family?
(3) How cohesive is this family? Is it more enmeshed or disengaged?
(4) How adaptable or rigid is this patient in the family system?

In addition to the therapeutic strategies suggested by family life-cycle theory, Minuchin's model, and Doherty and Baird's work, an approach to systems-oriented counseling is proposed along with descriptions of its four goals and the counseling skills required for the attainment of each goal. Transcripts of doctor-patient interviews, with parenthetical notations of the physician's thinking and behavior, illustrate how the skills are applied in clinical situations.

Family-Oriented Primary Care: A Manual for Medical Providers (McDaniel et al., 1990). This recent textbook authored by Susan McDaniel, Thomas Campbell, and David Seaburn declares at the outset that it focuses primarily on developing skills at Levels 2 through 4 of the five levels of physician involvement with families described by Doherty and Baird (1986). The emphasis of the book is Level 4, with mention of Level 2 and encouragement of Level 3. At Level 4, "the physician not only gathers information and deals with family affect, but intervenes in ways that may alter the family's interactional patterns. The physician at this level has an understanding of family systems theory and a grasp of the skills to counsel families to make constructive changes" (p. 12). Convening the family and conducting a family conference are cornerstones of the authors' family interventions. Family systems concepts are reviewed, and a systematic protocol for assessment is proposed. Though not explicitly acknowledged, the systems concepts presented reflect the influence of Minuchin, Bowen, McMaster, and family life-cycle theory. The systems interventions, as summarized in protocols, are tailored for each of the clinical problems presented. These protocols are meant to summarize the "practicalities and skills involved in day-to-day family-oriented primary care" (p. xiii). They are viewed as the operationalization of theory in practice, and describe in detail the counseling skills required for Level 4 family-oriented primary care.

Although the focus of this critique is the family medicine literature, authors in other clinical disciplines have written about the family in their clinical practices (e.g., psychiatry, behavioral medicine, family therapy, social work, and nursing). Three books from the nursing literature are relevant here, for they too describe primary care models of practice for "medical" patients: Hymovich and Barnard (1973), Miller and Janosik (1980), and Bradshaw (1988). These works are reviewed briefly to highlight the similarities between the family medicine and nursing literatures. In the remainder of this chapter, however, I will continue to limit discussion to family medicine; the parallels for nursing will be obvious.

Nursing

Family Health Care (Hymovich & Barnard, 1973). Debra Hymovich and Martha Barnard wrote and edited this book for nurse clinicians interested in family nursing. Family developmental theory expands the background for family interventions by building on an overview of

family structure and major tasks and functions. Crisis theory and behavioral therapy provide most of the specific recommendations for
assisting family units through common crises relating to health. Assessment questions are specified, as are the seven ways to help another in
crisis. The authors advocate anticipatory guidance; usually both parents
are included in the suggested interventions. Clinical cases illustrate the
general principles.

Family Focused Care (Miller & Janosik, 1980). This book was
written for upper-level undergraduate and master's students in nursing,
social work, counseling, and community service. Jean Miller and Ellen
Janosik have produced a work that includes virtually every theoretical
framework: developmental theory (Erickson & Duvall), structural theory (Minuchin), communication theory (Stair, Jackson, Haley, & Bateson),
psychoanalytic theory, and Bowen theory. These perspectives are con-
densed into assessments of family structure and family function. This
assessment model is applied to both family developments and challenges
(including physical and mental illness). Crisis theory is introduced in
the challenges section as well. In addition, behavioral interventions are
described as useful for some problems, and finally, family anticipatory
guidance is described. Family group sessions appear to be the dominant
mode of recommended clinical practice.

*Nursing of the Family in Health and Illness: A Developmental Ap-
proach* (Bradshaw, 1988). This book, edited by Martha Bradshaw,
primarily confines itself to developmental theory, but includes systems
and interactional perspectives in its six-point family assessment. Chapters outline family and individual tasks, potential stressors, coping
mechanisms, nursing assessment of family and individual, alterations
in health of individuals, and nursing responsibilities for each family
stage. Family units and individuals are the subjects of interventions.

CRITIQUE OF MODELS

The works described above are impressive. It is apparent that a great
deal of time and thought went into the development of the theoretical
models and assessment frameworks they present, which are based not
only on the writings of others, but also on the clinical experience of the

various authors. The elegance of the assessment frameworks is noteworthy, from the simplicity of the four questions of Doherty and Baird (1983) and Crouch and Roberts (1987), to the more elaborate PRACTICE acronym of Christie-Seely (1984b), to the very detailed Primary Care Family Assessment of Sawa (1985), to the thorough protocol outlined by McDaniel et al. (1990), to the problem-specific evaluations of Henao and Grose (1985). The complexity of the proposed frameworks parallels the theoretical foundations upon which they are based in that Doherty and Baird's and Crouch and Roberts's models are based primarily upon Minuchin's model, the frameworks of Christie-Seely and Sawa are derivatives of the McMaster model, and the approach of McDaniel et al. stems from both. Those of Henao and Grose combine Minuchin with Bowen and Weakland and Fisch. Regardless of theoretical orientation, each of these assessment frameworks presumes that the family is seen as a unit and that formal assessment precedes intervention, as Christie-Seely (1984b) underscores: "Family intervention without assessment is like treatment without diagnosis" (p. 216). Although the contents of the interventions may be different, owing to the variations in theoretical foundations, the family counseling skills proposed in all the texts are remarkably similar.

Even as elegant and impressive as these works are, annoying questions keep coming to mind: Do these exemplars really work with families in this way? Are these theoretical models, assessment frameworks, and counseling skills ideals toward which one strives, or are they used routinely in the exemplars' work? Are the clinical cases and transcripts "classic textbook" examples or are they representative of the typical daily encounters of these exemplars of family-oriented care? Even if the exemplars follow these frameworks to the letter, is this an everyday occurrence or reserved for a small fraction of their patients and families? How do they do family-oriented care for those who do not have indications for family conferences or complete family assessments? How did they come to embrace and adapt these particular theoretical models? How is it that they know that this is how they do their clinical work? How do we know that this is what they do? How do they know that this is what their learners do after completing the training?

Although the emphasis of these textbooks is on assessing and counseling families as units, each discusses the issue of how a systems perspective can be brought to clinical care without convening the family. Doherty and Baird (1983), however, note that "the key difference between a family physician who *thinks* in family terms and one who *practices* a family approach is that the latter regularly sits down with families in the office and hospital" (p. 19). These textbooks provide little guidance to physicians who want to "think family"; the work of Michael Glenn (1984) speaks more directly to this issue. Rather than describe a formal assessment framework, Glenn indicates that the practical approach to diagnosis is to begin with the "biomedical core" and to combine this with the "psychosocial envelope." Although he does not explicitly propose a theoretical model, Glenn's discussion of a comprehensive nosology, and the addition of family typologies from Olson's circumplex model and Beaver's systems model to the DSM-III axes, again reveals the assumption that theory drives practice. Glenn's work provides some guidance as to how one can think family and not necessarily practice a family approach, yet it leaves most of the same questions unanswered.

The six above-described works on family-oriented care from the family medicine literature were written to provide guidance for those family physicians choosing to work with families as units. The questions about how to apply systems thinking to the care of individuals are interesting, but cannot be considered a criticism of these exemplars' works, since this focus was not their intent. It is also not these authors' intent to address questions about how well their learners are able to master the material, or how well they apply it in their subsequent clinical practices. These are, however, some of the most interesting questions that arise out of reviewing these textbooks and are of crucial interest to educators.

Data are available on education outcomes for one of the frameworks, the Primary Care Family Assessment and counseling skills described by Sawa. Sawa, Henderson, Pablo, and Falk (1985) have reported long-term effects of the curriculum, in family functioning and assessment, in a study of self-reported attitudes and behaviors of residents who had completed the curriculum as well as other family or general physicians who had not completed the curriculum but who practiced in communities similar to those of the graduates. Sawa and Goldenberg (1988) also studied current residents before and after the training and compared them with residents from other family medicine training programs, as well as experienced physicians practicing in the same community as the residents receiving the family assessment training. In the long-term study, the trained family physicians "appeared to have a better understanding of the theory of family functioning, are more likely to recognize a family problem, and were more likely to take appropriate action toward solving that problem than the controls" (Sawa et al., 1985, p. 55). In the second study of current residents, there appeared to be a beneficial impact of the family assessment training program on residents' level of comfort and confidence in interviewing couples and families (Sawa & Goldenberg, 1988).

As noted earlier, the framework proposed by Sawa (1985) is based upon the McMaster model, as is the family assessment framework presented in Christie-Seely's (1984b) book. The McMaster model of family functioning (Epstein, Bishop, & Baldwin, 1982) and the corresponding treatment framework, problem-centered systems therapy of the family (Epstein & Bishop, 1981), have been well described. The authors of this framework have reported the results of a preliminary study that had three goals: "1) to develop a short, intensive training program which would train family physicians to carry out brief, systems-oriented family treatment based on the clearly defined model; 2) to evaluate the impact of this training on physicians' practices; and 3) to test the effectiveness of this treatment approach in managing psychosocial problems" (Bishop et al., 1984, p. 391). Bishop and colleagues report that the "training went well and was well received. However, in spite of ongoing contact and support from the research group, the physicians were not able to recruit families successfully" (p. 382). The family physicians were subsequently interviewed by one of the investigators. The physicians reported that they were using the skills they had learned, but not in any systematic or documented way. They did not bring families in for formal assessment, but "applied informal treatment interventions in an irregular fashion" (Bishop et al., 1984, p. 382). The family physicians appeared to provide interventions regardless of the patient's reason for the visit and irrespective of whether the patient contracted for or desired family interventions.

In their discussion, Bishop et al. (1984) report that their findings are similar to those of a study by McLean and Miles (1975) of a training program for family physicians in behaviorally oriented couple therapy for the treatment of clinical depression. McLean and Miles suggested that family practitioners act inconsistently and/or illogically, but Bishop et al. note that while the physicians were indeed inconsistent and incomplete in their approach, they were not illogical. McLean and Miles noted that the family physicians were idiosyncratic and individualistic in their application of the concepts and techniques and observed that the physicians' approach to the family problems seemed to be similar to the approach they utilized when dealing with biomedical problems. Bishop and colleagues even suggest that the approach taken by the family physicians may be more appropriate and effective for their type of practice than the systematic assessment and treatment framework presented in the training program. They offer several possible explanations for their observations: potential differences in the cognitive styles between family physicians and family therapists, economic and role constraints affecting the use of formal family assessment models in family practice, the particular trainees chosen for the project, resistance of the trainees to research procedures, and frank ineffectiveness of the training procedure.

The observations and comments of Bishop and colleagues produced lively discussion (see, e.g., Bishop & Epstein, n.d.; Hochheiser & Chapados, 1985; Weston, 1987). One of the most useful products of this debate has been the observation that "one of the tasks for academic Family Medicine is to develop a conceptual model of the discipline which describes what effective family doctors actually do in their practices" (Weston, 1987, p. 9). This statement relates directly to the questions raised above about how the clinical assessment and treatment frameworks were developed. Are these idealized frameworks or actually what the family physician authors do? How did the authors come to know that this is what they do? These questions are absolutely critical, for until we have adequate answers for them, we will not know whether the results noted by Bishop et al. (1984) were due to problems with the training program or problems with the clinical framework—a rather fundamental distinction in education.

The authors of the texts on exemplary family-oriented care comment that their approaches are based upon theoretical foundations described by others and their own clinical experience. The methods by which "their own clinical experience" was studied and analyzed in order to produce the clinical frameworks is not described. This is understandable, given that these texts are intended as clinical works and not research reports on the thinking and practice of family-oriented practitioners. Although not specified, it is assumed that the authors developed their frameworks in part by reflecting upon their clinical experiences. Through reflection and introspection, the practitioners became consciously aware of their problem-solving processes (P. E. Johnson, 1983; Kassirer, Kuipers, & Gorry, 1982).

Descriptions of how to perform successfully certain tasks that are developed through reflection and introspection have been called "reconstructed methods of reasoning" (P. E. Johnson, 1983). According to

P. E. Johnson (1983), these reconstructed methods are usually "rules for how a task might be done that seem plausible to a practitioner or group of practitioners in some domain of problem solving. These rules are often fairly general and are usually intended to apply to a variety of forms of a given task" (p. 91).

> Reconstructed methods of reasoning are usually developed by experts in order to codify what they know; often the methods appear in the writings of a practitioner group. . . . Reconstructed methods of reasoning are typically validated by acclamation. That is to say, they are claimed as sensible and indeed, elegant descriptions of the problem solving methods of a field by its practitioners. . . . The advantage of reconstructed methods of reasoning is that they are a means of constructing expert algorithms for doing a problem solving task. Reconstructed methods are typically understood and accepted by a problem solving community and as such they frequently serve as a means of justifying a series of problem solving steps. The disadvantage of these methods of reasoning is that they do not always work, sometimes not even in the hands of those who devised them. (p. 82)

The implications of these observations are obvious. The clinical models proposed in these textbooks on exemplary family-oriented care have been validated by acclamation. They are seen as being sensible and elegant. They are even well received by the students who learn them. But, as Bishop et al.'s (1984) results suggest, they may not work.

This issue is not isolated to the area of family-oriented care, but involves virtually all of medical education, which "consists of experts teaching students reconstructed methods for doing tasks. The fact that many students have difficulty solving problems successfully upon leaving medical school suggests that reconstructed methods are not adequate" (P. E. Johnson, 1983, p. 83). This issue may be particularly important, however, in the field of family-oriented care, because reconstructed methods of reasoning may work quite satisfactorily with well-structured problems, but for more ill-structured problems, such as those in the psychosocial and family domains, reconstructed methods are often unsuccessful (P. E. Johnson, 1983).

The problems with reconstructed methods of reasoning are not limited to these textbooks, but also affect the clinical practicum part of the curriculum. One of the primary pedagogical principles of teaching family systems is that exemplary models must be involved in clinical practicums. The views that these exemplars take toward the "kinds of knowing essential to professional competence" have a direct bearing on the suitability of reconstructed reasoning to the training process (Schon, 1987, p. 38). If professional knowledge is seen as facts, rules, or procedures that can be routinely applied to problems, then reconstructed methods may be legitimate. If, however, professional knowledge is seen in part as "thinking like" a family-oriented practitioner, then the learning will also include "the forms of inquiry by which competent practitioners reason their way, in problematic instances, to clear connections between general knowledge and particular cases" (Schon, 1987, p. 39). Even within this type of practicum, the exemplar may presume that there is a right answer for every situation and thereby emphasize the *rules* of inquiry.

Alternatively, the exemplar may assume neither that existing professional knowledge fits every case nor that every problem has a right answer, in which case the exemplar allows for "reflection-in-action," during which learners may develop new rules of inquiry. Learning to "think like" a family-oriented practitioner presumes that the existing rules of inquiry, or the new ones developed through reflection-in-action, can be made explicit. "Depending on one's view of 'thinking like a __ ,' coaches may emphasize either the rules of inquiry or the reflection-in-action by which, on occasion, students must develop new rules and methods of their own" (P. E. Johnson, 1983, p. 39). The appropriateness of variability among clinical coaches is not being questioned, but the method by which rules of inquiry and reflection-in-action become explicit is in question, given the observation that introspective reports often produce inaccurate or misleading inferences about thought processes (Kassirer et al., 1982).

For the benefit of both the writings about family-oriented health care and the exemplars who teach during clinical practicums, the assessment frameworks and rules of inquiry need to be made explicit. The most commonly used method of making this professional knowledge explicit, introspection, produces reconstructed methods of reasoning that are often unsuccessful when dealing with ill-structured problems (Schon, 1987). Of all the problem-solving domains confronted by family physicians, the family area certainly is characterized by ill-structured problems. By what methods, then, do we produce professional knowledge that can be transmitted through textbooks and clinical practicums in such a way that learners use the knowledge and are successful at solving clinical problems? How do we capture what have been called "authentic methods of reasoning"? ("Authentic methods of reasoning are developed by those who practice them and are validated by evidence demonstrating that they are operative in the behavior of the members of a problem solving community;" Johnson, 1983, p. 82).

METHODS OF
PRODUCING PROFESSIONAL KNOWLEDGE

These alternative methods of producing professional knowledge are described as process-tracing studies, in that the focus is on the forms of decision making that involve processing of information to make judgments (Elstein, Shulman, & Sprafka, 1978). "In the process tracing tradition, human thinking and problem solving are typically viewed as a series of operations susceptible to verbal characterization and perhaps restatement in a computer simulation program" (Elstein et al., 1978, p. 11). "Thinking aloud" and other verbal reports are considered to be legitimate data that are collected and transformed into information-processing models (Kassirer et al., 1982). The major unit of study is the process by which a problem is solved, and the major output is a detailed verbal, and perhaps quantitative, model that is proposed as an explanation of the observed problem-solving processes.

Process-tracing studies differ by the type of decision task, such as whether it is simple or complex, and whether the total task or particular parts or subtasks are examined. Total task investigations vary in their fidelity, which is a description of the degree to which the study task approximates the tasks confronted by the decision maker in actual practice. High-fidelity formats most closely resemble decision tasks in the natural setting, whereas low-fidelity formats are less realistic (Elstein et al., 1978; Kassirer et al., 1982). Several different formats of process-tracing studies have been used; these are briefly reviewed below.

Ethnography

Atwood Gaines (1979) undertook an ethnographic study of the psychiatric residents providing consultation for psychiatric emergencies identified by hospital emergency room physicians. He collected data from each of four residents during interviews that focused on aspects of the resident's ideology related to emergency psychiatric diagnosis. He solicited the resident's definition of the emergency situation, including the resident's conception of his role in the emergency room and the kinds of people the resident saw there. Gaines also gathered information on how the residents organized their knowledge about mental illness, especially the causes of mental problems. To obtain a graphic portrait of these conceptions of mental illness, he asked each resident to draw a diagram portraying his conceptual organization. Finally, he collected and analyzed case materials from at least one-fourth of all emergency cases handled by each resident.

Despite formal training in the same program, the residents all held different conceptions of mental illness that were readily apparent. These models ranged from impaired abilities in the area of human personality and cognition due to a biological flaw or deficiency; to difficulties in reasoning, problem solving, and reality testing due to thought disorders; to problems in handling or coping with current situational problems or levels of stress; to complex problems that may be medical, mental, social, or a combination of these, requiring a consideration of the patient's social context. The residents' perceptions of their roles and definitions of their therapeutic options were derived from these conceptions of mental illness.

Although Gaines "did not observe these residents actually making diagnoses, or making different diagnoses of the same patient" (p. 405), he was able to use verbal reports to develop a verbal, and even graphic, model that explained some of the residents' problem-solving processes that were apparent even to their peers. It is of considerable interest to note "that none of the residents' records indicate any shift in perspective during the course of their residency" (p. 408). Gaines points out that this is consistent with the work of others, showing that residents have the very same work style at the beginning and end of their training and that training serves only to provide acceptable linguistic codes with which the residents can express their already established perspectives on mental illness and its treatment.

Encounter Recordings

The second format for process tracing is to record actual encounters between physicians and patients (Crouch & McCauley, 1985, 1986; Kassirer et al., 1982; Lawler et al., 1985; Pridham & Hansen, 1980; Rogers & Durkin, 1984). These can be analyzed to determine the types of family information solicited and how this information appears to be used in decision making (Crouch & McCauley, 1985, 1986; Rogers & Durkin, 1984). Alternatively, such recordings can be coded to record several phases of verbal problem-solving behavior in order to describe the sequencing of these behaviors (Pridham & Hansen, 1980). Finally, these recordings can be used together with the physicians' "talking aloud" about internal thought processes as well as attributions and evaluations being made (Kassirer et al., 1982; Lawler et al., 1985). These data then can be used to develop "maps for action" that represent the behaviors people use to design and implement their actions (Argyris, Putnam, & Smith, 1985; Lawler et al., 1985). These maps represent the causal scripts that individuals use to inform their actions.

Recordings of Simulated Patients

The third format is to record, on audio- or videotape, encounters between physicians and simulated patients (Barrows, Norman, Neufeld, & Feightner, 1982; Kassirer & Gorry, 1978; Lutz, Schultz, & Litton, 1986; Neufeld, Norman, Feightner, & Barrows, 1981). The doctor-patient interview can be accompanied by "thinking aloud" on the part of the physician, who provides reasons for asking questions during the interview (Kassirer & Gorry, 1978). Alternatively, the tape can be reviewed immediately after the session, with the physician recalling his or her thinking processes during the encounter, using the tape to stimulate recall (Barrows et al., 1982; Lutz et al., 1986; Neufeld et al., 1981). The transcripts of the encounter can be reviewed and coded in a variety of ways to provide an analysis of the apparent decision making of the physician. In addition, the thinking-aloud or stimulated-recall protocols can be analyzed to understand the physician's account of his or her decision-making processes.

Simulated Encounters Without Recordings

In the fourth format, encounters with simulated patients are conducted without recordings, but data are self-reported by the physicians after the encounters or recorded by trained observers of the live interviews (Elliot & Hickam, 1987; Hampton, Harrison, Mitchell, Prichard, & Seymour, 1975; Harasym et al., 1980).

Case Simulations

The fifth format for process tracing has been used most frequently in a variety of studies of clinical decision making, but has the lowest fidelity of any of the formats considered thus far (Babbott & Halter, 1983; Benbassat & Bachar-Bassan, 1984; Berner, Hamilton, & Best, 1974; Donohue & Shumway, 1983; Eddy & Clanton, 1982; Feletti & Gillies, 1982; Harasym et al., 1980; Hickam, Sox, Marton, Skeff, & Chin, 1982; Leahey & Tomm, 1982; Margolis, Barnoon, & Barak, 1982; Marshall, 1983; Scherger, Gordon, Phillips, & LoGerfo, 1980; Silverman, Gartrell, Aronson, Steer, & Edbril, 1983; Simpson, Gjerdingen, Dalgaard, & O'Brien, 1982; Spiegel, Kemp, Newman, Birnbaum, & Alter, 1982; Stephenson & Bass, 1983; Voytovich, Rippey, & Suffredini, 1985; Wigton, Hoellerich, & Kashinath, 1986). This procedure consists of paper (Babbott & Halter, 1983; Benbassat & Bachar-Bassan, 1984; Berner et al., 1974; Donohue & Shumway, 1983; Eddy & Clanton, 1982; Feletti & Gillies, 1982; Harasym et al., 1980; Hickam et al., 1982; Marshall, 1983; Scherger et al., 1980; Simpson et al., 1982; Spiegel et al., 1982; Stephenson & Bass, 1983; Voytovich et al., 1985; Wigton et al., 1986) or taped (Leahey & Tomm, 1982; Margolis et al., 1982; Silverman et al., 1983) case simulations being presented to problem solvers who then respond to instructions. Typically, clinicians are asked to state their clinical hypotheses, request additional diagnostic information, develop a problem list, state the likelihood of a specific diagnosis, and outline treatment plans for the case. These studies rarely involve psychosocial or family issues. Those that have included these issues confirm the results of Crouch and McCauley's (1985, 1986) study based on taped doctor-patient encounters; namely, physicians rarely solicit psychosocial or family information and often ignore information of this type when it is spontaneously offered by patients (see also Silverman et al., 1983).

Questionnaires

The sixth format is not formally a process-tracing methodology, but has been used to capture clinicians' attitudes and practice policies regarding various family or psychosocial issues (Kushner & Meyer, 1989; Steinert & Rosenberg, 1987). This is the administration to physicians (Kushner & Meyer, 1989; Steinert & Rosenberg, 1987) as well as to patients (Clark, Schwenk, & Plackis, 1983; Frowick, Shank, Doherty, & Powell, 1986; Good, Good, & Cleary, 1987; Hansen, Bobula, Meyer, Kushner, & Pridham, 1987; Kushner, Meyer, & Hansen, 1986, 1989; Schwenk, Clark, Jones, Simmon, & Coleman, 1982; Steinert & Rosenberg, 1987; Yaffe & Stewart, 1986) of questionnaires about family and psychosocial problems. The results of these questionnaires are often used to determine the level of training residents may require in the family or psychosocial arena (Frowick et al., 1986; Schwenk et al., 1982; Steinert & Rosenberg, 1987; Strain, Pincus, Gise, & Houpt, 1986).

Case Presentations

The seventh and final format that has been used is the taping and analysis of case presentations during ward rounds, morning reports, teaching conferences, and clinical care settings, such as intensive care units or emergency rooms (Klos, Reuler, Nardone, & Girard, 1983). The one report of this methodology does not deal at all with family-oriented care, but the ubiquity of case presentations in the clinical writings reviewed earlier and in other works (Doherty & Baird, 1983; Houts & Leaman, 1983; Kushner, Mathew, Rodgers, & Hermann, 1982) indicates that this may be a fruitful approach to process tracing.

COMMENT

As noted earlier, the textbooks on exemplary family-oriented care discussed in this chapter include a number of case presentations and a few interview transcripts. It is apparent that some appropriate verbal data were available to the authors for classical process-tracing studies. The determining factor is whether the cases and transcripts were reviewed to produce the assessment and counseling frameworks or whether the cases and transcripts were chosen because they nicely demonstrated the frameworks previously developed by other means, such as introspection. The issue is whether "reconstructed" or "authentic" methods of reasoning characterize the type of professional knowledge contained in these textbooks of exemplary family-oriented care.

Our exemplars of family-oriented health care have expended considerable time and energy codifying their professional knowledge, presumably through the process of introspection. The scholarly works that describe their working frameworks have been acclaimed by their peers. Questions linger, however, over the credibility of the frameworks and the ability of learners to use them successfully. One source of this uncertainty is the very nature of reconstructed methods of reasoning vis-à-vis authentic reasoning. Process-tracing studies of family-oriented health care are a necessary part of the solution to these difficulties. The alternative methods by which information-processing models and action maps can be derived have been reviewed.

Education presumes an idea about the desired outcome, or product, of instruction. Exemplars embody the desired outcome. Knowing what exemplars do and how they do it is essential for meaningful teaching. For research to guide our instruction, the work of the future must address two questions: How well do the current frameworks for family-oriented health care work? Do process-tracing studies produce frameworks that work better?

TWELVE

Three Ways of Thinking

RUSSELL J. SAWA

STUCK IN FIRST GEAR

A 22-year-old Italian man, Mario, and his mother, Maria, came to the hospital emergency room requesting that Mario be prescribed narcotic analgesics and be admitted as a patient. His complaint was abdominal pain. This would have been his seventy-fifth admission in less than two years, during which no diagnosis had been established. A diagnosis of porphyria had recently been ruled out. The physician was on call for the regular physician, who had mentioned the case briefly during the day. A resident, who was on call, reported that the patient was lying on a stretcher and groaning.

This patient had a highly recurrent problem that resisted resolution by the usual methods of treatment (hospitalization, narcotics, and many repeated investigations). The clinician adopted a new approach. He asked that the patient be allowed to dress and that mother and son be asked to meet him in the emergency department's family meeting room.

The on-call physician then went into the room and began questioning Mario about his perceptions of his illness and its meaning to him. As the clinician listened to the story, he noted the degree of the mother's emotional upset and the very close way in which the two seemed to be emotionally allied, mother and son both exhibiting very similar nonverbal expressions of emotion. So cued, the physician inquired about the closeness of their relationship and those of other family members by asking who was most concerned about Mario's illness. Mario and Maria agreed that Maria was the most worried (even more than Mario himself). The doctor also learned that Mario's father had a chronic illness (chronic back pain), for which he had been on a disability pension for 30 years, and that Maria showed her love (as did her mother before her) by caring for her family when they were ill. The physician also learned that Mario's usual symptoms—nausea, vomiting, and abdominal pain—were often brought on by stress, and that Maria was very concerned that some awful illness that might kill her son was not yet diagnosed by the doctors.

With this limited information, the physician hypothesized a completely new formulation of the problem: that Mario's symptoms served a useful function in the family. The symptoms allowed Maria to be a good mother. They kept Mario bound to the family, since the illness and the family's response to it interfered with his schooling and his development of intimate peer relationships. However, the symptoms also were viewed with such high concern by the family (especially Maria) that the family may have organized itself around the illness, thereby limiting the development and differentiation of its members. The clinician concluded that the family was involved in dysfunctional patterns and needed help, regardless of whether a diagnosis for the illness would be found in the future.

The physician noted that as the discussion went on, Mario stopped groaning, began to take on a normal facial appearance, and then sat up quite normally by the end of the interview—in no apparent distress, despite being given no analgesics. This further supported the physician's hypothesis that interpersonal (systemic) issues were tied into the symptoms. In making this assessment, the physician was "thinking family," noting how the mother's emotional state fed into Mario's and vice versa, and noting that the family's balance had incorporated the illness and medical system into itself through the frequent involvement with health care personnel.

The physician then made a judgment based on the data. He informed mother and son that he felt the family was an important unit in helping to solve Mario's problem. This reframed the situation in an entirely new way, removing the exclusive focus on the symptoms and the search for a diagnosis. Mario left the emergency room looking and feeling well, without the usual analgesic. By suggesting that the family should be involved in a future meeting about Mario's illness, the physician was reframing the situation by sending the message that the family was important in the resolution of Mario's illness.

The on-call physician shared this information with Mario's regular physician, who initiated several sessions of family therapy. The therapy was discontinued by the family, as it was interpreted by them as meaning that the family was abnormal or at fault. The family was later invited to meet with the on-call physician, who routinely worked with families in his practice. The purpose of the meeting was to share medical information or talk about Mario's illness, a topic the family was eager to pursue. The physician's agenda was also to learn about the family's perceptions of the illness and its meaning and to correct any misconceptions the family might have. Through several such meetings, the family came to recognize that Mario was not seriously ill, and that the feelings and interpretations they had of the illness were not in keeping with the medical facts. They also learned that the strong feelings of anxiety felt by Mario and other family members about the illness were now contributing to his distress. At the same time, they learned about how normal such reactions can be under the circumstances, thus relieving them from any burden of blame. Mario accepted some behavior modification sessions to help reduce his stress.

THREE WAYS OF THINKING

The usual approach in Mario's case had been to strive to find the diagnosis of a specific organic disease. I will refer to this as the *mechanical* way of thinking. In the hospital, when the on-call physician changed the environment to the family room and began paying attention to Mario's perception of his illness and what it meant to him as a person, the physician was using a *personal* way of thinking. By inquiring into relationship issues, he moved into a *systemic* way of thinking. Switching to the personal and systemic ways of thinking allowed the family to become unstuck therapeutically, and subsequently the family and patient were able to become unstuck in their persistent view that some body part was diseased and was gravely threatening Mario's health. I will now discuss each of these ways of thinking in more detail.

The Mechanical Way

When a person, such as Mario, comes in to see a physician with abdominal (or any) pain, the clinician may, after a brief greeting, begin immediately to think of the emerging problem or illness in terms of underlying anatomy, pathophysiology, and possible diagnoses. The physician's attention is focused on parts of the body in a reductionist fashion, using linear cause and effect between illness and possible causative factors. This is thinking in the mechanical way.

The mechanical way, which may be no less caring than the personal mode, but in a different way, focuses on disease as a thing. The doctor-patient relationship is primarily parent-child (with doctor as the authority) or I-it (person to body part). The underlying epistemological (what constitutes knowing) assumption is empirical (knowledge is limited to immediate sensory experience). Patients are viewed in a dualistic fashion, with a mind/body split. Answers to illness are usually sought in the body before the mind, psyche, or spirit is considered as causing or contributing to the illness. The workings of the mind itself are reduced to biochemistry and neuroanatomy. The clinical method involves clarifying problems and solving them.

In using the mechanical way of thinking, we come to know through sense observation. The process results in data or facts that can be analyzed to develop a definition of the problem or a diagnosis. The mechanical way of thinking forms the basis of the biomedical model.

The Personal Way

We are persons by virtue of our relationships to one another. The goal of personal development is individual psychosocial development (Erickson, 1963), intimacy in relationships, appropriate and just relationships in society, and ultimately self-transcendence, in which the individual finds meaning and fulfillment through caring for others in some way. There may be a spiritual dimension to being a person in a relationship that has been described by Buber (1958) as an "I-thou" relationship. Any loving relationship is a healing relationship. The personal is the foundation for some forms of psychotherapy (Perls, 1970; Rogers, 1961; Yalom, 1980).

In the realm of the personal way of thinking, knowledge is obtained through personal interaction. It involves both feeling and intellect, and thus involves the whole person. Change occurs through growth, by innate developmental stages that involve differentiation and integration of knowledge together with transformations achieved through relationships with other persons and groups. Two persons in a relationship do not lose their individuality to become functional elements in a larger entity that includes them both, like cogs in some larger machine.

When the physician pays attention to the patient's feelings, worries, expectations, and fears and integrates this personal information with data about the illness, he or she is using the personal way of thinking. The meaning the patient attributes to the illness is a reflection of the inner world of the patient.

During clinical encounters, the physician is relating in the role of physician to the patient as a person. A physician employing this way of thinking tries to encourage the appropriate level of autonomy in the patient. Thus the physician invites collaboration rather than blind obedience to his or her authority.

In his clinical method, McWhinney (1986) refers to the development of the physician as a person. The transformation of clinical method from its present form to a patient-centered approach would require the physician to have self-knowledge, moral awareness, a reflective habit of mind, and a capacity for empathy and attentive or active listening (McWhinney, 1986).

The clinical method at the personal level involves clinical problem solving, but from a patient- or person-centered approach, rather than a doctor-centered approach (Brown, Weston, & Stewart, 1989; McWhinney, 1986; Stewart, Brown, & Weston, 1989; Weston, Brown, & Stewart, 1989).

Because family medicine also encourages personal responsibility and personal development of the patient, it implies a psychology that depicts persons as free to choose (with varying degrees of limitation) and a corresponding responsibility to be accountable (Rogers, 1961). Implicit in the above are both values and norms. Family medicine also values intervening preventively. To do so, it recognizes objective norms of development and prognosis based on current status of health or disease. A way of knowing (epistemology) consistent with this approach will thus allow for objectivity and norms as well as for feelings and the activities of internal consciousness (Lonergan, 1967, 1972).

The Systemic Way

Mario, in the case that opened this chapter, lives in a family that relieves interpersonal stress by expressing that stress somatically through one of its members. When thinking about the stresses and supports that are present in the families and social contexts of our patients, we move into the systemic way of thinking.

The systemic way rests on an analysis of living beings in the context of an ecosystem (MacMurray, 1933). Whether or not the social sciences will accept this theory as a basis for methodology remains to be seen.

In any event, it provides an excellent (and essential) theoretical foundation for understanding systems such as the family.

Knowledge in systems is about harmony and balance or, conversely, in some systems, about disharmony or conflict and imbalance. Change is seen as a process of growth through development, differentiation, and coordination of parts. Since the unity of what is alive is a unity of differences, not a reduction to some nonliving entity, it follows that the organic whole cannot be represented as the sum of its parts, as in the mechanical way of thinking. In the systemic way of thinking we cannot understand living creatures adequately when we see them only in terms of themselves; they must be viewed in terms of their larger environment.

In systems thinking, no part of an organic whole can be really individual (i.e., a child cannot be fully understood unless considered in the context of the family). Only the whole possesses true individuality. For this reason the person can become "lost" (in the mind of the clinician) in the larger system of which he or she is a part when the clinician is thinking in the systemic way, unless the personal way of thinking is the foundation for the physician's thinking as a whole.

POTENTIAL CONFLICT INHERENT TO
THE THREE WAYS OF THINKING

It should be recognized that the underlying assumptions of the three ways of thinking may differ radically from one another. For instance, some systems theorists find the norms (Dell, 1985) and linear causality inherent in the mechanical way of thinking (Dell, 1985, 1986) to be contradictory to their assumptions. In the same vein, a completely materialist empirical position found in the mechanical way of thinking denies the spiritual dimensions of personhood. This is one reason the biomedical model in itself is limited and is often extended by a biopsychosocial model. The personal way of thinking itself may be rejected, as Bateson does when he states, "The individual mind is immanent, but not in body. It is immanent also in the pathways and passages outside the body; and there is a larger mind of which the individual is only a subsystem" (quoted in Dell, 1985, p. 17). For these thinkers, there is no objective system, only distinctions that different observers draw.

At the same time, the personal must also contain or include the mechanical and systemic. But the world is not a machine or an organism. If the world were primarily a machine (i.e., if the mechanical way of thinking were foundational and thus best able among the three ways of thinking to provide understanding), then Mario could have been helped to attain health with a mechanical approach alone, since *health* would refer to the function of his bodily parts, which, mechanically speaking, were working (no abnormalities were found, despite extensive investigations).

If the world is to be understood with the systemic as foundational, as a system made up of other systems, then the concept of personhood would have to be understood as contained within our understanding of *system.* Yet systems thinking itself may lose sight of the personal, with the personal's freedom, love, dignity, autonomy, responsibility, and so on; in such thinking, health would be achieved by having Mario conform to the larger systems of his family, the health care system, or society as a whole, as determined by the rules of the system.

Examples of this thinking occur regularly in the political sphere: In totalitarian societies, authority decides the rules of how society is to be and forces people to behave or be a particular way. Under totalitarianism, individuals and groups are integrated into a closed, compulsory system defined in terms of a future order of the state and society, and dynamized by an ideological sense of mission of a better society or race (Bracher, 1973). Ethnic or cultural values may also be imposed on family members. This can be problematic, especially when a family moves to a new culture where restrictions and expectations are different. An application of this system in a clinician-client relationship would be the imposing of values by the clinician onto the client or patient, together with the use of power or manipulation to attain the goals or changes decided upon by the clinician. Even though the purpose of the intervention may be to stimulate positive change as judged by the therapist, this practice does not conform to the ethical guidelines in the personal way of thinking.

AN INTEGRATED APPROACH: FOUNDED ON THE PERSONAL

A systemic way of thinking that has the personal way of thinking as its foundation would regard the values inherent in the personal way of thinking as primary. Respect for individual persons would have a higher claim than the perceived welfare or good of the larger system. Thus the person could not lose his or her individuality and become a cog in some larger machine, as happens in political systems where the system or state is the primary value. By respecting the personhood of its members, the larger system would then presumably have its purpose accomplished as well, since the purpose of the system would be to achieve the good of its members. The dignity of the person would be an inviolable right.

The three ways of thinking may be conceived in an integrated fashion, with unopposed underlying assumptions if the personal way is the comprehensive and foundational source from which the others are derived. From this point of view, the world of human relationships, however complex, is personal. The personal way is foundational, in that persons are intrinsically in relationship (in a systems context). Also, persons have bodies with internal body parts that can be discerned in mechanical thinking, and thus the personal can contain within it the mechanical. One can also apply the principles of how systems function to machines, people's bodies, as well as to systems of relationships. Systems thinking can be applied to anything that is a part of a larger whole in which the whole is greater than the sum of the parts that have relationships with one another.

It is only when the world is comprehended through the personal way of thinking that the most comprehensive understanding occurs. The mechanical nature of the human body can be understood without contradicting the personhood of the individual within the body.

Similarly, the system of relationships a person has is well understood in personal terms. In fact, when systemic thinking is an extension of the personal, the elements that make up an ordered or functional system, as opposed to a dysfunctional system, naturally and lucidly unfold. An ordered or functional personal system will contain meaning, purpose, knowledge, love, freedom, respect, and hope. Through a personal way of thinking, a universe of meaning arises.

Applying this integrated approach clinically in the above case, the therapeutic goal with Mario and his family is to help their personal system (family) behave more personally (freely, mutually, out of love and knowledge rather than merely out of habitual patterns), so that there is no further need for them to bind themselves together in fear or ill-founded concern for Mario's health.

Psychoeducational approaches (Anderson, Reiss, & Hogarty, 1986) and family therapy models (Epstein, Bishop, & Levin, 1978) built on complementary ways of thinking with primary care principles may provide rich interdisciplinary dialogue through recognition of common underlying assumptions that take into account the personal way of thinking as primary.

FROM THEORY TO PRACTICE

It is important that a conceptual framework for clinical practice that includes persons, families, and larger systems be as simple, cogent, easy to teach, and consistent with clinical experience as possible. It should also be easy to adapt to the clinical setting.

In Chapter 14 of this volume, Becker points out that for innovations to be adopted (and for most contemporary physicians, including families in health care is an innovation), they must be compatible or must fit with the values, experiences, and needs of the practitioner; they must be simple rather than complex; they must be able to be tried out on a limited and experimental basis; and they must be observable. It is my experience that the three ways of thinking constitute a simple concept, in that it is readily understood and validated by students and practitioners; it expresses the values and experiences of practitioners and can be readily applied in practice. It also helps to define which of the theories and skills developed and used in other disciplines such as family therapy and the social sciences can be adopted by family medicine. Such theories and skills would fit with the values of the personal way of thinking and have the qualities Becker describes.

Family medicine will continue to evaluate and adopt what is applicable from the rapidly evolving disciplines of family therapy and the social sciences until authentic models, as discussed by Rogers in Chapter 11 of this volume, are developed. The concept of three ways of thinking can be used to help students extend their thinking, and also provides a framework that they and their teachers can use in evaluating the applicability of theories and skills that might be adopted in family practice.

Family physicians often have long-term professional relationships with their patients; they foster patients' growth and development toward wholeness, encouraging independence wherever possible. They establish relationships of trust that endure through time. This involves, at times, advocacy for patients. These assumptions can be applied in any context where problems of any sort need to be solved. Let us examine how the three ways of thinking can be used clinically.

In Mario's case, the fact that clinicians, his usual physician as well as others who had seen Mario prior to the emergency room visit described above, had remained in the mechanical way of thinking for several years may have arisen because the physicians did not ask themselves if the illness might have meaning beyond the mechanical level (i.e., through exploring its meaning at the personal and systemic levels). This illustrates the limitation of being stuck in the mechanical way. Even if a diagnosis had emerged, the family's growing frustration around the illness and the medical care received would have been ignored if this way of thinking alone were used. Because they had not moved into the personal way of thinking, the physicians attending and consulting apparently had not recognized or communicated clearly enough to Mario or his family how stress could be leading to many of his fears and symptoms. They were also prevented from beginning stress management for Mario, which did occur once the personal and systemic ways of thinking were used that made clear many of the dynamics in this illness.

It must be emphasized, however, that moving too quickly from the mechanical way of thinking can be fraught with danger. Examples of this include the cases of many women whose painful endometriosis resists diagnosis for years while they are told that all their symptoms are "in their heads." A recent case in Canada resulted in the death of a child whose abdominal pains were dismissed as psychological. An 8-year-old boy was admitted to the hospital with abdominal pain and vomiting. He was, at one point, made to clean up his own vomit as "therapy." A week after admission, surgeons discovered a section of his bowel was twisted, causing his pain and forcing him to vomit. Before the condition could be corrected, he had a cardiac arrest and died.

Once Mario's case was perceived from all three ways of thinking, the clinicians continually had to judge about the reality of the situation. Were the symptoms of organic, emotional, or systemic origin (or all three)? The approach that moved exclusively into a systemic family therapy mode may have failed because it did not take into account the family's interpretation of the meaning of the illness (i.e., Mario might die) or the family's interpretation of what it means to go into therapy (i.e., We are a bad family, and we have caused Mario's problems). Mario's parents spoke only very poor English, and this may have further impeded communication.

The use of all three ways of thinking completes the picture. The physicians always maintained a firm belief that the facts (data) can be known and used to intervene. Ideas about family function were simply tools that permitted the formation of a coherent picture that could lead to insight and understanding. Judgment that the hypothesis was correct and should be acted upon was also a critical step.

A physician who operates only out of the biomedical model may not recognize the personal or systemic ways of thinking. A family therapist, using a constructivist framework (appropriately), might find the reductionism of the biomedical model and its focus on disease antitherapeutic.

Clinical Application: A Team Approach

Mario's case could have been handled by three cooperating clinicians working together: a biomedical expert, a psychologist, and a family therapist. Each might hold radically different assumptions, yet the three could make contributions collectively to get the case unstuck. An interdisciplinary team can work together to get beyond stuck situations. Problems to be avoided include the following:

(1) Two clinical team members are involved and one uses only the mechanical mode of thinking, refusing to accept evidence from another way.

(2) A family therapist takes only a systemic approach while ignoring the importance of the mechanical and personal.

(3) A family therapist working with a primary care clinician adopts a manipulative systemic intervention that ignores or offends the personhood of the patient or family and leads to disengagement with the therapist and clinician.

(4) If the personal way of thinking is ignored by team members, there might be dissonance between them and a primary care clinician who has become Mario's advocate.

(5) The attending physician asks the help of the team, but persists in the mechanical way of thinking while team members wish to move into the other ways.

This last instance indeed appeared to occur in Mario's case. While the two family sessions with the on-call physician that consisted of sharing medical information diffused the anxiety of the family, the attending physician continued to view the problem as fundamentally and primarily physical. This removed any reason to explore family issues further. Mario was seen fairly regularly in the office for what were thought to be his abdominal migraines.

Ultimately, the usefulness of any hypothesis generated by any physician will be decided through all of the following steps (Barden & McShane, 1969; MacMurray, 1933):

(1) Check the validity of perception of the experiential data.
(2) Correctly manipulate the ideas with the use of a valid model for understanding such ideas.
(3) Correctly judge the sufficiency and validity of the data.

Restriction to the first step and to only measurable data is a materialist-positivist limitation and is inadequate to get Mario's case unstuck or moving again. Limitation to the second step reduces the kind of essential information obtained in the first. And judgment not based on the data will likely be fallacious. Norms and objectivity are assumed in order to decide where the case is off track.

A medical specialist could function solely in the mechanical way, as long as he or she worked with a family physician and perhaps a family therapist. Collaboration would be required.

As Mario's case unfolded over time, knowledge grew richer. Different opinions and suggestions emerged, determined by the breadth of experience of those involved. Mario and his family were discussed among all the physicians who might see Mario in after-hours, on-call situations. Ultimately, the attending physician made the judgments about what should be done clinically and how the group of physicians should relate to the patient and his family. Collaboration was achieved. Biases among team members were questioned and discussed.

Clinical Application: A Single-Physician Approach

Mario's case illustrates that a clinician (on-call physician) can move from one way of thinking to another freely. In order to do so, the clinician must assume that he or she can and does know a real world, and that, in order to come to know it, his or her intellect is involved in a dynamic process that involves experiencing, understanding, and judging the validity of relevant data (Lonergan, 1967). By remaining true to the assumptions of the personal way—personhood as the ultimate value, freedom, respect, autonomy, and so on—and by applying systemic thinking, the on-call physician was able to switch from one way of thinking to another, remaining radically open to any data, physical or emotional, objective or subjective. The methodology employed demonstrates that experiences may lead to understanding, and understanding to correct judgment about events in the real world. The physician also made the assumptions that Mario is responsible for his own actions, that he has freedom of choice, and that his personal development is enhanced by the physician's fostering his autonomy as much as possible.

Having made the case that all three ways of thinking are necessary if a single physician is to be able to get out of a stalled or stuck situation as in Mario's case, I must note that it is important to realize that physicians functioning exclusively in one of the three ways of thinking might hold assumptions that are diametrically opposed to some of the assumptions necessary for an individual to function in all three. The opposed assumptions might be contradictory epistemologies or assumptions about how knowledge is gained or understood, theories of causality, or views of human nature. In order to adapt techniques or theories from disciplines such as family therapy, we should openly recognize and celebrate the presence of such contradictions, since these differences may be cues to expanding our understanding of the world in which we live. However, they should be adopted in family medicine only if they are compatible with the personal way of thinking.

The most important insight is perhaps that of the potential complementary nature of the three ways of thinking, as long as each is being applied in the appropriate circumstance. The "shifting of gears" to the systemic (family) way allows one to contemplate initiating change in the patient's problem by changing the system in which the problem is embedded.

Practical Suggestions:
How to Use the Three Ways of Thinking in the Office

McWhinney's (1986) clinical method utilizes the personal way of thinking. In this method the clinician strives to encounter the patient as a person by inquiring into the meaning of the illness from the patient's point of view. Kleinman and Katon (1981) also encourage the inclusion of the personal by suggesting that clinicians explore the patient's perception and personal understanding (explanatory model) of illness. This can be fleshed out by obtaining the patient's ideas on the cause of the illness, its severity, the kind of treatment it might need, the anticipated results of the treatment, and what problems the sickness has caused the patient. The world of the patient is further explored through discussion of the meaning the illness has for him or her, and what the patient fears most about it.

One can move into the systemic way of thinking with the patient by inquiring about the most important or difficult experiences he or she associates with the illness, and how these experiences are important to or affect family and friends (Good & Good, 1981). One can also inquire what the patient thinks other people think about the patient's illness, how they react to the patient, and how he or she feels about those reactions. The patient's perceptions of the problems the illness has caused for others might enrich this view of the patient's world.

In a family interview, the physician can gain a deeper understanding of the relationship system by asking difference questions (e.g., Who is most concerned?), triadic questions (asking one person to comment on some aspect of the relationship between two other people), and interpersonal perception questions (what one person thinks another thinks or believes about the illness). Questions can be used to investigate, explore, or facilitate change (Tomm, 1987a, 1987b, 1988).

A systemic way of thinking that remains personal is appropriate for a primary care physician. If an intervention violates the dignity or lessens the autonomy of the patient for no adequate reason, it is probably inappropriate.

Some clinical situations may require switching gears more than others. It is valuable to be able to recognize such situations in advance. The following is an initial list; clearly, this list will be expanded as we learn more about what causes physicians and patients to get stuck.

(1) When one way of thinking is not succeeding (Be sure patient and physician have the same agenda.)
(2) Somatization
(3) Life-style change
(4) Chronic or terminal illness
(5) Vague and ill-defined problems
(6) Chronic pain

SOMATIZATION: CAN THIS BE WHY MARIO'S CASE IS STUCK?

In my opinion, Mario's case is one of somatization (Lipowski, 1988). Somatizing patients are "those who frequently complain of physical symptoms that either lack demonstrable organic basis or are judged to be grossly in excess of what one would expect on the grounds of objective medical findings" (Lipowski, 1988, p. 1358). Somatization is very common worldwide. Somatizing patients such as Mario account for a disproportionately high number of visits to physicians' offices and outpatient clinics, laboratory investigations, prescriptions, and surgical procedures (Lipowski, 1988). It should be noted that somatization does not imply that the patient may not have a concurrent illness. Somatization may coexist with, mask, and be facilitated by such an illness. Research suggests that a child exposed to much physical pain and illness behavior, as Mario was with his father, who had chronic back pain since before Mario's birth and throughout Mario's formative years, is at risk for somatization as an adult. A child who learns that being ill or complaining is likely to be rewarded by increased attention or avoidance of some obligation is predisposed to develop somatization as a coping strategy in later life (Lipowski, 1988). Mario had the entire family's attention whenever he was ill, especially his mother's.

Cultural/ethnic considerations may come into play as well. Mario's family emigrated from Italy to Canada, both Western countries. Somatization is most often found in Western countries. As Mario's regular physician pointed out to me, Mario's mother was much like many other Italian and Slavic mothers in his practice, who also seem to be overly concerned about their children's health. Somatization appears to be particularly prevalent in cultures in which expression of emotional distress in psychological terms is traditionally inhibited (i.e., Canada and other Western countries). In my opinion, any case of somatization requires intervention using all three ways of thinking.

It should be noted that criteria for diagnosis of somatization disorders as defined by the American Psychiatric Association (1980) in the DSM-III require that the symptoms be of several years' duration and have at least 12 of a possible 37 symptoms, including nausea, abdominal pain, vomiting spells, bloating, intolerance of a variety of foods, fainting, and dizziness. (The DSM-III is used for research purposes and sets the standards for diagnosis in North America. Europe uses the ICD-10.) By these criteria, Mario has not yet acquired a fully developed case of somatization disorder, but he does have somatizing symptoms. Without intervention he would undoubtedly acquire the full disorder. It is recognized clinically that the number of symptoms builds over time, as the personal and familial anxieties persist and mount. Mario was first seen with his symptoms at age 21. If interventions had not occurred to curtail the overly concerned and exaggerated responses of Mario and his family members, the symptoms would have continued to persist and other symptoms of somatization would have appeared.

TEACHING THE THREE WAYS OF THINKING

Medical students vary in their openness to the social sciences, arts, and humanities, as do medical schools. Often, the empirical sciences are seen as producing "good" knowledge, with the underlying assumption of positivism (knowledge is attainable only through sensory experience). The social sciences, however, are sometimes seen as "soft" or second-rate in importance. When teaching the family to medical students, it is necessary to integrate information from the physical sciences, the social sciences, and the humanities. It is important for teachers to recognize the resistance of some students to the psychosocial area, so they can adopt an approach that opens the mind rather than inhibits learning. The concept of the three ways of thinking allows an integration of the humanities and sciences because it is a useful and readily acceptable metaphor for the ways clinicians in primary care actually think as they help people with the wide variety of problems that arise in the context of a doctor-patient relationship.

Our Western society is also often biased toward the notion that objectivity is good and subjectivity, particularly subjective feelings, is not to be trusted. This attitude may also be common among medical students. Medical schools generally do not expose students to the various methods of answering the questions that have been discussed by philosophers over the centuries—What is knowledge, or truth, or acceptable evidence?—nor do they even provide guidance in how to think critically. Nonetheless, to formulate more comprehensive theories and skills, medicine must integrate knowledge from the sciences and humanities. On the one hand, the adoption of positivism would reject data from the social sciences and humanities; on the other hand, the adoption of subjectivity without norms (i.e., idealism/constructivism) would undermine the biological and physical sciences. Adopting a phenomenological approach to looking at the doctor-patient relationship and other relationships (which necessarily involve subjectivity) is useful and necessary, but any outright denial of some degree of objectivity and its norms would be a major stumbling block for the adoption of a family perspective by family medicine and primary care. Thus, for the teacher and/or theoretician, a way of knowing (epistemology) that allows for both objectivity and subjectivity (Lonergan, 1967) is essential. Both objectivity (to allow for norms) and subjectivity (to express the personal) must be retained, as well as a recognition that we can have differing viewpoints, stemming from our different experiential and intellectual backgrounds, that can all nonetheless be correct.

Differing Viewpoints or Horizons

Teachers should be aware that all persons have deep, fundamental assumptions, which are often unconscious (Lonergan, 1972), that may preclude their adoption of one or more of these ways of thinking. Our basic assumptions are often hidden, even from ourselves. We can discover these assumptions by observing and reflecting on how we behave in given (clinical or other) circumstances.

How can there be both the "objectivity" of norms, yet validly differing experiences of the same reality or phenomena? This occurs when two individuals each possess excellent reasoning skills and a dedication to "the truth" and yet have differing breadths of experience. The intellectual life can be compared to a person standing on a mountain looking out in all directions (Lonergan, 1972). That person would have a particular view. As the person moves down the mountain, his or her perception of the shapes and contours of all the surrounding objects would change. If the person were to move to a second mountain, again the shape and the total expanse of the horizon would change. What I can see relates to where I stand (the breadth of my experience). Where I stand in the intellectual life is also associated with my fundamental, deep assumptions. I am often unaware of what these may be. Each person has his or her own horizon that delimits the scope of that person's knowledge and experience. So, too, do scope of knowledge and range of interest vary with the period in which an individual lives, social background and milieu, and education and personal development.

In the above case example, the two clinicians may have differing underlying assumptions and differing experiences that account for their fundamentally differing horizons. However, irrespective of this, Mario improved. After more than 100 admissions in a little more than 2 years, he has been in the hospital for the above-mentioned symptoms only twice in the last 10 months. Whether this is due to the family interventions or an improvement in the migraines (despite absence of successful response to specific antimigraine therapy) is left for the reader to decide. Mario's treatment is decided by his regular physician, and other on-call physicians follow his protocol. At the present time, Mario is treated with Demerol and intravenous hydration when he presents in the emergency ward with his symptoms. He settles and is discharged in 2 days.

An educator might be required to encourage clinical students to open their minds in recognition of wider domains. Clear articulation of the three ways of thinking may help a student clinician gain facility in moving from one way of thinking to another. When the underlying assumptions differ between individuals, this may be used to engage in generative learning (see Smith, chap. 10, this volume).

The likely first step in teaching would be to help student clinicians to become aware of their particular assumptions. They could be exposed to clinical situations in which it is necessary to shift from one way of thinking to another. Severe whiplash (acute and chronic pain with disability), terminal cancer, quadriplegia and paraplegia, type one diabetes, depression, old age and inability to cope at home, dietary restrictions in at-risk situations (coronary artery disease and diabetes), disabling neurological disease from cerebrovascular accidents, multiple sclerosis, and Parkinson's disease are all good examples of diagnoses for which all three ways of thinking are necessary for optimal clinical management. Somatization as in Mario's case provides dramatic illustration of the relevance of these concepts.

By presenting these kinds of cases, ideally with videotape as well, teachers can help students to achieve the insight that they need to open their minds to thinking that goes beyond the biomedical. Pointing out the benefits of including the personal and systemic ways of thinking in terms of actual clinical scenarios can quickly help students gain the insight that all three ways of thinking are included in good medical care. Teachers should remember that medical students are often overwhelmed with learning facts, and they need to see the relevance of this theory.

Our current medical care systems have been biased historically by the wonderful achievements of the biomedical model and its mechanical approach. It is the task of this generation of young clinicians and scholars to continue to integrate the healing art of medicine with its science, for surely healing is the core of what being a physician is all about.

THIRTEEN

Family Medicine: A Time for Clarity

MACARAN A. BAIRD

As demonstrated in the chapters of this book, there is reason to embrace a family-centered approach to medical care as an important theme for family medicine. People do, after all, still commonly live and function within and relate to family units (however defined and in changing forms), in spite of shifts in family economic status, social mobility, and widened definitions of *family*. Nevertheless, for more than two decades family physicians have been unclear and ambivalent about our *family* label.

THE FAMILY IN FAMILY MEDICINE: WHY THE AMBIVALENCE?

From our roots in general practice, we have evolved into a viable medical speciality on the North American continent, with recent successful experiments in many other countries in Asia, South America, and Europe. Why, then, is the family theme of family medicine still controversial? My response to this quandary of ambivalence relates to several factors that have worked together to make us unsure and unclear about the clinical and educational implications of adopting the family in our name.

First, family medicine is the only medical specialty to identify itself with something other than an organ system or bodily function, disease

AUTHOR'S NOTE: I would like to acknowledge gratefully the editorial and motivational support provided by Dr. Russell Sawa. Without his diligent efforts, this chapter would not have been possible.

167

entity, or age group. Instead, we are named after a social and functional unit. Indeed, the name is ambitious! It has both liberated us from certain limits of other specialties and tied us to the quintessential generalist role in the face of powerful opposing forces. The name selection was simultaneously brilliant strategically and unrealistic politically. No other medical specialty is likely to challenge our title to a generalism that reaches even beyond the individual. Specialists are fighting for the right to smaller and smaller "pieces" of individuals! However, the political notion of family is changing with the evolving social definition of what a family is. Unlike an organ system, which does not change its role within the body, families evolve rather quickly as they try to cope with rapidly changing social and economic forces. Therefore, functional definitions for *the family* will continue to change with time. At least we have some consolation that there is little competition for our name.

A HISTORICAL PERSPECTIVE

Let me recount our first two decades. Most of the early pioneers in family medicine came directly from general practice. In those early years, some family-oriented family physicians adopted what at times sounded like angry and strident voices, proclaiming that the family should be "the center of family practice." Perhaps in response to this, in the past I have preferred an understated approach to teaching and promoting the incorporation of the family in the care of our patients. I realize that these early well-intentioned voices wanted to distinguish the new specialty of family practice from the generalist without residency training. I realize that the generalists in the past often practiced with longitudinal knowledge of each patient and took for granted that they knew each patient's family because of their style of practice. These same practitioners were often highly involved in many procedures and surgical operations. This part of their clinical activity was challenged by competitive specialties. Faced with battles for hospital privileges and issues of direct consequence to their earning potential, these doctors assigned a low priority to the importance of involvement with families as a reasonably efficient way to gain better understanding of individual patients, and this aspect of their practice was lost. They lost sight of how frequently the family either supported or undermined the physician and a movement to health, especially during difficult interactions.

It is understandable that during those years the political leadership of family practice had more powerful economic issues to address than whether or not family physicians were either skilled in thinking about families or significantly involved with patients' families. Although a legitimate pragmatic and academic part of family medicine, family issues did not generate intense interest at the political and economic levels. It seemed that only angry and strident voices could attract attention.

During the second decade of family medicine the academic faculties of the specialty became actively involved in writing about family themes within the scope of this medical specialty. At national meetings, slowly increasing numbers of family physicians began discussion with other academic disciplines, such as family social science, family nursing, family therapy, and psychiatry. Regional workshops and continuing medical education courses often included topics related to "working with families" and family therapy in the context of family practice. Each residency developed an approach to the behavioral science objectives of the curriculum, often with a family systems orientation. Academic leaders and a few private practitioners published numerous articles and books relating to families and health. In fact, family themes have become a primary focus of academic textbooks published by family medicine faculty. The family in family medicine has been a most stimulating topic for academic family physicians. However, the specialty as a whole remains ambivalent about family issues being clearly stated as central to our specialty.

I believe that understanding the patient clinically usually involves understanding the patient's context, relationships, and support systems. The patient's family is important because it has shaped that patient's health beliefs, genetic vulnerability, and economic survival, and it is a major support system. Given all this, why must we strive to understand our patients' family themes? It is simply pragmatic to do so. It saves us time and energy. Often, we can learn and benefit from both questions and answers offered by family members.

A CLEAR, FIRM STAND:
LIVING UP TO OUR NAME

Without being strident, we can now confidently state that for us to be excellent family physicians, we must often seek information from and about our patients' families. Sometimes we inquire about family members' feelings about the primary patient's medical condition. On some occasions we attempt to intervene in family interaction patterns that impede our patients' well-being. For example, for an alcoholic patient, a family physician may ask for family support to seek specific assistance for an alcohol-related problem that the patient cannot easily address alone. Of course, the physician would respectfully ask for the patient's permission to seek this family participation. On rarer occasions, family physicians may suggest that patients with particular problems would be most aided by seeking consultation with or referral to family therapists.

None of these activities is inappropriate for a family physician. Many can be useful to the patient and his or her family. These concepts are not incompatible with other daily activities that also define the broad specialty of family medicine. Family thinking and interactions need not be more or less important than other basic activities within this specialty. No boastfulness is needed. Our adolescent rebellion from general practice can move toward a more mature self-definition. Reactivity against others or our history is no longer essential for our specialty. We know who we are now, after more than two decades: We are *family physicians.*

All of clinical medicine has struggled with the problems of how to use basic research findings in direct clinical care. How do we apply new knowledge? Drs. Rogers, Smith, and Sawa, in their chapters in this volume, have undertaken the problem of reconciling early basic theory on the treatment of families in primary care with realistic physician education and applied research. Each author approaches the problem from a different perspective.

RECONSTRUCTED METHODS OF REASONING

In his summary of some of the major publications that contributed to the formulation of family-centered care in family medicine, Rogers's analysis of reconstructive methods of reasoning outlines the limitations of the first efforts to describe family-centered care and family medicine. There are indeed limitations in the current literature and models of teaching family-oriented family medicine. We must collectively and heartily support research using different formats, such as "process-tracing studies" or direct observation of exemplary physicians who claim to practice in a new model. This careful observation could lead to clearer understanding of family-centered models.

The purpose of earlier reviews of literature has been to propose a model for talking with and treating patients in a more complex manner than that encouraged by the biomedical model. As Rogers has pointed out, we can generate one or several research protocols to evaluate the practice of several of the "exemplars" in actual practice. In this way we might learn more precisely the nature of the gap between written expression of these concepts and actual practice by the exemplars.

As Rogers suggests, we might use process-tracing studies to understand more clearly the gradations of involvement with families in family medicine. The "levels of involvement with families" concept has not been adequately researched. I believe that expanding the studies (using Rogers's suggestions) already done by Kushner and Meyer (1989) and Kushner, Meyer, and Hansen (1989) on this concept would be a useful enterprise.

I will now expand upon the development of our models (Doherty & Baird, 1983, 1986). I do so in order to expand upon and make clear how the existing models have been derived. As will become evident, there is an element of introspection on my personal experience both as a family physician and a family therapist. However, there is also a strong element of trying out my ideas, in both clinical and teaching situations, and modifying the model I was working on based on feedback from patients and students. I will also comment on the various influences on my own thinking. I should also point out that I began my personal journey toward developing a new way of practicing by observing a clinician and patient encounter and having an insight that something was missing in the model of that clinician. The idea that this was the contextual or family dimension occurred to other colleagues (R. J. Sawa, personal communication, November 9, 1991) who also developed models at about the same time, and to family physicians who also integrated family therapy and family medicine clinically (Christie-Seely, 1984b; Sawa, 1985); this suggests to me that our discipline had developed to the point where it was ready to evolve in this new direction.

FAMILY THERAPY AND FAMILY MEDICINE

In the publication *Family Therapy and Family Medicine* (1983), William Doherty and I offered a direct confrontation of the status quo. That book was anything but mainstream in family medicine and was greeted with a wide continuum of responses, both negative and positive. It is interesting that this work has now been identified as a seminal work for guiding the future direction of family medicine. When my key chapters of this text were developed, they reflected my own anger and my own (unknown at the time) desire to be recognized as different from most family physicians. And yet I felt that this new model of practice (and I) should be recognized as legitimate.

Once I entered academic medicine, I became directly concerned about the teaching limitations of our proposed family-centered model. After listening to residents' and students' frustration with the model, Doherty and I modified the model (and thus added an experimental component to our model-making method) to demonstrate gradients of involvement with patients' families (Doherty & Baird, 1986). In our first effort to teach primary care family counseling, *Family Therapy and Family Medicine,* we used a language that we discovered later was not always intelligible to residents in family practice. Subsequently, we modified the term *primary care family counseling* (again using feedback to correct deficiencies in our model) in order to help residents and physicians in practice value the intermediate steps from no involvement with family to heavy involvement with family. These gradations, or *levels of involvement with families,* both permitted trainees to reward themselves for behavior they were already doing and encouraged them to seek more challenges if they chose to become more involved with patients' families. In this manner, we employed the generative learning model that Smith describes in Chapter 10; however, we did not use her more precise educational language to describe it.

The concept of levels of involvement with families has since become well received and used in family medicine and is outlined in several other chapters in this volume. Research is now beginning to show that the "developmental levels of involvement with families" concept applied to working with families does have validity, as demonstrated by Kushner et al. (1989; Kushner & Meyer, 1989).

MY PERSONAL JOURNEY
TOWARD FAMILY-CENTERED CARE

I became interested in including families in the care of individual patients when I was a medical student on a nine-month rural elective in

Minnesota. During that process I could be included in the medical interview and not be primarily responsible for the decisions made by the physician (see also p. 1 in this volume). In that experience it became apparent to me that the routine medical encounter sometimes left both physician and patient moderately dissatisfied. This occurred most frequently when the patient's complaint was not well focused or was complicated by conflicts with family members. Sometimes this would surface with statements such as, "My mother doesn't agree with you, doctor, about this medicine." Such a statement was usually not addressed directly by the physician, who would continue with the medical treatment plan undisturbed. However, in weeks to come the patient would return to the physician unimproved. The physician would focus attention on alternative diagnoses or treatment plans, but never would return to the prior concerns of the patient that a respected family member had originally (and perhaps still) disapproved of the management plan. By staying within the traditional approach, the physician would continue to try to persuade the patient of the validity of that approach. What would happen if we inquired about the other family member's reasons for disagreement? At that point in my training I did not know the answer, but I was determined to find out.

During my residency I was involved in learning "office counseling" and only indirectly was approaching the above-identified dilemma. The training as a family therapist was to help me become useful to couples and families facing internal conflict, which I had also come to appreciate while a student. However, at that time I did not anticipate that the family therapy training would confound my thinking and behavior toward every patient. It was not then clear to me that as a family physician with longitudinal contact with patients I was inexorably intertwined with patients and families as if we were all part of an extended family. Once I gained insight into working with families as a family therapist, my approach to patients was modestly different. Specifically, whenever I felt something important was happening I would ask if the patient would permit me to include at least one other family member in the interaction. It seemed perfectly natural to me to do so. Only much later did I realize that few "family physicians" actually saw families. These meetings usually occurred in the hospital, at first, to discuss a patient's serious diagnosis or treatment plan. These would occur once or twice per week to once or twice per month. Later I would convene a family meeting in the office usually to discuss some more chronic illness. The office meetings were usually briefer (20 minutes versus an hour) and could be done as part of a routine visit.

Soon after I entered practice I was excited to find that the McMaster model of family functioning was published in the *Journal of Marital and Family Therapy* (Epstein, Bishop, & Levin, 1978). This was the most clearly explained model of comparative healthy family functioning versus problematic functioning that I had seen. I was so convinced that this model would help me explain my new interests to other physicians that I ordered 100 copies of it for a presentation that I was giving. To my despair, other physicians did not immediately see its relevance to practice. I had not yet appreciated that I was thinking and acting in a manner that was qualitatively different from other physicians in family practice. Slowly I began to realize that very few family physicians actually "saw families."

The McMaster model was helpful because it teased out specific dimensions of family activities and roles that could lead to either adaptive or dysfunctional responses to challenges. It led well past the description of a family as "well" versus "dysfunctional" to more discrete descriptors. I could then develop an internal language for myself when I encountered families that were stuck in some interactive pattern that had become problematic. I did use the model to organize my thinking about families and to describe to others in a more specific manner how families function. Specifically, the domains of direct and clear communication, affective response and involvement, and roles within the family were helpful constructs for me. However, I did not (and never have) used that formal instrument for a clinical assessment of a family.

Then, as now, I directed my work with families from a symbolic/experiential model (Whitaker), guided as much by my sense of intuition as by any of the other classical models of family assessment or therapy. In this model the experience of therapy is encoded in symbolism and metaphors that cradle the meaning of the therapeutic interaction. The remembered symbolism is more important than the specific words that created the symbol. For example, if a couple is struggling with the impact of the loss of elderly parents through illness and also learning slowly to cope with an emancipating teenager, they may be stimulated to see the teenager as moving toward adulthood—thus predicting their own impending death in the future. The symbolism might be discovered by the process of the therapist stating what he or she associates with the family dilemma, for example, "Mr. and Mrs. X, I just had a fantasy that if you allow your son to grow up you may be inviting your own funeral! I know that sounds a little odd, but I just thought I would mention it." If this is too direct or too far afield, it will be quickly rejected as irrelevant by the family. If the metaphor is close, it allows the family to model it to their own interpretation and create a new meaning for their conflict. Perhaps they could see themselves as courageous to allow their son to grow more independent rather than view such changes as "caving in" to his wishes.

Rogers is essentially correct in his suggestion that in our introductory book, *Family Therapy and Family Medicine,* Doherty and I used reconstructive methods (but with a combined use of student feedback to rectify it as needed) to create our "new model" of primary care family counseling. In fact, Doherty and I discussed Doherty's experience as a family therapist/family social scientist teaching family physicians and my efforts to learn pragmatic new options for patient care as a dually trained family physician and family therapist.

My experience in practice (5 years in rural Minnesota) was essentially my personal experiment with inviting families into the discussion with the patient when major medical events were occurring. Having been trained to invite families into a therapeutic contract as a family therapist (I trained in family therapy while doing my family practice residency, and became certified by the American Association of Marriage and Family Therapists just before graduating from my residency), I was empowered and willing to risk their involvement when I was in the role of a family physician caring for the individual identified patient. However, I had not yet become conscious that I was breaking from a traditional approach. (No one told me that family physicians don't frequently include the family in the care of patients!) Through our discussions, Doherty and I discovered that there was, indeed, a concrete sense of a functional "therapeutic triangle" made up of patient, family, and physician. This insight, along with the insight that it was most reasonable to have family members join the patient and to discuss the patient's illness, forms the basis of both the model in our textbook and the model of levels of involvement with families. Doherty would bring the insights and experience I had in my medical practice into the language and conceptualization of family theory.

A case we described in that first book will serve as an example. I was caring for an elderly widow who had been hospitalized repeatedly for angina pectoris. The tempo and urgency of the admissions were accelerating. During one admission I invited the patient's family to discuss this repeated experience. They explained their terror at the prospect of being the one who would respond too slowly to their mother's report of angina and be responsible for her death. As this was explored, the patient became aware that *any* complaint from her had eventually become interpreted as her indirect request for medical evaluation to rule out her next potential infarction and risk of death. A quick trip to the hospital would result. Upon inquiry, I found that she actually would prefer to report her discomfort but be involved in deciding whether or not to seek medical attention for a given episode. She felt that some events could be managed at home. What she really wanted to do was play the piano, even if she did get angina. She wanted to live a little and worry less about waiting to die. Subsequently, her admissions became infrequent. She was admitted for her final infarction and died peacefully in the hospital as she had wished. Her family mourned her loss, but did not suffer guilt over not responding appropriately. Through this process I slowly learned that a family interview could change the meaning and impact of the illness for everyone: patient, family, and physician.

By processing such cases together, Doherty and I cogenerated this alternative model of interacting with patients and families in a purposeful manner. Doherty's theoretical background and teaching experience and my clinical-experimental style of medical practice contributed equally to this newly constructed model. We cocreated the model and were energized by the collaborative process.

However, when we began to write the text, we concluded that teaching an intuitive style to physicians was not going to be helpful. Therefore, we used the structural model of family assessment (Minuchin) to create an understandable framework for family physicians who would be unfamiliar with almost any model of family assessment. In retrospect, I do not think that our suggestions for assessing family function were as helpful to family physicians as was the basic concept of the "therapeutic triangle" in medical practice. With the triangular concept in mind the idea of the "informal family health adviser" was easily received by most physicians.

DEVELOPMENT OF THE
LEVELS OF INVOLVEMENT WITH FAMILIES

We developed the levels concept because we learned from residents' feedback that they thought that if a physician was not doing whatever they viewed as therapy (whatever that "magic" is), it was not valid. They were so humble about their interactions that they did not realize that it was useful to be with families to discuss their medical conditions.

Levels 2 through 5 of our model are described below. Level 1, the basic, baseline level of involvement, needs no explanation.

Level 2

The goal of Level 2 involvement is sitting down, with confidence, and discussing medical matters with both the patient and his or her family. If a member of a patient's family has a problem, especially a serious or chronic one, or one that has psychiatric overlay, it would be useful for the physician to meet with the family to share medical perspectives. Ideally, this would be a collaborative experience in which the patient, family, and physician could educate one another. (Sharing information with the patient and family in this manner would be a minimum competency level expected of a resident and clinician in family medicine.)

Why would the physician be interested in participating in such a session? Because the one-on-one patient-doctor dyad is an optical illusion as a communication experience. It looks like a dyad, or two people conversing. But the "dyad" commonly expands beyond the bounds of the one-on-one conversation because either person may say something controversial, unacceptable, or painful. In such a situation, it is normal for the patient (or the physician) to go talk to someone else. Family communication theory suggests that the most stable communication unit is a triad, not a dyad. When two people are in conflict about something, one or both of them will find it comforting to talk to a third party and discuss what just happened. For the patient, the third person may or may not be trained in medical matters. As a result of these consultations, each person's belief system about the medical issue will be either verified or challenged. For example, the unseen family member could say: "That doctor's exactly right and I'm glad that you went" or "That's nonsense, you don't look sick to me." In the latter case, the patient comes back a week later and has not done anything about the treatment.

If, during the dyadic interview, the physician does not check out both the patient's belief about what this current illness or diagnosis means to the patient, as well as other information sources the patient may use, misunderstandings may arise. As physicians, we want to persuade our patients that we are right and, in this case, they are wrong. What do we do? We talk louder and faster, or we stand up with medical diplomas behind us on the wall and act more powerful! Of course, this is about as effective as trying to make a French-speaking person understand us by speaking louder and more slowly in English. It effectively blocks communication. In this manner, we persist in pursuing the individual patient when, in fact, the primary fulcrum here would be identifying who else is "in the room." It could be a consulting physician, a nurse, a spouse, or other "family health expert." By asking, "Is someone else advising you about this health problem?" we could discover this "informal family health adviser."

It is often very difficult for patients to confront their physicians when there is a conflict in medical beliefs. Few patients can comfortably say, "Maybe you're wrong, doc!" Thus the discomfort is not spoken and the triangulation happens silently. If we understand that this triangular pattern of communication is normal, we can explicitly inquire about it to allow everyone a voice in the medical interaction. For example, the physician might ask, "Mr. Smith, is someone else advising you about this? Who is that?" If he answers, "My mother-in-law, she's a nurse," or "My father-in-law, he's a neurosurgeon," the physician may then directly explore this: "Well, what does that person say?" Through such inquiry we may help all of us head in the same direction. In fact, in cases involving serious conditions, I would argue it is useful for the physician to meet with the patient and that (third) person. By doing so, he or she can create a therapeutic triangle and become decidedly less frustrated with patient dilemmas.

If I accept the therapeutic triangle as normal, then I may choose a positive direction and encourage that third person to come join the patient in the next interview. This is always done with the patient's permission. But if I do not accept the triangle as normal, and assume that the third person is just an extension of a quarrelsome patient trying to undermine my authority as a physician, I can erroneously choose to make a scapegoat of the uninvited third party. Once challenged, it is easy to blame the conflict on the absent member of the triangle. Defensively, I might say, "That person is wrong. Where is his or her medical degree? I'm the doctor here."

Loading the blame onto the third party who is not in the room is a process of scapegoating. While this may initially solve the conflict, it does not resolve the problems. Unfortunately, scapegoating is seductive. When we in family medicine have conflicts among ourselves, it is easy to blame them on the Department of Medicine or on the Department of Surgery. This becomes an easy way to relieve the tension between parties who are in conflict face to face. In the clinical setting, once the physician scapegoats the absent "family" member of the doctor-patient-family triangle, the patient later consults that person and the physician becomes the absent party and is discounted. We contribute to the problem by modeling for the patient how to make a scapegoat of the one who is absent. Unfortunately, once the patient is home, the physician is the absent member of the triangle. If we share information collaboratively with a patient and another family member, we may form a therapeutic triangle, and we can avoid the entire painful process.

Level 3

Level 3 involvement with families adds the discussion of feelings to the interactions of Level 2. Take, for example, the case of a woman with newly diagnosed breast cancer, facing a life-threatening illness and disfiguring surgery. The diagnosis and its implications induce a full range of images and fears. If I do not inquire of this patient and her family what the diagnosis and its implications mean to them, I will have no sense of the range of responses they might have. During the process of inquiry, however, there will be significant release of emotion. I must be prepared for this release and my own response to it. If I am not prepared to handle my own emotions about this situation, and because it is so awful to see someone uncomfortable, I could choose to cut off the discussion by inappropriately reassuring the patient and her family prematurely. This undermines the patient's and family's sense of reality and treats only my needs, not theirs. Unfortunately, this happens all the time in clinical medicine. I would argue that we need extra training about our own feelings, including how to be aware of them and how to deal with them in a healthy way, in order to manage such situations most helpfully.

In my clinical practice, I need someplace to talk about my feelings about difficult clinical situations. When I was in private practice, I picked up the continuing habit of connecting with my partners during hospital rounds. There I talk about the cases I am most worried about, such as the ones that kept me awake last night, or last week, or last month. This serves me functionally as a Balint group.

Approximately one-third of what physicians do is totally unrelated to what the patient needs. It is primarily related to what the doctor needs—not defensive medicine or greed as the motivating factor, but rather our affective needs. Physicians are human, and if we are upset, anxious, nervous, angry, or sad, may order more tests or fewer tests, or involve more consultants or fewer consultants, depending on our interactions with given patients. If we do not have a way to process our reactions to patients, we can become unbalanced in our professional interactions.

Some of what we do as human beings in the role of physicians is take care of ourselves. That we experience countertransference is not necessarily a problem unless we are unaware of it. Without a way to process our feelings, we run the risk of thinking we are being balanced and objective when we are being emotionally reactive toward the patient and unbalanced in our decision-making processes.

It has taken a support system and training for me to understand the importance of my own affect. It is very helpful to have someone (a nurse, a medical colleague, or a therapist) with whom to discuss my reactions to a given patient. It is also helpful, before I go into a patient's room, to evaluate if I need to be on guard—because I don't like this person or I do like this person too much, because I'm angry, or whatever. If I do not work to understand my feelings about my patients, my decision-making process will be negatively influenced and possibly incomplete. I have come to understand that although I may be angry with one patient or drawn too much to another or intimidated by yet another (who initially unknown to me wants me to be a "super doc"), I also have to be myself and be a physician.

Level 4

Level 4 involvement includes the use of short-term directed intervention. Consider a patient who initially presents with abdominal complaints. Over a series of interactions, it is apparent that her condition is primarily related to abuse of alcohol. A series of purposeful interactions might follow, with the first task being to convert her general complaint of abdominal discomfort to a specific diagnosis of gastritis due to alcoholism. At this point, it is important to persuade the patient that it would be appropriate that we collectively (her spouse/partner, herself, and the physician) discuss her drinking patterns and behavior. The short-term change of helping the patient to accept a mental health diagnosis and not just focus on the medical complaint means the physician must challenge the patient's and family's belief system about the illness. When we challenge belief systems, we have to connect with the patient's primary sources of support, which is usually (but not always) a family. Finally, in the total process, the patient would be assisted in enrolling in a recovery program. This entire scenario, while "short term" in concept, may take 2 years or more to accomplish.

The effective use of short-term directed intervention involving both patients and families is a fairly high-level skill. Even as a trained therapist,

I sometimes find it a difficult challenge to conduct such interactions in a respectful and honest manner. It is understandable that many physicians never learn to feel competent in this type of situation. To learn such skills as a resident or practicing physician takes dedicated extra effort.

Level 5

Level 5 involvement is equivalent to providing ongoing family therapy to patients. It clearly requires specialized training. Detailed discussion on this degree of involvement is beyond the scope of this chapter. Alternative resources may be helpful to clarify this role for a physician (see, e.g., Doherty & Baird, 1987b).

Most physicians take pride and satisfaction in working at Levels 2 and 3. Such interactions with families are both valuable and therapeutic. A few physicians function at Level 4, with fewer still trained to do family therapy.

A NEW WAY OF BEING A PHYSICIAN

Now that I have experimented with this method of viewing patients, I have become comfortable with a new set of assumptions about being a physician. My new assumptions are as follows:

(1) Patients' beliefs about a symptom or illness are important and discoverable if I am patient in my inquiry.

(2) Under ideal circumstances, it is helpful to understand the patient as a human being (connected to a wider context) before I invest in pursuing the medical diagnosis.

(3) Sometimes I am wrong.

(4) It is important for me to discuss troubling cases with colleagues or a therapist on a regular basis. For this reason, I have helped to create an academic environment enriched with multiple family therapists, psychiatrists, interested nurses, clergy, and so on.

(5) If I am enjoying myself in the process of providing care, I am doing something right. When I feel overworked and oppressed in this role, I have begun to become part of the problem.

(6) Bodies don't lie. If a patient's complaint cannot fit into any understandable medical diagnostic category, it is useful to state: "I believe that

bodies don't lie. If you could imagine some way to explain your conditions outside of medical 'stuff,' how would you do it? For example, although you may not be currently upset about anything, if you could pretend you are upset about something, what would it be like for you?" Corollary: medical treatment is not always helpful.

GENERATIVE LEARNING MODEL

Smith's generative learning model is parallel to learning through formative evaluation. We become better teachers if we listen to the feedback from those we are teaching. Much of the controversy about the appropriate role for family physicians as we care for families would be solved by providing feedback to academia and changing the teaching model.

Smith's different portraits of medical practice are similar to what Doherty, Baird, and Becker (1987) describe in the split biopsychosocial model framework. This suggests that we are still in a "split" biopsychosocial model, where clinical problems are viewed as either "bio" or "psychosocial" in content. An "integrated" model would not accept the definite separation of bio from psychosocial content. This is also consistent with the difference between Levels 1 and 5 in the levels of involvement model. The conflict between models offers an outstanding opportunity for learning. It is, as Smith notes, most helpful to use role conflicts and professional understandings that conflict in order to explore limits and mistakes in different views.

By adopting a generative learning style, both educators and trainees will learn from each other. We would do well to train trainers to understand and become proficient in the generative learning model, and also help them learn how teachers can constantly learn from the "learners."

A new area for research exploration is describing and understanding the limitation of the role of the primary care physician (family physician) as he or she tries to apply family therapy (Level 5). As outlined by McDaniel, Campbell, and Seaburn (1990), activities short of family therapy (Levels 2-4) seem most applicable to family medicine. Discoveries in the last several years have shown me that there is an inherent role conflict between the nurturing, yet challenging, role of the family physician and the more fundamentally provocative and challenging role of the family therapist. Since this is a new idea in the "generative process," I offer it for its ability to challenge models that we have been teaching for 10 years, including those models that I have helped create, in which the family physician is also family therapist.

THREE WAYS OF THINKING

It is clear that Sawa's concept of shifting gears is directly applicable to family medicine. So too is the concept of horizons that both limit our understanding and also allow us to discover new ideas. The concept of horizons is primarily useful to the teacher as he or she uses clinical cases to expand the horizon of the student who has limited experience. It is to be hoped that all of us expand our horizons with daily experiences. We need to continue to do research in a reductionist biomedical model (mechanical way of thinking) as well as research integrating personal-level experiences (personal way of thinking) that address psychological and social issues (systemic way of thinking). We would also be wise to research the complex interplay among the biological, psychological, and social/environmental levels of interaction.

Rather than *limit* or reduce the "dissonance" between these sometimes conflicting concepts of biomedical model versus biopsychosocial model, clinicians of different backgrounds should *celebrate* our differences and *enjoy* the dissonance created in different models! We learn the most when there is dissonance among our assumptions, models, and interpretations of experiences. When clinicians have different training, we often generate different, more creative, hypotheses on clinical cases. The potential for new discoveries and useful new interactions with patients multiplies. I would argue that it is extremely useful to expose trainees to these conflicting assumptions (often between "therapist types" and "medical types"). We should encourage trainees to explore these differences. In this way we can help them recognize the breadth of their own horizons as learners and also encourage them to broaden their view. It is for us as educators to provide the learning environment in which students are enabled and encouraged to express their dissenting views.

The concept of shifting gears is easily understood and readily applicable to a person in clinical training. Before I inquire about symptoms that might lead to a diagnosis, I first must understand why the patient is here today with this specific complaint, and what the meaning of this complaint is to the patient. After that, I shift gears into the way of thinking that is perceived by me to be most appropriate for a given case.

I agree with Sawa that it is helpful to assist students in developing an awareness of their own assumptions about reality (the content of their horizons). It is useful to expose trainees to clinical situations in which it is necessary to shift from one way of understanding to another. There is a potential complementary role for biological, psychological, and social/environmental influences in any problem. Thus Sawa's "three ways of thinking" do represent a clinical reality.

CHRONIC ILLNESS CENTER

A functional application of the theory presented in the three preceding chapters can be found in the Chronic Illness Center of the Department of Family Medicine in Syracuse. At the Chronic Illness Center, a team of physicians and therapists see frustrating cases together in order to reexamine the nature of the doctor-patient-family relationship. The physician identifies and brings his or her own cases (cases that are "stuck" in one way or another) to the program, where the physician is directly observed and/or videotaped, allowing us to inquire into his or her "on-the-spot thinking and feeling."

Why do we get stuck in the first place? We unwittingly begin to recycle through ineffective interactions. If we did not care at all about people, we would not get stuck. If we were not willing to suffer, we also would not get stuck. When we reach our limit of struggling with patients we limit our pain by not investing ourselves in the next difficult patient. I think this is wise. We do have limits to our energy. However, we have rarely found a way to get unstuck, even with a few patients. My informal discussions with family physicians around the continent have taught me that the average family physician has about 6 stuck situations with patients at any given time. Even if it were 20 cases, that is a small number compared with most of our panels of 1,500 or 2,000 patients. Yet these few patients are what give us our sense of satisfaction or dissatisfaction in practice. If we find a way to interact constructively with these few challenging patients and get unstuck, it changes our whole sense of what it is to practice medicine. We have learned through our Chronic Illness Center that physicians gradually learn what being overly responsible means; they are able to back up and share different beliefs about an illness with families. Once a physician does that two or three times, frequently that physician can generalize to the next patient and gain a new perspective. If we could teach our residents how to handle the stuck patients, they would find practice more satisfying. They would burn out less frequently. They might sleep better!

The goal of our Chronic Illness Center is to help physicians, patients, and families struggle more collaboratively when facing chronic illness. A secondary benefit is the realization that patients do function in families. That is where ideas about health matters are shaped. That is where the support system is for our patients. Eventually, the family physician begins to function like part of the extended family and may become stuck in a nonproductive role, just as do other family members. If we could engage our residents with stuck clinical situations and find a way to help them change, they would practice better medicine in the future. Who knows, they could be happier people 30 years later!

Accomplishing all of this often requires a team. Usually, we are unable to see our own blind spots, which lead to being stuck, without help. We need colleagues who are trained differently from physicians to be right with us in practice, so that we can turn to them and say, "I'm frustrated with Mrs. X and Mr. X" and have a conversation about the problem. We need to set up a system so that we have such support available. This is important; it can prevent us from managing our own personal issues and reactions indirectly through patient care. One human (whom we label a physician) cannot do all this in primary care. It is too complicated. If we are smart we will set up systems slowly, cautiously, so that we have other people in our midst who understand relationships. These other professionals may have various different titles in mental health or they may be nurses, social workers, Ph.D.s, or clergy. We need people with training unlike the training doctors receive to be right beside us so we can process our interactions, while still understanding that as physicians we have the core medical responsibility. This kind of training will help the trainees of the future, and, where resources are available, will become one kind of collaborative model for our clinical practice.

Management of medical issues as well as their psychosocial aspects is so challenging that nearly all medical clinicians would benefit from such helpers, colleagues beside us with different "lenses," to give us binocular vision. If we use that vision to solve the problems of our stuck patients, we can be more receptive and helpful in meeting the needs of both physician and patient. Once we create proper multidisciplinary teams, I think we will be more comfortable with the term *family physician*.

PART IV

Practice

FOURTEEN

Issues in the Adoption of a Family Approach by Practicing Family Physicians

LORNE A. BECKER

Although many family physicians believe that a family-oriented approach to patient care leads to better outcomes, and in spite of a growing literature on the principles and theory of working with families in primary care, most physicians have been very slow to move from an individual to a family approach with their patients. This chapter examines some of the issues involved in the adoption of innovations by practitioners and explores their implications for the increased inclusion of the family in medical practice.

Investigators who have examined what actually happens in a family practice have found little evidence of a family approach to care. What little family information is obtained is frequently incomplete or inaccurate and does not seem to influence clinical decision making (Pless, 1984). While some family physicians obtain more family information from some patients than from others, in general, "the level of knowledge about families of patients they treat is remarkably limited" (p. 338). How well the family physician knows the family seems largely unrelated to satisfaction, compliance, or outcome. Physicians are often mistaken in their beliefs about their patients' marital status and personal circumstances, and thus place their patients "in a family context not of their own experience but of the doctor's invention" (Marinker, 1976, p. 116). In other studies, less than 5% of problem lists in a family medicine residency practice contained any family data (Crouch & Theidke, 1986), and discussion of family issues took up less than 6% of the time spent in assessing a family medicine patient at a first visit. Explorations of family dynamics were rarely used (Crouch & McCauley, 1985), few patients were referred to family therapists (Detchon & Storm, 1987), and even when family information was provided to physicians (Mengel, 1987; Rogers & Cohn, 1987), their clinical decisions did not appear to change.

Special training programs have been ineffective in improving family physicians' skills in working with families (Bishop et al., 1984; McLean & Miles, 1975). Thus, at first glance, there would appear to be ample ammunition for critics, such as Merkel (1983), who argue that family medicine is ill suited to a family approach, and suggest that the marriage of family and family practice is not worth further investment. While I do not share Merkel's pessimism, it is clear that the inclusion of the family in the routine care delivered by family physicians is not likely to be a simple task.

Many reasons have been advanced to explain family physicians' slow adoption of family techniques to date. Poor reimbursement for time spent in family conferences, lack of appropriate office space, lack of training, lack of acceptability to patients, and lack of incontrovertible proof of the benefits of a family approach to health care have all been cited. While all of these factors may impede the provision of family-centered care, none presents insoluble problems. Indeed, identical factors have not inhibited the adoption by family physicians of other innovations such as flexible sigmoidoscopy. This procedure also requires reorganization of office space and special training. It is not exactly welcomed by patients, and (at least as a screening tool for early detection of gastrointestinal cancers) has not been shown to be beneficial. In spite of these barriers, 24% of primary care physicians in the United States own flexible sigmoidoscopes and an additional 12% plan to obtain them (Holleb, 1985). Reimbursement for flexible sigmoidoscopy is higher than for family counseling, although this must be offset against the expense of purchasing and maintaining the required equipment. However, financial issues are likely a small factor in Canada, where reimbursement for family counseling is virtually identical to that for other types of office visits. Indeed, Canadian family physicians continue to provide services, such as house calls, that are less well reimbursed than family counseling.

Further, it is particularly unlikely that physicians are awaiting proof of efficacy for family approaches before adopting them, given the way medical innovations are usually adopted. Contrary to popular belief, most medical innovations are adopted before proof of effectiveness exists. Young (1981) suggests that CT scanning was adopted in this way, with physicians making wide use of the technique long before solid evidence was available to support its accuracy and benefits. In fact, the U.S. Office of Technology Assessment has estimated that only 10-20% of the interventions physicians currently use are supported by evidence from randomized controlled trials, and there are many examples of innovations that have been eagerly embraced only to be abandoned when more careful evaluation showed them to be ineffective.

Thus there are many examples of successful dissemination of medical innovations in spite of similar barriers to those proposed as explanations for the failure of family physicians to adopt a family approach to care. Are there other reasons that should be considered? The question of how innovative procedures are adopted by individuals and groups is not unique to family studies or family medicine. Over the last four decades, the "diffusion of innovations" has been carefully studied; a large body of research has produced a literature encompassing thousands of publications, most dealing with nonphysicians and nonmedical innovations. A number of the findings from this body of research suggest that family physicians may find if difficult to begin to "think family" in general terms while caring for an individual patient. However, dissemination of a limited number of family interventions related to specific health care problems may be more feasible. Rogers and Shoemaker (1971) have written extensively on the "classical diffusion model" and have outlined five important characteristics of the innovation itself that influence the ease with which it is adopted: relative advantage, compatibility, complexity, trialability, and observability.

RELATIVE ADVANTAGE

Relative advantage refers to the degree to which an innovation is seen as better (in terms of economics, prestige, convenience, satisfaction, and so on) than whatever it is designed to replace. While there are philosophical and theoretical reasons to expect family-oriented health care to be more effective and to provide benefits for patients, there is little to suggest that a family approach will necessarily provide family physicians with greater professional satisfaction, more appreciation from patients, or enhanced prestige. In fact, the approach has many potential disadvantages. Patients and families may resist or become angry if they feel that they are being blamed for their problems rather than helped. Some family interventions may be very time-consuming and thus may limit the physician's ability to care for other patients.

These relative disadvantages seem more prominent when we speak of family interventions in general. Physicians may find it easier to see the relative advantage of a specific family intervention for a biomedical problem. For example, one might propose that family physicians should "include the family" when an individual is diagnosed as hyperlipidemic by encouraging all family members to consider adopting a lipid-lowering diet.

This problem-specific innovation has several relative advantages. It offers the opportunity to provide preventive counseling to a number of individuals who are likely to share similar cardiovascular risk factors (Venters, 1986). Raising the issues of dietary change with the family as a group may avoid some of the doctor-patient-family power struggles that can result when life-style changes are prescribed (Hoebel, 1977). In addition, this family intervention escapes some of the relative disadvantages family physicians may view as disincentives to working with families. Family members are unlikely to feel blamed or stigmatized by an invitation to discuss their shared diet. A discussion with the family may require no more time than a similar discussion with the patient alone. Instead, the approach may save time, since a single meeting with the entire family may decrease requests for the physician to discuss the same material repeatedly with individual family members.

COMPATIBILITY

Compatibility refers to the fit between the innovation and the values, experiences, and perceived needs of the potential adopters. The least compatible innovations require adopters to change their views of the world and how it works. Thus physicians will prescribe a new member of a familiar class of drugs more readily than they will prescribe a drug from a new class with a different mechanism of action (Fennell & Warnecke, 1988). A family approach requires just such a change, depending on a systemic view of health and illness—an approach to practice that has not been seen as necessary or feasible by all physicians (Doherty, Baird, & Becker, 1987). Family approaches may appear to be in conflict with individual doctor-patient relationships if attempts to achieve the best outcomes for the family are seen to result in less than optimal care for individual family members. Some physicians are reluctant to raise family issues, fearing negative reactions from the patient. Traditional medical education, with its focus on the biomedical, has reinforced this feeling that family issues are beyond the limits of the physician and are most appropriately handled by referral to a nonphysician. Studies of patient preferences suggest otherwise, with patients often indicating that they would welcome a family conference, at least for some health problems (Kushner & Meyer, 1989; Kushner, Meyer, & Hansen, 1986).

As with relative advantage, compatibility may be more apparent when one considers a specific family intervention such as the family approach to lipid lowering outlined above. It makes sense to involve all of the family members who share meals in discussions of dietary change. It makes particular sense to involve the person who usually serves as the family's shopper and meal preparer. A family approach is compatible with the perception of the family as a nurturing institution with interest in providing a healthy diet for all its members.

COMPLEXITY

Complex innovations, not surprisingly, are less readily adopted than simpler ones. The most complex family interventions involve intensive family therapy or attempts to resolve psychosocial problems. Family therapists spend many hours mastering the concepts and skills of their discipline. Family physicians who have family therapy training describe a prolonged and difficult time of adaptation of the family therapy approach to the everyday realities of a busy practice (Weston, 1987). Not all families need family therapy, however. Doherty and Baird (1986) have outlined five levels of physician involvement with families, ranging from family therapy to much less complex interventions such as simply providing information (Level 2) or facilitating discussion of feelings (Level 3). These less complex Level 2 or 3 interventions are the ones family physicians are likely to use for family approaches to commonly encountered biomedical conditions such as hyperlipidemia. (For a more complete overview of Doherty and Baird's levels of physician involvement with families, see the appendix to this chapter. The explanations provided there are the result of a collaboration between Thomas Campbell and myself.)

TRIALABILITY

Trialability refers to the degree to which an innovation may be partially adopted or experimented with before a full commitment is made. Trialability is essential for all but the simplest innovations, since the innovation must be tailored to fit with individual practice circumstances and preferred modes of operation. This expectation that the new user will make substantial modifications to the intervention stands in marked contrast to the presumption in much of the family medicine literature that physicians will rigidly follow protocols proposed by family therapists or behavioral scientists. For example, in the "unsuccessful" attempts of Bishop et al. (1984) and of McLean and Miles (1975), physicians' efforts to find their own ways to use their newly learned skills were seen as evidence of misunderstanding or noncompliance. Trialability of family interventions could be addressed by providing physicians with a range of options when first trying an innovation. For example, a family approach to lipid lowering might involve a family meeting, a series of one-on-one meetings with family members, a session with only the husband and wife, or some written material sent home with the patient. Physicians using the family meeting approach could choose to work exclusively at Level 2 (providing information to the family), could also use Level 3 strategies (encouraging family members to express their emotions about the diagnosis and the proposed diet), or could include Level 4 (actively problem solving with the family as they try to come up with changes that will fit with their needs). This wide range of options with plenty of opportunity for tailoring by the physician leads to more "trials" and more ready adoption.

OBSERVABILITY

Observability refers to the degree to which the adoption of an innovation by the more adventuresome members of a group is visible to the other group members. Physicians, like other professionals, depend heavily upon the opinions and observed behaviors of particularly respected colleagues—even when these opinions conflict with available scientific evidence (Rogers & Shoemaker, 1971; Williamson, German, Weiss, Skinner, & Bowes, 1989). This explains why adoption of medical innovations usually precedes clear evidence of benefit. Family physicians often learn of innovations first from specialists with whom they have consulted about specific patient problems. Innovations found useful with one patient are then generalized and applied in the care of other patients managed without consultation. Unfortunately, working with families is not seen as a priority by any of the medical specialties. Thus family physicians must take the major responsibility for passing family innovations on to family practice colleagues.

Many family interventions are not particularly observable. They frequently involve discussions of confidential issues, performed in the privacy of the physician's office and requiring no highly visible equipment or extra staff. A family physician may practice in this mode while drawing very little attention or interest from peers or patients. Furthermore, most family physicians practice alone or in small groups and have few occasions to discuss innovations in their individual practices with one another. Ransom (1986a) has contrasted this situation with the many opportunities family therapists have to observe their peers in action via workshops, video recordings, written transcripts, and cotherapy.

Family physicians may be in a position to gain more visibility among peers and patients with family approaches to common biomedical problems such as elevated cholesterol levels. Patients will not hesitate to tell one another of this new approach (assuming they are pleased with it) because, unlike family therapy for identified psychosocial problems, there is no perceived stigma. Family physicians may be less reluctant to discuss it among themselves because they will feel less concerned about the need for patient confidentiality.

CONCLUSION

Given these issues in innovation diffusion, how likely is it that family physicians will adopt innovations that include the family unit in the delivery of health care? While most family physicians are unlikely to begin in-depth family therapy with large numbers of families in their practices, relatively simple family-oriented approaches for specific clinical problems might well be welcomed by both physicians and patients. Biomedical problems should be the first targets for a family approach, since many of the problems with dissemination are less evident with biomedical than with psychosocial innovations. Some evidence is available from medical research that family approaches may be particularly effective for some disorders, such as obesity (Brownell, Heckerman, Westlake, Hayes, & Monti, 1978; Pearce, LeBow, & Orchard, 1981; Saccone & Israel, 1978), hypertension (Levine et al., 1979; Morisky et al., 1983), and asthma (Clark et al., 1981; Lask & Matthew, 1979). However, as noted, formulation and dissemination of family approaches need not await incontestable proof of effectiveness (because no other area of medicine proceeds with that particular expectation).

Finally, those who wish to be innovators and promoters of a family approach must realize that with this, as with any other innovation, dissemination will not happen on its own; it must be promoted. Development of a new set of family interventions will require hard work by family therapists and family physicians working together. The innovations must be described and presented in a fashion that encourages practicing physicians to modify and experiment with them. The advantages of the intervention to the family physician must be considered, along with the advantages to the patient. They must not be seen as so complex or so different from current clinical activities as to be incompatible with everyday practice. Active efforts to promote the adoption of family interventions must focus not only on the nuts and bolts of how to deliver the intervention, but also on the principles of innovation dissemination.

APPENDIX: LEVELS OF
PHYSICIAN INVOLVEMENT WITH FAMILIES

Level 1: Minimal Emphasis on Family

This baseline level of involvement consists of dealing with families only as necessary for practical and medical/legal reasons, but not viewing communicating with families as integral to the physician's role or as involving skills for the physician to develop. This level presumably characterizes most medical school training, where biomedical issues are often the sole conscious focus of patient care.

Level 2: Ongoing Medical Information and Advice

At a minimum, family education involves teaching at least one family member about the patient's illness, but can include extended family and friends. It can be a one-time intervention or an ongoing series of education sessions. It may be provided by the physician, another health professional, or an advocacy agency, such as the American Heart Association or the Arthritis Foundation.

Knowledge base: primarily medical, plus awareness of the triangular dimension of physician-patient-family relationships

Personal development: openness to engage patients and families in a collaborative way

Skills:

(1) Regularly and clearly communicating medical findings and treatment options to family members

(2) Asking family members questions that elicit relevant diagnostic and treatment information

(3) Attentively listening to family members' questions and concerns

(4) Advising families about how to handle the medical and rehabilitation needs of the patient

(5) For large or demanding families, knowing how to channel communication through one or two key members

(6) Identifying gross family dysfunction that interferes with medical treatment, and referring the family to a therapist

Level 3: Feelings and Support

To provide support, families must receive some education and have a basic understanding of the illness. Family support can be enhanced by simply convening the family and encouraging them to discuss their concerns. The provider must be comfortable dealing with the feelings expressed by family members. Specific suggestions for eliminating nonsupportive behaviors and developing supportive behaviors can be provided.

Knowledge base: normal family development and reactions to stress

Personal development: awareness of one's own feelings in relation to the patient and family

Skills:

(1) Asking questions that elicit family members' expressions of concerns and feelings related to the patient's condition and its effects on the family

(2) Empathically listening to family members' concerns and feelings and normalizing them where appropriate

(3) Forming a preliminary assessment of the family's level of functioning as it relates to the patient's problem

(4) Encouraging family members in their efforts to cope as a family with their situation

(5) Tailoring medical advice to the unique needs, concerns, and feelings of the family

(6) Identifying family dysfunction and fitting a referral recommendation to the unique situation of the family

Level 4: Systematic Assessment and Planned Intervention

This level of involvement involves systematic assessment and intervention and is focused on the specific problems related to the illness or risk behavior. The health care provider elicits the problem (e.g., an Alzheimer's patient wandering at night) and helps the family develop a solution. Some basic knowledge of family dynamics and functioning and skills in family assessment are necessary to facilitate family coping.

Knowledge base: family systems

Personal development: awareness of one's own participation in systems, including the therapeutic triangle, the medical system, one's own family system, and larger community systems

Skills:

(1) Engaging family members, including reluctant ones, in a planned family conference or a series of conferences

(2) Structuring a conference with even a poorly communicating family in such a way that all members have a chance to express themselves

(3) Systematically assessing the family's level of functioning

(4) Supporting individual members while avoiding coalitions

(5) Reframing the family's definition of their problem in a way that makes problem solving more achievable

(6) Helping family members view their difficulty as requiring new forms of collaborative efforts

(7) Helping family members generate alternative, mutually acceptable ways to cope with their difficulty

(8) Helping family members balance their coping efforts by calibrating their various roles in a way that allows support without sacrificing anyone's autonomy

(9) Identifying family dysfunction that lies beyond primary care treatment and orchestrating a referral by educating the family and the therapist about what to expect from one another

Level 5: Family Therapy

This level of involvement is usually reserved for highly stressed or dysfunctional families that need more intensive interventions than are provided by

Levels 2-4. The goal of family therapy is to change dysfunctional patterns of family interaction that interfere with coping. It requires specialized training that few health care providers receive. Health care providers need to be able to identify and refer highly dysfunctional families to therapists.

> *Knowledge base:* family systems and patterns whereby dysfunctional families interact with professionals and other health care systems
>
> *Personal development:* ability to handle intense emotions in families and self and to maintain neutrality in the face of strong pressure from family members or other professionals
>
> *Skills:* (The following is not an exhaustive list of family therapy skills, but a list of several key skills that distinguish Level 5 involvement from primary care involvement with families.)
>
> (1) Interviewing families or family members who are quite difficult to engage
>
> (2) Efficiently generating and testing hypotheses about the family's difficulties and interaction patterns
>
> (3) Escalating conflict in the family in order to break a family impasse
>
> (4) Temporarily siding with one family member against another
>
> (5) Constructively dealing with a family's strong resistance to change
>
> (6) Negotiating collaborative relationships with other professionals and other systems who are working with the family, even when these groups are at odds with one another

FIFTEEN

Psychoeducation: A Potential Model for Intervention in Family Practice

WILLIAM R. McFARLANE

Expanding insights into the critical factors determining course in schizophrenia have radically transformed the nature of family therapy in this devastating disorder. Family psychoeducation and multiple-family groups have demonstrated remarkable effects on relapse rates and rehabilitation outcomes. The components of this approach include techniques for (a) establishing an empathic collaboration with family members, (b) providing information about the illness and specific guidelines for ongoing management, (c) problem solving to enhance coping skills, and (d) expanding the patient's and family's social network. Because these elements are intended to deal with specific factors influencing the disorder, and because some of those factors are present in chronic medical disorders, the general approach, with carefully designed modifications, seems likely to be applicable in many family practice settings.

RECENT CHANGES IN THE TREATMENT OF THE FAMILY IN SCHIZOPHRENIA

During the last decade, family therapy in schizophrenia has undergone a dramatic shift of strategy, to the extent that it is no longer valid to use the term to describe what many clinicians are now practicing.

Present practice has become biologically based; the work with families is now described as *family management* or *psychoeducation.* Although this shift has been accompanied by controversy, studies of outcome in these newer strategies have provided the most consistent evidence to date for the efficacy of a family treatment (Leff, 1989).

These approaches have all proceeded from empirical studies of family interactional influences on chronic psychiatric illness and have been developed within an outcome research context. In this regard, the family models for treating schizophrenia resemble medical treatments and rehabilitation more than other psychotherapies. They are based on a relatively simple "biosocial" paradigm: Course and outcome are the result of known, though circumscribed, interactions between aspects of the patient's environment and specific biological processes. This new definition has significant parallels with many chronic medical disorders that are often treated in family practice. For that reason, family psychoeducation may have relevance and utility in that context.

This chapter describes (a) the current understanding of the biological and social factors associated with schizophrenia; (b) the rationale for, and the key elements of, the psychoeducational model of treatment for this disorder; and (c) ways in which psychoeducation may apply to family practice. The psychoeducational multifamily group model is presented because it seems to hold great promise as a template for the design of family treatments for medical illnesses. The fundamental assertion here is that new family-based treatments for medical disorders might be constructed in a manner similar to those for schizophrenia.

CURRENT CONCEPTS OF SCHIZOPHRENIA

Schizophrenia is currently viewed as a complex phenomenon, in which onset and course are determined by factors at several levels: biochemical, physiological, psychological, family, and social network. Like many chronic medical illnesses, it is disabling, has a poorly understood etiology, is incurable, has treatments that are only partially corrective, and is complex, confusing, and stressful to family members and recruits their concern and assistance. Further, it has become clear that it is heavily influenced by specific social factors, most of which seem to be the result of the illness and its disabilities.

Psychobiological Factors

Schizophrenia is best defined as a disorder of central nervous system functioning, with interrelated defects in ventral tegmental arousal centers, dorsolateral frontal cortical association areas, hippocampal attention areas, and limbic affective areas. Weinberger (1987) offers a comprehensive model that involves deficient dopaminergic activation of the dorsolateral frontal cortex. He proposes that, in response to stress, limbic and possibly the hippocampal cortex become hyperactive, leading to deterioration of attention and to more primitive affective and behavioral responses. This is an attractive model because it is consistent with a large body of existing neurophysiologic and neuroanatomic findings. It also places the brain in context, seeing it as responding aberrantly to certain forms of stressful input, generating cognitive, affective, and behavioral symptoms that in turn elicit major disruptions in the immediate social environment. The etiology of the tegmental-frontal disruption is unclear, but could lie in inherited chromosomal defects, perinatal trauma, or early viral infection.

This pervasive dysfunction of cerebral activity leaves the individual sufferer vulnerable to a variety of stimuli, all of which tend to increase uncontrollably the level of physiological arousal, leading to widespread deterioration in mental functioning. Disabling stimuli include high rates of change in the environment (Chung, Langelluddecke, et al., 1986; Steinberg & Durell, 1968), negative interpersonal interaction (Vaughn & Leff, 1976), high levels of complexity in communication and task demand (Linn, Caffey, Klett, et al., 1979), and physical and chemical influences (Janowski et al., 1973). Stated another way, these patients have a lowered threshold for cognitive disorganization in response to a wide variety of commonly encountered stimuli.

The Social Environment and
Its Influence on the Course of the Illness

The family and the social network of the patient, especially insofar as they are sources of disabling stimuli, influence the course of schizophrenia. In schizophrenia, problems occur both within the social network and within the family.

Social Network Factors

Stigma. In view of the public rejection of patients, it is remarkable that most families do not report feeling stigmatized by the emergence of schizophrenia in one of their members (Freeman & Simmons, 1961). On the other hand, many family members act as if they have been stigmatized. They attempt to conceal the presence of the illness from friends and more distant relatives and, in many cases, drop friends following the initial episode (Yarrow, Clausen, & Robbins, 1955). Lamb and Oliphant (1978) report that many parents find it difficult to talk to other parents about their children's achievements—the contrast is too painful—and gradually see less of them. In contrast to other kinds of crises, schizophrenia does not tend to induce a rallying of support and empathy in the patient's social network.

Network size and structure. The social networks of patients with schizophrenia and their families have been studied extensively, with a singularly consistent finding: Patients and, to a lesser extent, families are more isolated than their peers, even those with other psychiatric disorders. Pattison, Llama, and Hurd (1979), Hammer (1981), and Garrison (1978) have documented smaller network sizes in schizophrenic cases, as have Brown, Birley, and Wing (1972). Patient social networks are constricted and more dominated by kin at first admission (Tolsdorf, 1976), while the entire network decreases in size as the illness becomes chronic (Anderson, Hogarty, Bayer, et al., 1984; Lipton, Cohen, & Katz, 1981). Explanations for these findings include withdrawal of contact and support by friends and extended kin and reduced social initiative by family members because of shame and preoccupation with the patient. Attenuated social support leads to the loss of adaptive resources coming from outside the family (e.g., information, concrete assistance, relief, and advice) and depletion of caretakers' emotional reserves.

Life events. Although there is some disagreement in the literature, life events seem to provoke symptomatology in schizophrenia. Specifically, events that require a major increase in information processing and adaptation or that are perceived as subjectively unpleasant seem to trigger decompensation. Steinberg and Durell (1968) found that a majority of first episodes were immediately preceded by entry into military service or college, events that also disrupt social networks. Life events appear to be a primary factor in precipitating relapse in stable and medicated outpatients (Leff & Vaughn, 1980).

Family Factors

Families attempting to cope with a mental illness in their midst are faced with an overwhelming set of challenges. The resources that a given family can bring to bear on this most chronic of illnesses vary widely, but seem to be critical to the patient's later condition. Four factors that have been useful for predicting the course of the illness are lack of information, burden, inadequate coping skills, and expressed emotion.

Lack of information. Schizophrenia, like other major illnesses, appears to family members as threatening, confusing, and unpredictable. Because it varies widely over time, it does not even appear to be a single entity, let alone an identifiable illness, but rather a set of alternating states and vacillating, unstable phenomena. Vaughn and Leff (1976) found that those relatives who are most critical of the patient tend to ascribe more subtle symptoms, unknowingly, to personality defects or character traits. Many family members are completely unaware of the extent and causes of the mental disruptions and aberrations that are besieging their ill relative. Diagnosis and treatment often appear mysterious and sometimes arbitrary or erratic. It is not surprising that one of the primary complaints of families in surveys is that they have been left uninformed and unguided by clinicians (Hatfield, 1983).

Burden. The difficulties schizophrenia patients pose for their families are multiple (D. J. Johnson, 1990). Remarkably, few translate their complaints into outright rejection and abandonment. Nevertheless, relatives commonly report economic drain, sleep disruption, interferences with daily routine, exacerbations of medical conditions, depression, tension from fear of unpredictable behavior and difficulties in communication, and strained family and marital relationships (Grad & Sainsbury, 1963). Parents, especially, appear to resent having become captives of the situation, but are also beset by feelings of guilt, inadequacy, and anger.

Inadequate coping skills. As experience has accumulated, it has become apparent that much of what previously was seen as family pathology is actually misguided attempts to help the patient. What looks like overinvolvement can be seen more usefully as vigilance, protectiveness, and anxiety in the face of the unknown, reasonable responses to dangerous behavior or a result of uninformed guilt. The stress of caring for a chronically mentally ill person can lead to depression, high levels of anxiety, and exacerbation of existing chronic medical disorders. The end result is that many family members find themselves with markedly diminished capacity to manage the illness successfully, especially when unsupported by the professional treatment system (Holden

& Lewine, 1982). To make matters worse, many preferable illness management techniques are largely counterintuitive and would not appear to be helpful or even reasonable to the majority of the population.

Expressed emotion. The most well-researched factor is termed *expressed emotion* (EE), a construct originally developed by Brown and his colleagues (1972), who hypothesized that environmental affective factors might account for relapse. It consists of an attitudinal aspect (highly critical views of the patient) and a behavioral component (a tendency to be "overinvolved"; i.e., highly protective of, or attentive and reactive to, the patient). Having assessed the level of EE in key relatives, they found that when EE was higher, relapse occurred much more frequently, at rates from 54% to 92% within 9 months, with and without medication, respectively. In low-EE homes, the comparable rates were 12% and 15%. That is, some families seemed as protective against relapse as medication. Leff and Vaughn (1985) documented the central role played by misunderstanding in the genesis of high-EE interaction; in their study, nearly 75% of family members' critical comments concerned functional disabilities that they attributed to character defects. Thus a view has emerged of family interaction as a powerful influence, promoting either recovery or relapse and disability. Further, some evidence suggests that levels of expressed emotion may be higher in more isolated families (Brown, Monck, Carstairs, & Wing, 1962).

FAMILY PSYCHOEDUCATION: KEY COMPONENTS

A number of investigators have developed clinical intervention models that attempt to ameliorate the effects of these network and family factors on the course of the illness and the status of the patient. These approaches can be grouped together as "psychoeducational" intervention models. Put simply, family psychoeducational treatment is a set of well-described and structured interventions having the factors described above as their targets. The family management (Falloon & Liberman, 1983), psychoeducational (Anderson, 1983), and multifamily group approaches (McFarlane, 1990) to treating schizophrenia have been developed using a common strategy—to influence clinical outcome by providing families with information, coping and interaction skills, and social supports that appear to be lacking in most cases. We turn now to a short review of the components of the psychoeducational approach and their intended effects on the problems outlined above.

Engagement of the Family and Patient

In all family treatments, creation of a treatment system is the first necessity (Minuchin, 1974). The engagement process includes several crucial elements: (a) delineating the family's existing coping methods, especially those that work; (b) eliciting each family member's reactions to the illness and the treatment system; (c) exploring each member's understanding of the disorder and its causes; and (d) making a brief evaluation of the family as family. In addition, the stresses leading to relapse and early prodromal signs are explored and clarified. It is crucial to describe explicitly what the family's role will be in treatment, as well as the role of the professionals. If a given family member needs to share unacceptable and/or suppressed feelings, there is value in allowing that, without the patient's presence.

The goal is to establish a *collaborative* alliance with all family members, alleviating guilt, anxiety, and implicit blame. These structured sessions are useful to normalize the family's experience, comparing it with those of others in the same situation or with well-known social support models, such as Al-Anon, crime victims' support groups, or organizations of families of the mentally retarded.

Education

Sharing information and illness management techniques with families has proved to be an enormously helpful and therapeutic strategy in schizophrenia and mental retardation. Education can be defined along a continuum from simple suggestions and the distribution of pamphlets to comprehensive educational workshops lasting several hours. Psychoeducational models cluster along the more ambitious end of the spectrum, primarily because schizophrenia is so complex and poorly understood.

Education in the psychiatric disorders includes clarifying (a) behaviors that are actually symptoms of illness, (b) the inner subjective experience of the ill individual, (c) the biological rationale for medication and social interventions, (d) the expected outcomes of treatment, and (e) the best strategies for day-to-day management and interaction at home. The desired effect is to create a shared frame of reference within the patient-family-clinician network.

Enhancing Coping Skills

Experience with family approaches in schizophrenia has emphatically confirmed the importance of assisting families to improve coping skills. This has been necessary because intuitive approaches—providing protection, reasoning with the patient about delusions, pressuring the patient to work as an antidote to his or her deterioration, and so on—tend to exacerbate the condition. In practice, enhancing coping skills has taken several forms. The psychoeducational model provides families with management guidelines that are quite specific, but that require individualizing for each family. The guidelines themselves are derived from a well-validated psychophysiological model of schizophrenia (Neuchterlein & Dawson, 1984; Tecce & Cole, 1976) that suggests the need for (a) a calm, affectively warm, and low-pressure social environment and (b) carefully graduated increases in expectations and role functioning. These guidelines are used to develop suggestions for new strategies that are practiced at home and refined as necessary. The procedure involves ongoing, biweekly sessions, preferably in multiple-family groups, in which the goals are avoiding psychotic relapse, buffering the effects of life events, and gradually promoting functional recovery.

Falloon and Liberman's (1983) family management approach uses in-session problem-solving methodology and structured training in communication skills. Here the goal is to deal with more general family phenomena, especially distorted, overintense, or negative communication, overinvolvement by a family member, and conflicts precipitated by the illness. Falloon and Liberman have developed behavioral interventions in which the clinician makes a careful assessment of interaction patterns and works with family members, using repeated-practice and problem-solving procedures, to change key behavior patterns used by the patient and interactions between family members.

Social Network Expansion and Multiple-Family Groups

Because family isolation seems to be so common and so pernicious in its effects on the family and the illness, a number of intervention models have included means for expanding and strengthening the family's social networks. The most ambitious of these is the multiple-family group (MFG), in which the clinical team attempts to create a new, prosthetic social network among similarly afflicted families. I have developed a psychoeducational MFG model that stresses lively, positive social interaction among participants, a group-based problem-solving approach, and the gradual conversion of the group into a natural social network. Families and clinicians consistently describe these groups as more useful, enjoyable, and meaningful than single-family work. A recent study comparing multiple- and single-family models demonstrated superior outcomes in the MFG format (McFarlane, 1990). The parsimonious explanation is that the difference results from the additional support, resilience, and problem-solving capacity inherent in the larger network.

TREATMENT EFFECTS
OF FAMILY PSYCHOEDUCATION

A distinguishing feature of the development of psychoeducational approaches is that they have been based on empirical research. The basic designs have attempted to capitalize on previous studies of effects of various factors on outcome, and they have been rigorously tested in experimental studies. The results in these studies have been remarkable in the size of the main effects. Table 15.1 presents outcomes, measured by relapse rates, from seven studies undertaken during the last decade. While the intervention strategies and relapse criteria vary across studies, there is sufficient similarity that the summation of rates, comparing family to no-family treatment, is meaningful. It is also telling. The average relapse rate for family-based treatment is roughly 12%, compared with 48% for individual-based treatment, in seven studies with samples totaling 217. There are altogether eight studies reported; all but one strongly replicate each other. The eighth, which found no difference in a comparably designed experiment, is widely regarded as irrelevant, because the intervention involved a psychodynamically oriented family therapy that provides almost none of the crucial elements detailed previously (Kottgen, Sonnichsen, Mollenauer, et al., 1984). The present record represents one of the most successful and consistent clinical research efforts in the history of the field.

TABLE 15.1 Relapse Outcome in Family Intervention Trials (in percentages)

Author	n	Test Treatment	Comparison Treatment	Test Interval (months)
Goldstein et al. (1980)	49	FCT	IST	6
		0	17	
Leff et al. (1982)	24	RGT	IST	12
		8	50	
Falloon et al. (1985)	36	BFM	IST	24
		11	83	
Hogarty et al. (1986)	50	FPE	IST	12
		19	41	
Leff et al. (1989)	23	RGT	BFM	12
		17	8	
McFarlane (1990)	41	PEMFG	FPE	48
		50	72	
Tarrier et al. (1988)	48	BFM	IST	9
		12	53	
Average rates/year		family intervention	IST	
		11.5	47.5	

NOTE: FCT = family crisis therapy; IST = individual supportive therapy; RGT = relatives' group therapy; BFM = behavioral family management; FPE = family psychoeducation; PEMFG = psychoeducational multiple-family group.

POTENTIAL APPLICATIONS
TO FAMILY PRACTICE

The extension of the experience with family intervention in schizophrenia to medical conditions with both biological and social determinants seems natural and promising. It also faces a number of problems. Many medical conditions seem amenable to one or another of the treatment elements described above. However, we generally lack the basic studies of family or network predictors or course indicators that have been so useful in designing treatments for schizophrenia. Further, in schizophrenia the patient is assumed to be a somewhat passive recipient of intervention. In medical disorders, this is rarely the case: The patient could more actively collaborate in developing new coping solutions or, on the other hand, could be more capable of sabotaging interventions. This difference has been taken into account in existing treatment models in ways that seem promising (Gonzalez, Steinglass, & Reiss, 1987).

210   PRACTICE

It is likely that the family factors reviewed above—lack of information, social isolation, expressed emotion, stigma, and, especially, insufficient coping skills—play a role in many medical disorders. Because the components of the family psychoeducational approach have been designed specifically to address these illness-induced problems, applying them, in appropriate combinations, seems likely to yield superior outcomes. A small number of studies have tested this proposition and have generally found positive effects. The targeted disorders have included sexual dysfunction (Kuriansky, Sharpe, & O'Connor, 1982), attentional deficit disorders of childhood (Dulcan, 1985), bulimia (Connors, Johnson, & Stuckey, 1984), rheumatoid arthritis (Schwartz, Marcus, & Condon, 1978), myocardial infarct (Frank, Heller, & Kornfeld, 1979), breast cancer (Spiegel & Yalom, 1978), senile dementia (Zarit & Zarit, 1982), childhood asthma (Abramson & Peshkin, 1979), essential hypertension (Eustaugh & Hatcher, 1982), seizure disorders (Flora, 1977), cystic fibrosis (B. Johnson, 1974), and juvenile diabetes (Koukal & Parham, 1978). Note that in all such conditions, the common denominators are (a) major, chronic biological dysfunction that induces changes in social and family interaction and (b) some evidence that focused intervention to alter that social interaction positively influences biological and behavioral processes and secondarily the course of the illness.

Clinician-Family Collaboration

The experience with schizophrenia has provided at least three general guidelines for application of psychoeducation in family practice. First, in the psychoeducational approach concentrated effort is expended on developing an empathic and collaborative alliance as much with family members as with the patient. Simply including family members, if only as adjunctive clinical supports, in discussions of treatment recommendations and ongoing management appointments appears essential to maximizing outcome in many chronic disorders, especially those that induce depression, anxiety, or persistent disability in the patient and exasperation, demoralization, or exhaustion in the family. Because anxiety and depression arising from disability are often contagious within families, including family members in the face-to-face contacts between the physician and patient acts to focus their energy on supporting treatment, enhances their sense of efficacy, and serves to mobilize hope and morale. That alone makes it worth the extra effort, without necessarily making this intervention family therapy.

Education and Training in Illness Management

Another generalizable lesson has been that social interventions to reduce the arousal and anxiety level in the patient have proved invaluable in preventing relapse in the psychotic disorders; the same may be true in many chronic medical illnesses. The educational component in psychoeducation has been critical to this success. The majority of families demonstrate significant alterations in their attitude toward the patient, reductions in the tendency to criticize and reject, and enhanced interest and ability in collaborating in the treatment and rehabilitation effort. Reductions in family expressed emotion immediately after comprehensive educational workshops are usually dramatic. Given the common role of arousal and anxiety in mediating outcome in a variety of medical disorders, negative family reactions to these disorders could be alleviated by the same sort of educational programs.

Problem Solving in Multifamily Groups

The third generalizable treatment element is well-organized problem solving in multifamily groups. Studies of family educational and management approaches suggest that enhanced coping skills form the variable that most powerfully predicts improved clinical outcome (Falloon, Boyd, McGill, et al., 1985). The capacity of several families, patients, and well-trained clinicians to jointly develop highly refined and individualized solutions for problems related to management and/or treatment of a given disorder has been impressive. By combining these with empirically based general strategies for management, it is possible to create nearly optimal social environments for recuperation, recovery, and maintenance of remission. This format also allows for careful construction of comprehensive treatment plans that take into account the contributions and limitations of the patient's family and social network. For instance, in schizophrenia, it is clear that patients need much more physical and psychological space than unaffected family members. This has been translated into a guideline for families that encourages reduced interpersonal intensity, pressure, and frequency of contact, as well as allowing withdrawal when social stimulation has become excessive. The goal is to keep physiological arousal at a manageable level.

In a multifamily group problem-solving session, the entire group will make and evaluate many suggestions for means of implementing the general parameters of the guideline, in ways that are specific, useful, and feasible for a given family and patient. These solutions often are surprising to clinicians and family alike, because they arise from a broad pool of human experience and the creative influences of large-group brainstorming. Given the often complex effects on family functioning of a variety of common medical disorders and the requirements for unpleasant and unaccustomed life-style modifications, the need for innovative, individualized ideas for family management may be as great as in schizophrenia.

Practical Considerations

The issues that have been left out of consideration until now are those of efficiency and feasibility. One of the strongest arguments for developing variations on the psychoeducational multifamily group is that it is so efficient: Families can be educated in larger numbers, management strategies can be developed and shared collectively, and brainstorming about methods is more effective with more participants. Also, the value of the newer family strategies is that they lend themselves to "dose packaging"; that is, components can be assembled based on a reasonable estimate of what is relevant and feasible, with a fairly clear idea of what the expected outcome, and its limitations, will be.

CONCLUSION

To summarize, accumulating experience with psychoeducation in treating schizophrenia has demonstrated the efficacy of including the family in ongoing psychiatric management and providing comprehensive education and problem solving in multifamily groups. These elements could constitute the starting point in designing family-oriented interventions for the family practice setting, in whatever ways appear feasible for given disorders and the specific circumstances of the practice setting. The other lesson from schizophrenia work is that interventions should be empirically tested and continually refined on the basis of that evaluation. What remains is to undertake trials of these methods in the family practice setting to determine their efficacy and feasibility.

SIXTEEN

Family Interventions in Physical Health

THOMAS L. CAMPBELL

Clinicians and researchers in the mental health field have long been interested in the role of the family in psychiatric disorders, but interest in families and physical health has been more recent. Over the last decade there has been an increasing amount of research on families and health (Campbell, 1986; Doherty & Campbell, 1988), and several major texts have been published that have advocated and described family-oriented approaches to medical care (Christie-Seely, 1984b; Doherty & Baird, 1983, 1987a, 1987b; McDaniel, Campbell, & Seaburn, 1990; Sawa, 1985). Despite these advances, there has been little research on family interventions in health care, and the research that has been undertaken has been inconclusive (see Table 16.1). There are no proven effective family interventions in physical health. This chapter reviews existing research on family interventions in physical health and proposes guidelines for developing, implementing, and studying family interventions.

AN EMPIRICALLY BASED APPROACH TO FAMILY INTERVENTIONS

McFarlane (1991; see also Chapter 15, this volume) has presented schizophrenia as a disorder that parallels many chronic medical illnesses and can serve as a model for developing family interventions for other disorders. He describes a treatment approach developed from empirical studies of family influences on schizophrenia. While there are important

TABLE 16.1 Randomized Controlled Trials of Family Interventions in Physical
                Illness

Study	Illness	Intervention	Results
Lask and Matthew (1979)	asthma	family therapy	improvements in symptoms and thoracic gas volumes
Clark et al. (1981)	asthma	family education	less fear and better management of illness
Gustafsson et al. (1986)	asthma	family therapy	improvement in overall pediatric assessment
Baranowski et al. (1982)	cardiovascular	multifamily support groups	more supportive behaviors to change diet and exercise
Earp et al. (1982)	hypertension	family involvement	no effect in home visit
Morisky et al. (1983)	hypertension	family support	57% reduction in overall mortality
Brownell et al. (1978)	obesity	spouse involvement	maintained weight loss
Saccone and Israel (1978)	obesity	spouse reinforcement	increased weight loss
Wilson and Brownell (1978)	obesity	family involvement	no effect
Pearce et al. (1981)	obesity	spouse involvement	greater weight loss and maintenance
Brownell et al. (1983)	obesity	mother involvement	group with mother and daughter seen separately lost the most weight

differences between schizophrenia and many chronic physical disorders, this empirically based approach has proven to be very effective in schizophrenia and is likely to lead to the most pragmatic and effective family interventions for physical health problems. Even more than in schizophrenia, the research on families and physical health is largely atheoretical. There are currently no widely accepted theories of families and health. This chapter applies McFarlane's empirically based approach to family interventions to what we currently know about families and physical health.

The psychoeducational model for schizophrenia developed from the serendipitous finding that the family's level of expressed emotion at the time of hospitalization powerfully predicted subsequent relapses. This initial discovery by Brown, Monck, Carstairs, and Wing (1962) in

England has been confirmed by many other researchers, and several different psychoeducational interventions have been developed to reduce levels of family expressed emotion. A number of randomized controlled trials have demonstrated that family interventions are as important as antipsychotic medication in the treatment of schizophrenia and should become the standard of care (Steinglass, 1987a). Unfortunately, no such powerful psychosocial or family predictor has been found in physical health. Little is known about the role of many of the family factors described by McFarlane in physical health, such as family stigma, isolation, and expressed emotion. However, three family factors appear to be consistently related to poor physical health: family stress, inadequate social or family support, and family enmeshment. The research on each of these family variables is briefly reviewed and interventions developed from this research are discussed below.

FAMILY STRESS

Despite the methodological problems involved in studying stress, most reviewers agree that psychosocial stress has an adverse effect on physical health (Cohen, 1981; Rabkin & Streuning, 1976) and that the major sources of stress occur within the family (Campbell, 1986). While clinical interventions have been developed that help families to reduce or cope with stress (Figley, 1989), none has been shown to reduce the adverse effects of stress on physical health. Research on bereavement, the most stressful life event, shows the strongest and most consistent relationship between family stress and health (Osterweis, Solomon, & Green, 1984). Numerous well-designed studies have demonstrated an increase in morbidity and mortality after the death of a spouse. The adverse effects appear to be greatest in men during the first 6 months of bereavement and are associated with depressed immune response (Bartrop, Luckhurst, Lazarus, Kiloh, & Penny, 1977; Schleifer, Keller, Camerino, Thornton, & Stein, 1983). Brief interventions designed to help the bereaved have shown a beneficial effect on coping and overall mental health (Vachon, Lyall, Rogers, Freedman-Letofsky, & Freeman, 1980). No studies have looked at the effects of these interventions on physical health. Because death or serious health problems are relatively rare during bereavement, such an intervention study would require data from thousands of subjects before any effect could be detected. However, more sensitive measures of physical health and functioning are available (Stewart et al., 1989) and could be used.

Another promising area for developing family interventions is the impact of marital separation and divorce on health. Many cross-sectional studies have shown that separated and divorced individuals have poorer health and higher death rates than single, married, or widowed persons (Verbrugge, 1977), but there have been no prospective studies of divorce and health to determine whether this is a causal relationship. However, recent studies have shown that divorced men and women, as well as those with low marital satisfaction, have poor immune responses (Kiecolt-Glaser et al., 1987, 1988), which may be partially responsible for their poor health.

These studies suggest that at least two transitions in the family life cycle, bereavement and divorce, are associated with high stress and poor physical health, and that family interventions may help to reduce or buffer this stress and prevent stress-related health problems.

FAMILY AS SOCIAL SUPPORT

Research on social support and health research provides the most powerful evidence that families influence physical health. Numerous carefully controlled prospective studies have demonstrated that low social support results in higher mortality, and that family members are the most important source of social support (Cohen & Syme, 1985; Ganster & Victor, 1988). In a recent review, House, Landis, and Umberson (1988) conclude:

> The evidence regarding social relationships and health increasingly approximates the evidence in the 1964 Surgeon General's report that established cigarette smoking as a cause or risk factor for mortality and morbidity from a range of diseases. The age-adjusted relative risk ratios are stronger than the relative risks for all causes of mortality reported for cigarette smoking. (p. 543)

For middle-aged adults, the spouse is the most important source of social support, but for the elderly, the presence of adult children has the greatest impact on health. Again, it appears that men are more susceptible to the effects of inadequate social support than are women. Social supports have similar influence on the onset and course of specific health conditions, such as pregnancy (Nuckolls, Cassel, & Kaplan, 1972), heart disease (Medalie & Goldbourt, 1976), and hip fractures (Cummings et al., 1988). Spousal support is also associated with the implementation of healthy behaviors such as smoking cessation (Mermelstein, Lichtenstein, & McIntyre, 1983) and weight reduction (Barbarin & Tirado, 1984).

These large epidemiological studies of social support use simple and crude measures of social networks and social support. While there is evidence that social supports both buffer the effects of stress and have an independent influence on health (Blake, 1988), little is known about how social supports improve health (House et al., 1988).

Social support can be conceptualized as being provided from within or outside the family. Interventions designed to enhance social support have focused on either increasing extrafamilial supports through support groups or increasing the support provided by a patient's partner (intrafamily support) (Gottlieb, 1988). Most of the work on support groups has been individually focused and has not included the family. Exceptions to this include multifamily groups for schizophrenia (McFarlane, 1983) and chronic medical illness (Steinglass & Horan, 1988a).

Intervention studies developed to enhance intrafamily supports have come primarily from behavioral psychology and have used spouses as reinforcers of healthy behaviors, especially for weight loss and smoking cessation. Several randomized trials of spousal support in weight reduction programs have demonstrated that involving the spouse helps obese patients to maintain their weight loss (Barbarin & Tirado, 1984). One study found that preventing critical or unsupportive comments or behaviors by the spouse is as effective as encouraging supportive behaviors (Pearce, LeBow, & Orchard, 1981). While there is a consistent relationship between spousal support and successful smoking cessation, intervention studies have failed to demonstrate any improvement in outcome (Mermelstein et al., 1983). The authors of these studies report that they had difficulty changing spouse behaviors within the context of their smoking cessation program and suggest that more intensive interventions are necessary to improve spousal support.

The most effective family intervention in physical illness carried out so far involved a very simple approach to providing family education and enhancing family support for hypertensive patients. Morisky et al. (1983) at Johns Hopkins studied the impact of three different educational interventions (brief individual counseling, family education during a home visit, and small patient group sessions) on appointment keeping, weight control, blood pressure, and overall mortality in black hypertensive patients in the inner city. The family intervention consisted of a single home visit during which a significant family member (usually the spouse) was educated about hypertension and encouraged to support the patient's medical regimen (taking medication, keeping appointments, losing weight). At 2- and 5-year follow-ups, the experimental groups had a significant improvement in all outcome measures, including compliance with appointments and medication, lowering of systolic and diastolic blood pressure, and overall mortality. At 5 years, the experimental groups had a 57% reduction in overall mortality compared with the control group. Family education and support, either alone or in combination with other interventions, appeared to be more effective than the other interventions, but the groups were too small to detect any significant differences between experimental groups.

This landmark study demonstrated that a very simple family intervention can have major impact on overall mortality. Unfortunately, because of the design of the study and the number of patients in each group, the effective ingredients of the interventions could not be determined. Morisky et al.'s study is a major breakthrough in the field of family interventions and may be analogous to the work on expressed emotion in schizophrenia. Not only was the intervention relatively simple and easily incorporated into routine health care, but the effect may be generalizable to other medical conditions. The family intervention was included in the study because a survey conducted in the Johns Hopkins medical clinic indicated that 70% of the hypertensive patients expressed a desire for family members to learn more about their illness. Most surveys of families with chronic illness indicate that one of their greatest needs is to receive more information about the illness.

As a result of this study and others linking social support with compliance, the National Heart, Lung and Blood Institute (1987) issued a booklet recommending that all physicians use the following as one of three basic strategies for increasing adherence to prescribed antihypertensive regimes:

> Enhance support from family members—identifying and involving one influential person, preferably someone living with the patient, who can provide encouragement, help support the behavior change, and, if necessary, remind the patient about the specifics of the regimen.

This government guide, sent to all physicians in the United States, gives specific suggestions on how to enhance family support for each of the five most frequent behavior changes recommended for hypertensive patients: taking medication daily, maintaining desirable weight, reducing dietary sodium, increasing vigorous exercise, and moderating alcohol consumption.

Research on social support and health is beginning to have an influence on the care of medical patients, perhaps analogous to the influence of the research on expressed emotion on the care of patients with schizophrenia. Unfortunately, Morisky et al.'s study has never been repeated, nor have similar interventions been tested with chronic illnesses.

FAMILY ENMESHMENT

While many studies have found an association between overall family dysfunction and numerous physical illnesses, family enmeshment or high cohesion is the specific component of family functioning that is most consistently related to poor health outcomes. Family cohesion has been defined as "the emotional bonding that family members have towards one another" (Olson, Sprenkle, & Russell, 1979), and enmeshment is a pathologically high level of cohesion in which there is a lack of autonomy and family members overreact to the stress of another family member. The concept of enmeshment comes from the work of Salvador Minuchin, and much of the research on enmeshment and health is derived from his psychosomatic family model. Minuchin and his colleagues (1975) at the Philadelphia Child Guidance Center observed a specific pattern of family interaction in the families of children with brittle diabetes, severe asthma, and anorexia nervosa, which consisted of enmeshment, overprotectiveness, rigidity, and conflict avoidance. Minuchin et al. hypothesized that these patterns of family interaction lead to physiological arousal and worsening of psychosomatic illnesses in susceptible children. While Minuchin did not measure family cohesion and its relationship to the type or severity of illness, others have studied these relationships with conflicting results. Some studies of diabetes have found that poor metabolic control is associated with rigid and enmeshed families, while others have found that these families tend to be chaotic and disengaged (Doherty & Campbell, 1988). One study of asthma confirmed Minuchin's clinical observation that families of severe asthmatics are more enmeshed and rigid than normal families (Gustafsson, Kjellman, Ludvigsson, & Cederblad, 1987), while a second study found no relationship (Burbeck, 1979). Researchers at the University of Oklahoma have studied the relationship of family cohesion, as measured by Olson's Family Adaptability and Cohesion Scale to pregnancy outcome (Ramsey, Abell, & Baker, 1986) and susceptibility to influenza (Clover, Abell, Becker, Crawford, & Ramsey, 1989). They found that high cohesion was associated with delivering a lower birth weight infant and, in a separate study, with developing influenza. These researchers hypothesize that family enmeshment has an adverse effect on immune functioning that results in more frequent influenza infections and perinatal infections that precipitate premature labor.

Family expressed emotion has been found to be a powerful predictor of the course of schizophrenia and other mental disorders and is associated with poor outcome in weight reduction programs (Fischman-Havstad & Marston, 1984). A key component of expressed emotion is the emotional overinvolvement of the family in the patient's life, a concept very similar to enmeshment. No studies have looked empirically at the relationship between family enmeshment and expressed emotion. One difficulty is that there is considerable disagreement about what the concepts of cohesion and enmeshment represent and how best to measure them. The role of family expressed emotion and its relationship to enmeshment needs to be studied more carefully in physical health.

A number of investigators have developed family interventions designed to change family interactions in chronic physical illness. From their carefully articulated model, Minuchin and colleagues (1975) used structural family therapy to change the patterns of interaction they observed in psychosomatic families. They reported considerable success in using this intervention in 48 cases of diabetes, asthma, and anorexia nervosa. As a result of their work, the psychosomatic family model has become the most influential model of families and chronic illness, and structural family therapy the most widely promoted family intervention in physical illness (Griffith & Griffith, 1987). Recently, Minuchin's work has come under considerable criticism for conceptual and methodological problems (Campbell, 1986; Coyne & Anderson, 1988). By the researchers' own admission, these families were a highly selective group, and not representative of most families with these illnesses (Rosman & Baker, 1988). In addition, their studies lacked any control groups or statistical analyses.

Despite this interest in family therapy for physical disorders, there have been only two randomized controlled trials of family therapy in physical illness, both for asthma. Using the psychosomatic family model, Gustafsson, Kjellman, and Cederblad (1986) were able to demonstrate a greater improvement than in controls in overall health of 9 children with severe asthma whose families received 8 monthly sessions of structural family therapy. In a similar study, Lask and Matthew (1979) in England randomly assigned 33 families with 37 asthmatic children to experimental and control groups. The experimental groups received a total of 6 hours of family therapy designed to improve the families' coping skills in dealing with acute attacks. At the end of 1 year, the children who received family therapy reported less wheezing and a slight improvement in pulmonary function tests. Lask and Matthew used a psychoeducational approach that focused upon problem solving and developing skills to cope with the illness, rather than on changing family structure or functioning. In both studies, the benefits of therapy were quite modest, and the generalizability of the results to other families with asthma is questionable.

MECHANISMS:
HOW FAMILIES INFLUENCE HEALTH

In developing family interventions in physical health, the mechanisms or pathways by which family factors can influence health should be considered. Family interventions developed to improve health may block or enhance a specific pathway.

Excluding the direct transmission of infectious agents from one family member to another, there are two general pathways, psychophysiological and behavioral, by which a family can influence the health of its members. In the psychophysiological pathway, family factors such as stress or life events affect the emotional state of an individual family member, resulting in direct physiological changes that predispose the individual to becoming ill. With the behavioral pathway, the family influences the individual's health behaviors, such as diet, exercise, smoking, compliance with medical treatment, and visits to the physician, and these health behaviors affect the individual's health (see Figure 16.1).

Early research on the psychophysiological pathway emphasized the neuroendocrine connection. Stress researchers have demonstrated how

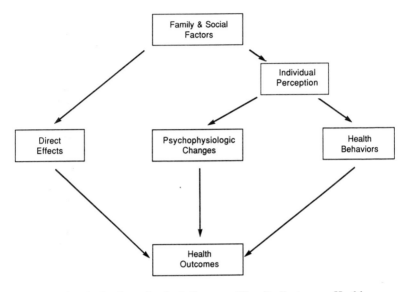

Figure 16.1. Mechanisms for the Influence of Family Factors on Health

stressful stimuli result in autonomic arousal with elevated catechola-
mine levels, which can cause arrhythmias, heart attack, or death in
cardiac patients (Lown, Desilva, Reich, & Murawski, 1980), or may
increase glucose and free fatty acid levels in diabetic patients and
precipitate diabetic ketoacidosis (Minuchin, Rosman, & Baker, 1978).
Marital conflict and dissatisfaction have been shown to increase autonomic arousal and lead to poorer self-reported health (Levenson &
Gottman, 1983, 1985). More recent research in psychoimmunology has
revealed how stress can suppress the immune system and result in
illness (Ader, 1981; Calabrese, Kling, & Gold, 1987). Bereaved, divorced, and depressed individuals have been shown to have poorer
immune functioning than controls (Bartrop et al., 1977; Kiecolt-Glaser
et al., 1987, 1988; Schleifer et al., 1983).

The family may also influence health more indirectly by influencing
health behaviors (behavioral pathway). For example, while the stress of
bereavement may directly affect the immune system, it also results in
profound behavioral changes, including an increase in smoking, alcohol
consumption, and use of sedatives, all of which may result in poor
health (Osterweis et al., 1984). Cirrhosis, accidents, and suicide account

for a large proportion of the increased mortality after bereavement and are often the result of alcohol abuse.

Although more research has been done on the psychophysiological pathway, it is likely that the behavioral pathway is more important for the family's influence on health. Research suggests that health behaviors have a more powerful influence on health than emotional states. For example, behavioral cardiac risk factors, such as smoking, diet, and compliance with hypertension medication, are more important than emotional states, such as stress or Type A, in the development of heart disease. Similarly for diabetes, poor metabolic control appears to be primarily a result of poor compliance rather than emotional distress (Coyne & Anderson, 1988). Knowing the mechanisms by which families influence health will help guide clinical interventions.

DEVELOPING FAMILY INTERVENTIONS

Based upon three productive areas of research on families and health—family stress, social support, and family enmeshment—some recommendations for the development and testing of family interventions are possible. An empirically based intervention should help families reduce or cope with stress, enhance support, and facilitate effective family functioning. The components of family interventions designed to do this can be organized around Doherty and Baird's (1986, 1987a) levels of physician involvement with the family in health care. This model has proven to be useful for understanding how health care providers work with families in clinical practice. It can be adapted to describe different elements or components of family interventions derived from empirical research. (For a full explanation of the levels of involvement, see the appendix to Chapter 14 of this volume.)

Level 2 (educating the family) and Level 3 (enhancing family support) include interventions that are commonly provided by family physicians and require no additional training. Level 4 (facilitating family problem solving) usually involves systematically assessing the family's strengths and weaknesses as well as family members' styles of coping. To provide Level 4 interventions, a family physician generally needs additional clinical training in family assessment and intervention, either in residency training (McDaniel, Campbell, Wynn, & Weber, 1988) or in postresidency workshops (Bishop et al., 1984). Family therapy (Level 5) requires extensive family therapy training and supervision (American Association of Marriage and Family Therapy, 1986), which few family physicians have or are likely to obtain.

An advantage of Doherty and Baird's framework for family interventions is that it is based upon a family strength (versus family deficit) model that assumes that families are healthy and an important resource for helping the patient deal with health problems or illnesses. This approach focuses upon the illness, not the family, as the source of stress and difficulty. The physician usually begins with the simplest level of involvement, educating the family (Level 2), and moves up to higher-level involvement as needed. For example, after a myocardial infarction, the physician may meet with the patient and spouse to explain the cardiac rehabilitation, including the levels of physical and sexual activity in which the patient can safely engage. Because of the highly stressful nature of a heart attack, the physician might move beyond education and encourage the couple to discuss their feelings about the illness and their fears for the future (Level 3). If it becomes apparent that the couple are having difficulty coping with the heart attack (e.g., the patient is not limiting his activities and his wife is nagging him about it), the physician could decide to work with the couple for several sessions to help them deal more effectively with cardiac rehabilitation (Level 4). If during those sessions more chronic or severe marital problems surface, the couple would be referred for marital therapy (Level 5). A physician who is unskilled or not interested in primary care family counseling, or who detects serious marital difficulties earlier, might refer the couple to a family therapist sooner.

Each level of intervention may involve one or more members of the family or multiple families. In addition, the intervention may be provided by the primary health care provider or another professional. For example, the family physician may educate (Level 2) the cardiac patient and spouse about the patient's physical limitations, and the couple could attend family-oriented cardiac education classes provided by an organization such as the American Heart Association. Similarly, to enhance family support (Level 3) for smoking cessation, the physician can give the spouse specific suggestions on how to be more supportive (e.g., praising the patient) and how to eliminate nonsupportive behaviors (e.g., nagging the patient), and the couple could attend a support group run by a smoking cessation clinic or group such as Smokenders.

Level 4 (facilitating family problem solving) represents the core of a family psychoeducational approach. Based upon current research and the experience of working with families with schizophrenia, this approach is likely to be very effective in chronic physical illness. In addition to providing education and encouraging family support, the psychoeducational approach focuses on changing ineffective coping behaviors. It utilizes family strengths and family resources as well as community resources. It does not explicitly or implicitly blame the family for the illness or associated problem. The family is viewed as a crucial resource for helping to deal with the illness, rather than in need of therapy. Family dysfunction, when it exists, is assumed to result primarily from attempts to cope with the illness, rather than primarily due to family pathology. Family therapy is reserved for families that fail a psychoeducational intervention or are severely dysfunctional.

The psychoeducational approach may be most efficiently and effectively implemented in a multifamily group setting. All three components (education, support, and problem solving) can be provided by the group facilitator and other families in the group. Such groups can be developed within a single clinical practice or for an entire community. One problem in developing family interventions for chronic illness is deciding whether to make them disease specific or generic to all chronic disorders. Gonzalez, Steinglass, and Reiss's (1989) multifamily groups for chronic physical illness focus on generic themes (e.g., "putting illness in its place") that occur in all chronic illnesses. These researchers argue that the mix of illnesses represented in any group enriches the experience and encourages the group to deal with the broader issues of coping rather than the specific details of the particular illness. One approach to dealing with the wide range of chronic illnesses seen in clinical practice is to classify chronic illnesses according to their psychosocial demands, as Rolland (1984) has done, and develop interventions to fit groups of illnesses that have similar psychosocial characteristics.

CONCLUSION

Although more research is needed if we are to understand the relationship between family factors and physical health, current research findings suggest that we are ready to develop and test family interventions in physical health. Family interventions that focus on education, support, and problem solving can be developed and implemented in practice. The two areas in which family interventions are likely to be most effective are those of promoting healthy behaviors and helping families cope with chronic illness. Enhancing spousal support for life-style changes such as smoking cessation, reducing cholesterol intake, weight reduction, or exercise programs can have a significant impact on these behaviors. Psychoeducational approaches for common chronic illnesses such as hypertension, heart disease, chronic lung disease, diabetes, arthritis, and cancer should be developed and tested. As shown by Morisky et al.'s (1983) study, these interventions need not be complex or intensive to be effective, but can be as simple as a single intervention to educate and enhance support from family members.

Studies of family interventions should measure multiple intervening and outcome measures. For example, a trial of family psychoeducation for a chronic illness should assess whether the family's knowledge, support, and problem solving improve and whether such improvements lead to better patient and family outcomes. In addition to measuring traditional medical outcomes such as compliance, complications, and overall mortality, sensitive measures of health status (Stewart et al., 1989) allow the researcher to measure much more subtle changes in health.

An important lesson can be learned from the research and clinical work that has been undertaken with families of schizophrenics. Clinicians and researchers should collaborate with the families involved and elicit their input and guidance in developing and testing family interventions. This process can begin by simply convening a group of families to discuss what kind of assistance they would find helpful and then forming a patient-family advisory group for the chronic illness. The most effective and successful family-oriented health care views families as an invaluable resource for patient care.

SEVENTEEN

The Family in Family Practice

REG L. PERKIN

Family practice arose out of general practice. It is mainly a North American phenomenon. In the United States, the term *family practice* is strongly preferred and *general practice* has almost a second-class connotation. In Canada, the two terms are used interchangeably in the practice setting, but *family practice* is preferred in the academic environment. *Family medicine* refers to the academic discipline on which family practice is based.

My premise is that the term *family practice* did not result from the initiative of practicing doctors. It is not a child of our colleagues in practice, and indeed has not yet been accepted by many of them. In the United States, *family practice* was chosen to achieve a distinct identity from other primary care providers, in a country where only 15% of the doctors are family physicians. In Canada, the name was chosen in an effort to leave behind the image of the general practitioner as a doctor who must know everything about everything, and allow the academic discipline of family medicine to define its limits and set its educational objectives. This was crucial to the introduction of departments of family medicine into the Canadian medical schools. Undoubtedly many of these same reasons also applied in the United States.

Elsewhere in the English-speaking world, in the United Kingdom, Australia, and New Zealand, the term *general practice* continues to be used in both practice and academic settings. There was no reason to change the name in those countries because there is not so much competition for the provision of primary care, and the postgraduate training programs are not so closely allied with the universities.

In North America it was realized that the general practitioner did look after families and knew them well. There was, therefore, good reason for choosing the terms *family practice* and *family medicine.* North American family physicians should be including the family in the care of their patients.

HISTORICAL PERSPECTIVE

In seventeenth-century England, the apothecaries were the forerunners of general practitioners, and the physicians of the day were the equivalent of today's consulting specialists. The Apothecaries Act of 1815 allowed apothecaries to charge for their medical care. By 1829, they were being called general practitioners.

In Canada, the first medical schools were formed in 1823 in Montreal and in 1843 in Toronto. Specialists have existed in Canada since the middle of the nineteenth century. The role of specialists was strengthened by the Flexner Report of 1910, which placed medical education totally under the control of universities and teaching hospitals.

The College of General Practice of Canada, as it was initially known, was founded in 1954. The American Academy had been founded in 1947 and the British College in 1952. Certification in family medicine began in Canada in 1969.

The College of General Practice in Canada changed its name to the College of Family Physicians of Canada in 1967. The reasons for the name change have already been alluded to. We still have members who prefer the old name. If we look at the general practitioner of a few decades ago, I believe we can identify intuitive reasons that led to the name change. General practitioners often worked alone and for long hours, which made them personally available to patients. Primary care was less competitive, so all members of the family would tend to go to the same physician. Medical life was less complicated, and it was easier for GPs to follow patients into the hospital and to deliver babies and provide a wide range of patient care services. There was less traffic, public transportation was not as well developed, community services were not as available, and therefore GPs made more house calls, thereby providing more close personal contact with family members. Today's sophisticated technology was not available, and there was more "laying on of hands" by physicians in providing care to patients.

It is easy to see why it was logical to change the name from *general practice* to *family practice,* particularly when we appreciate that this occurred a quarter of a century ago. But the changes that have subsequently occurred in family practice, particularly in the last decade, are taking us in the opposite direction. More competition for primary care from specialists and walk-in clinics, larger call groups and less direct after-hours coverage, fewer house calls, giving up obstetrics, less involvement with emergency departments and in-hospital care of patients, more pressure to crank up the volume in the office, patients more demanding, increased medicolegal risks, pressure to overinvestigate, pressure to get consultations—all these factors are escalating rapidly in the practice of family doctors, especially in urban areas. Add to these the complexities of modern life—both parents working, day care and other parental concerns, and the strong motivation for a better life-style, all personal factors affecting both patients and physicians—and it is no wonder many family physicians are questioning the system and their place in it.

Family medicine is not the only discipline that is experiencing an identity problem. General internal medicine is certainly an endangered species and close to extinction in some parts of the country. General surgeons are now limited to the area bounded by the diaphragm on the north and the iliac crest on the south, with the rest of what they used to do having been neatly amputated by a plethora of surgical subspecialties. We shall soon face a crisis in the rural areas of Canada when the existing GP surgeons retire and there is nobody to replace them. Even the subspecialties have been split into pediatric and adult halves, and some of the halves split again into even smaller pieces. To date, family medicine has remained more cohesive, although we do have small numbers of our colleagues splitting off into areas of special interest.

FAMILY MEDICINE

With the above as background, I would like to return to a focus on family medicine. One of our early difficulties was in defining *family.* The traditional definition of a legally married man and woman with children was too restrictive. When we established the Department of Family and Community Medicine at the University of Toronto in 1969, one of our first problems was overcoming patients' misconception that we were a family planning clinic. Once we got beyond that difficulty, we were faced with looking after a wide spectrum of social groups: We dealt with single-parent families, acted as a shelter for battered wives and as a halfway house for rehabilitated alcoholics, and more. We decided to define a *family* as "a group of people who sit down to one meal together each day." A few years later, in 1973, Ransom and Vandervoort defined a family as "a group of intimates with both a history and a future."

Family practice in 1990 demonstrates a pattern of illness similar, but not identical, to the pattern of illness in the community. The problems presented to the physician are often a complex mixture of emotional, physical, and social factors. Many clinical problems remain undifferentiated and never reach the point of being labeled with a specific diagnosis of the kind found in a pathology textbook. Illness is often seen in its early stages and must be followed over time before the diagnosis becomes clear. There is a high incidence of acute short-term illness. Much of the family physician's time is taken up with the management of chronic disease and problems related to life-style and behavior.

If one were to analyze the physician-patient contacts in the offices of family doctors across the country, one would undoubtedly conclude that it would be better to name this type of doctor a *personal* physician rather than a family physician. Even when the physician undertakes a "family" intervention, it is almost always done on a one-to-one basis with a single person, not with the entire family in the consulting room. Even though 50% of the doctors in Canada are family physicians, compared with 15% in the United States, and we do not have the same degree of competition for primary care in Canada, we still experience fragmentation in the care of family members. The development of group practice, even when all the members of the group are family physicians, tends to break up families because different family members prefer different doctors in the group. External primary care providers such as walk-in clinics and emergency departments increase the fragmentation of care.

I believe that the four keys to having more intact families in a family practice are availability, obstetrics, hospital involvement, and house calls. More personal availability to patients is achieved by working in smaller groups with more close-knit on-call arrangements. Physicians who do obstetrics are also far more likely to look after all members of a family. Patients bond to physicians when their need is greatest, and this is frequently when they are sick enough to be in the hospital. House calls put physicians in contact with family members in addition to the initial patient, and have the added benefit of providing information about the family a doctor will not learn in any other way.

These same observations are obviously important in family practice training programs as well. If medical students and family practice residents are not exposed to appropriate role models in their teachers, they will not come to understand the full scope of family practice. At least some of the faculty should be doing obstetrics and looking after patients in hospitals. House calls should be one of the ways in which health care is delivered. The family practice unit should not be signing out to the emergency department or a doctors' replacement service on evenings and weekends. Some of our teaching programs have fallen into these bad habits in the past, but there has been a great deal of improvement in recent years. Some 20 years ago, when family practice residency training was getting started in Canada, there was more focus on family and particularly the psychosocial aspects of care. Many of our detractors in those early years labeled residency training as "glorified social work." We were criticized for replacing practical procedural training with such "soft" skills as counseling and family therapy. Mind you, the family involvement taught in the early days of the residency programs was pegged more at Level 3, as defined by Doherty and Baird (1986), with some residents achieving Level 4 but very few trained to Level 5. (For discussion of these levels, see Baird, Chapter 13; Becker, Chapter 14, especially the appendix; and Campbell, Chapter 16, this volume.)

We have drifted away from some of the emphases that received a great deal of attention in the early years of family practice residency training in Canada. There have been signs in recent years that we are moving toward restoring a better balance in our training programs. That is what makes this book on the family in family medicine so timely and important.

RESPONSE TO THE
THREE PRACTICE CHAPTERS

At the beginning of this discussion it is important to review the five levels of family intervention as defined by Doherty and Baird (1986; see the appendix to Chapter 14 of this volume). Let me start by exploring further the reasons the concept of family is not as important a part of family practice as one might imagine. Some of the historical aspects have already been presented. Becker identifies a number of others in his Chapter 14 of this volume. These components of care are not as well reimbursed in the fee-for-service payment mechanism as are procedural items. Family physicians often do not have appropriate staff or physical arrangements in the office to accommodate family groups. Most graduates of family practice residency programs will have received training to Level 3 or Level 4 of family intervention, but few reach Level 5. Although there is significant evidence to support the contention that family intervention is of value in the care of patients, the proof of this has not been extensively developed and certainly has not been well publicized. Family physicians may therefore underestimate its value, or not appreciate the interest of their patients in the potential inclusion of family intervention in their care, or both. Undoubtedly, there are large numbers of patients who do not perceive medical care extending beyond their own person, and there is ample evidence of this in the widespread use of walk-in clinics and emergency departments for episodic care. Some patients may say, "I do not have a family involved," but almost everyone has a psychosocial context—that is, a partner or someone else who is close to him or her, a close friend if not a family member. Therefore, if we use one of the definitions of *family* referred to earlier, such patients are still amenable to family intervention.

Many parallels can be drawn between McFarlane's chapter on schizophrenia and Campbell's chapter on physical health to illustrate how factors that adversely affect health or interfere with healing can be helped by strategies that involve family intervention. McFarlane points out that high levels of expressed emotion (EE) in family members will make a patient's schizophrenia worse. Noncompliance with taking medication may be aggravated by family interaction. He also identifies other factors in the patient's social network that may aggravate the disease, including the stigma of schizophrenia, family members pulling away and thereby shrinking the size of the patient's support network, intervening life events or disabilities that cause family members to withdraw support, and family members who find the disease confusing or fail to grasp important information, who find the burden too heavy to bear, or who just do not have the coping skills to continue to support the patient.

In dealing with physical health, Campbell points out that the level of EE in family members at the time of a patient's hospitalization can be related to the frequency of subsequent relapse of the disease. He also notes that family enmeshment, a combination of a high level of EE with family cohesion, has an adverse effect on chronic illnesses such as asthma. Family stress related to such life events as bereavement or separation and divorce leads to poor physical health. Support from both within and without the family is important in achieving compliance in the treatment of common health problems such as obesity, smoking, and hypertension. Campbell observes that patients who lack family and social support have higher morbidity and mortality rates.

Becker, Campbell, and McFarlane also seem to agree that long-term outcomes of treatment are more favorable if the family is involved: Motivation and compliance are increased, and morbidity and mortality are reduced. The only obvious negative factor is that sometimes the welfare of the patient and that of the family may be in conflict.

McWhinney (1989), in his *Textbook of Family Medicine,* makes some other points that are pertinent to this discussion. Knowledge of the family can be used in treating the patient and can increase the number of management options. He observes that some families are vulnerable, and the family physician needs to look out for them, provide them with extra support, and be there at times of crisis. There are also individual family members who are vulnerable, the easily missed "hidden" patient, who may also be the family scapegoat. McWhinney cautions us not to take sides in family conflicts, but to be proactive in offering a family conference at times of stress.

My evaluation of the evidence presented at the Calgary symposium for which the chapters in this volume were initially written, supported by information from other sources and corroborated by an understanding of the historical perspective of our discipline, leads me to conclude that the advantages of including more "family" in family practice far outweigh the disadvantages. The major obstacle, obviously, is the lack of interest, awareness, and expertise in this area on the part of the majority of family physicians. What can be done about it?

STRATEGIES FOR CHANGE

I shall conclude this chapter with a discussion of strategies for change. The framework for this discussion will be McWhinney's patient-centered clinical method and the five principles of innovation diffusion outlined by Becker in Chapter 14 and drawn from the work of Rogers (Chapter 11, this volume).

The Patient-Centered Clinical Method

McWhinney's patient-centered clinical method, as contrasted to the traditional disease-oriented model, has an interesting historical perspective that goes back to ancient Greece. The school of Cos, in which Hippocrates was prominent, was the forerunner of the McWhinney model. These physicians linked the patient with the disease, treated each patient individually, and used a comprehensive regimen of therapy. The school of Cnidus was the prototype for the traditional disease-oriented model of modern times. The Cnidians believed that the disease has a reality independent of the patient, and they classified the patient's illness in a taxonomy of diseases, using abstractions and generalizations and applying specific remedies to each disease process.

In practicing a patient-centered clinical method, the physician attaches equal importance to following the traditional agenda and to understanding the meaning of the illness for the patient. This involves understanding the patient's perception of the illness and its causes, explaining treatment and outcome, and understanding the patient's feelings and fears. Some fear is nearly always present in the medical encounter, even when the illness seems to be minor: fear of the unknown, fear of death, fear of insanity, disability, and rejection. The meaning the illness has for the patient will usually be related in some way to that person's life. Relationships in the family may have contributed to the illness in some way and the illness itself will have an impact on the family.

In practicing patient-centered medicine, the physician tries to enter the patient's world, as well as to interpret the illness in terms of medical abstractions. Since between 25% and 50% of patients seen by family doctors do not have clinical diagnoses in a specific sense, the key to understanding the illness is understanding the patient. It is interesting that, before the modern era, *diagnosis* often referred to the diagnosis of a patient rather than a disease. In any serious illness, acute or chronic, an understanding of the person is crucial, and this inevitably involves an understanding of his or her important relationships.

The key skill for the patient-centered physician is active listening, a much-needed skill in modern medicine. The analytic style of the conventional clinical method has tended to encourage an interaction dominated by the physician, rather than one in which the patient is allowed to express thoughts and feelings. This transformation of our clinical method involves a radical change in the way physicians perceive themselves and their task. It may be the most revolutionary change in medical thought since our conventional clinical method first took on its present form in the nineteenth century.

Principles of Innovation Diffusion

The five principles of innovation diffusion are relative advantage, compatibility, complexity, trialability, and observability. In Chapter 14, Becker rightly points out the major difficulties that must be overcome in convincing family physicians to adopt family intervention procedures as an important part of their practice, as well as getting patients and families to accept this added dimension of care. Becker makes some suggestions about how the innovation might be spread, and I have used these ideas to build a discussion of strategies for change.

The first principle, *relative advantage,* is obviously crucial. We shall have to prove to family physicians that adding family intervention strategies to their therapeutic armamentarium will allow them to provide their patients with better care than they can provide now. Evidence to support the truth of this statement is rapidly mounting. Further research in this area and publication of the results will help. I believe the key factor in making this successful will be to link the family factor to discrete clinical interventions. I do not believe that family physicians will buy the concept in a generic global sense, but will see the wisdom and practicality of it when applied to specific clinical situations. Also, the family component must be woven into the clinical encounter, not just tacked onto the end of the patient visit, and this is where the McWhinney patient-centered clinical method becomes so important. If the strategies are to be accepted, they must be practical and cost-effective. This will require changes in the fee schedule or family physicians' embracing a different payment mechanism. Also, we must reach our trainees, especially those in the postgraduate programs. Family practice residents should be taught to "think family" and should be trained at least to Level 4, where they can do a systematic assessment of family function and plan an intervention.

The principle of *compatibility* refers to the fit between the innovation and the values, experiences, and perceived needs of the adopters. Here I perceive the physician as being concerned about potential conflict between the good of the patient and the good of the patient's family, in situations where the welfare of the patient may conflict with that of other family members. There is always the risk of "stirring up trouble" within a family by involving family members in the treatment of an individual patient. Family members may feel they are being blamed for the illness or other problems of the patient, especially when a child is the identified patient. Sometimes the family is not functioning in a healthy or functional way and requires a Level 5 intervention (family therapy). The physician must take care not to become judgmental, as this makes it impossible to help the family unit. Rather, the physician should support the family and empower family members to take responsibility to change where necessary. In promoting this help, the family physician must carefully define the illness so as to avoid placing blame on family members. The physician also needs to spend time just being friendly with family members, something the old-fashioned GP did so well and that now, with more pressure on time in the office, is working against us. We also need to remember McWhinney's cautions about "hidden" patients, scapegoats, issues of confidentiality, not taking sides, and being there in times of crisis. I believe these are all factors that can be researched, taught, learned, and communicated.

Complexity is an important principle. If an innovation is too complicated, it is less likely to be adopted. I believe the majority of family physicians function comfortably at Level 2 and do a good job giving information and advice. Residency-trained family physicians should be able to function at Level 3 (emotional support of families) and be capable of understanding and dealing with the affective aspects of family life. Our strategy should be, through residency training and continuing medical education, to interest family physicians in moving up to Level 4. If this is based on defined strategies related to specific clinical situations, I believe it can be successful. Family physicians who practice in groups, and those who are remunerated by some method other than fee for service, might be the best initial target audience. Those with the appropriate staff and office layouts could be encouraged to work with families or groups of families in a manner similar to the problem-driven treatment model outlined by McFarlane in Chapter 15. Some family physicians undoubtedly will get "turned on" and want to train up to Level 5 and become family therapists. Those who do will have to understand clearly the distinction between being a family physician and being a family therapist, and should read McWhinney's excellent dissertation on this subject in his textbook of family medicine. I believe, however, that the vast majority of family physicians will choose to stop at the level of identifying families that need formal family therapy and referring them, as they do with other specialized clinical problems.

Trialability is a principle that lends itself to group CME and group research. Increasingly, family physicians are working in groups and have more opportunity for dialogue among themselves during normal working hours. We are seeing a number of special interest groups emerging within family medicine. I see those interested in family interventions coming together to share ideas, learn from each other, engage in collaborative research, and, by publishing their results, spread the word to others. This volume and the conference from which it came are good examples. What we need to do is start a grass fire!

Finally, *observability* is essential if this idea is to catch on and become a grass-roots movement among family physicians. In his chapter, Becker refers to the importance of peers in the adoption of any innovation. The sackcloth and ashes that we have worn for so long in describing ourselves as "just GPs" is starting to disappear. Family physicians are relying more on other family physicians for consultation. At national meetings of the College of Family Physicians of Canada, more than 50% of the speakers are now family physicians, and the majority of the programs consist of seminars and workshops instead of lectures. Another good example is obstetrics, where family physicians who have stopped delivering babies are referring their low-risk obstetric patients to family physician colleagues who continue to do obstetrics. Medical record-keeping systems that include genograms and file the records of family members together increase observability for everyone working in that patient care facility. I believe we can build on these trends to increase the observability of the value of family interventions as an important component of what family physicians do in caring for their patients. Observability will be enhanced by disseminating, by every means possible, information about the importance of "family" in family practice.

CONCLUSION

I shall conclude with one final observation. A study of history makes one aware of the twist of irony that frequently comes to the surface when comparing the present to the past. The old-fashioned GP really was a family doctor, but was not called one. The majority of present-day family physicians do not fulfill the "family" part of the clinical picture as well as their predecessors, largely as a result of changes over which they have had very little control. However, I believe the intuitive sense of the importance of "family" is valid and still present in the minds of practicing family physicians. With the new knowledge that is emerging, and the innovative strategies available to us, I believe our family physician colleagues can be encouraged to expand their horizons to include more family interventions in their care of patients and achieve the objective of becoming family physicians in function as well as in name.

EIGHTEEN

Expanding Our Horizons:
Visions of the Future

RUSSELL J. SAWA

THE SYMPOSIUM ON
THE FAMILY IN PRIMARY CARE

At the symposium on the family in primary care that led to this volume, an evolutional dialectic was facilitated by a continual focusing and refining of the discussion (through group process) so that the result was a plan for future action that synthesized the most important ideas of the meeting. The group was challenged at the outset to undertake to move beyond the present state of the art to the agenda for the next decade. A number of themes emerged.

Themes

Practice

Physicians who adopt a family approach continue to work primarily with individuals, but do so in a significantly different way. There is a shift from a biomedical/technological/individual orientation to an aware-ness of the relationships the patient has, especially the doctor-patient relationship. This new way of thinking is facilitated through the use of genograms on patient charts. Firsthand knowledge of family members is often obtained through a conscious effort on the part of the physician to take care of the whole family by stating the desire to do so on the first visit. There will be times that the family is convened, such as when middle-aged children can no longer cope with the care of elderly parents, or when a family member is critically ill or dying. Just as a preventive approach requires a certain kind of practice organization, so does working with families. The family-oriented primary care clinician will recognize when a personal or systemic way of thinking is necessary to understand or manage a problem. He or she will also *utilize* the supportive strength of the family (however defined).

Many physicians were family oriented prior to the recent awakening of interest in family-oriented care. Without the benefit of the theory and skills that are now being delineated, these physicians were caring/ loving individuals who often knew the families of their patients because they took care of the whole family (for elaboration of the historical development of a family approach to health care, see Baird, Chapter 13; Perkin, Chapter 17, this volume). Care should be taken not to lose what these physicians modeled, such as participating in the dying process to help prevent or heal psychic wounds. They recognized that healing is not always curing, that dying is part of living, that pain can be redemptive, maturing, and a path to growth, and that finding meaning in life and its joys and sorrows is essential if one is to be fully alive. Joining in collaborative ways with patients and families, sharing information, and problem-focused counseling are natural extensions of the skills family physicians already possess (Sawa, 1986).

Theory

It has been noted that systems theory is not always accessible to the practitioner. Although systems theory may be our "general theory," we will need to develop "application theory" that addresses how and in what circumstances we put systems theory into practice (see Doherty, Chapter 4; Steinglass, Chapter 3, this volume).

The themes that have emerged around theory are well described in the four theory chapters of this volume and in the action statements of the group at the symposium, summarized below.

Methodology

The integration of qualitative and quantitative approaches will allow us to develop new methods. Crucial data often lie in patients' stories, rather than in formalized, data-gathering approaches. We need to focus on the patient's primary relatedness network, and shift our attention toward family health maintenance and promotion as well as illness, and toward investigating ways in which family physicians currently improve their patients' sense of wellness and control (Sawa, Jennett, & Elford, 1991). Another important area for research is that of the physiological and psychological mechanisms involved in stress, coping, and social support (Antonovsky, 1979, 1987; Milsum, 1984).

It will also be important to study the doctor-patient-family relationship, to learn how what we do helps the health of our patients, and how we can do it best.

Education

At the Calgary symposium we had a "fishbowl" experience after the education presentations. Several participants were asked to move into the center of the room, into the fishbowl, and several other participants were asked to seat themselves around those in the center to act as appointed observers and commentators. The larger group observed from the periphery but did not participate directly.

During this experience, a participant stated that he felt angry that family-oriented care had come to mean, for many, the idea of seeing whole families. This seemed to leave out those physicians who worked primarily at Levels 2 and 3 (see the appendix to Becker, Chapter 14, this volume). A number of participants responded by strongly supporting the value of working at Levels 2 and 3 and "thinking family" while working with individuals, clarifying that this probably is where primary care clinicians make their greatest contribution to the care of families. Physicians can be therapeutic with families without being family therapists. We need not be tyrannized by the notion of seeing whole families.

The importance of learning from our general practitioner mentors was underlined. An example of a man who had become psychotic in the intensive care unit environment was given to illustrate this point. His physician solved this problem by moving him into a regular room and having his wife get into bed with him for comfort. We might also learn a lot from allied health professionals such as nurses—for instance, in the area of using touch appropriately—by watching what they do and by being open to being challenged by them. Other examples of those we can learn much from are people working with chronic pain, rehabilitation staff, oncology workers, and those working in geriatrics hospices.

Some problems cannot be solved by logic and reasoning, but only transcended by love.

As was pointed out in the fishbowl experience, we can learn by "falling in love" with ideas and people. We need to add the context of love, respect, and caring to learning and discussions of patient care. Love in this sense means opening space for others. Love and caring have become almost as taboo as religion in scholarly professional scientific assemblies and writings. Yet love is crucial to our professional and personal activity. There has, however, been some wisdom in this verbal or linguistic detachment from the word *love*, since it has come to mean many things; some detachment has been necessary to preserve our professional boundaries. The symposium participants agreed that there must be ethical caring for our patients, which involves identifying with their needs and goals rather than imposing our own (Christie & Hoffmaster, 1986). Love or caring is balanced with mutual responsibility. The importance of boundaries that respect our own persons and the persons of our patients was acknowledged, yet being personally and emotionally available is the essence of being therapeutic. We touch people with our words as profoundly as we do with our fingers. We convey caring in our actions, by taking the risk of sharing ourselves with others. This opens up the possibility of caring.

Dehumanized educational environments, on the other hand, sabotage attempts to facilitate a caring mind-set in both teachers and trainees. We recognize that we are part of abusive systems, often based on hierarchy, autocracy, and power. Somehow we must create a loving work environment. We must respect our trainees (and they us) if we wish them to be receptive, and begin where they are. We recognized that there is a lack of a broad cultural mandate for the sensitive caring we feel is necessary. Unfortunately, it is often easier to be destructive or hateful than to love. We experience a struggle between trying to be perfect (or projecting the need to be perfect), or in control, and being whole. Showing and living wholeness may involve acknowledging we are sometimes wrong; sometimes we are not in control. These may be the keys to caring and connecting with residents.

"We've Only Just Begun"

Our discussion then shifted direction: Our models of family-oriented health care are not yet clearly defined or described. We have borrowed frameworks that neither describe our experience nor give us predictive accuracy. We have not yet worked out the philosophical basis of our discipline with clarity. In borrowing theory, we experience dissonance as we try to find out what fits and what doesn't. Given this situation, for the present, we are satisfied to teach theoretical frameworks that can be modified and built on by the learner. Primary care clinicians are required to decide when families need help, thus they need to have some set of norms to decide when families need counseling or therapy (Walsh, 1982). The McMaster model (Epstein, Bishop, & Levin, 1978) provides an excellent foundation for the clinician (medical or otherwise) who is working with families in primary care. Several family assessment models for primary care clinicians have been derived from the McMaster model (Christie-Seely, 1984b; Sawa, 1985) and used to teach primary care clinicians (for a discussion of primary care family models, see Rogers, Chapter 11, this volume). These models can be modified and built upon so that they fit students' own experiences and intuitions. Clinicians can revise them as they gain clinical experience.

By describing and researching interventions that are intended to share medical information (Sawa et al., 1991), we believe we will create more appropriate models (see Campbell, Chapter 16, this volume). The current models are reconstructed from the activities of those who have pioneered the integration of family therapy with family medicine. These will give way to models that will be derived from observation of clinicians doing family work that is integrated into everyday practice.

"What I Do Is Me"

As kingfishers catch fire, dragonflies draw flame;
As tumbled over rim in roundly wells
Stones ring, like each tucked string tells, each hung bell's
Bow swung finds tongue to fling out broad its name;
Each mortal thing does one thing and the same:
Deals out that being indoors each one dwells;
Selves—goes itself, *myself* it speaks and spells,
Crying WHAT I DO IS ME: FOR THAT I CAME.

In this poem, Gerard Manley Hopkins captures beautifully what followed in our discussion—that we model to our students by our behavior, attitudes, and values; we teach them by who we are. Family-oriented care is most effectively taught by modeling it. In order to nurture ourselves as models to our students, those of us in academic family medicine may, perhaps, choose to pay serious attention to creating environments that foster the development of well-rounded faculty: physically, intellectually, psychologically, socially, and spiritually.

An environment of trust facilitates growth. Faculty and administration may/must choose to respect their own boundaries and take on only the amount of work they can handle, so that they maintain strong personal, collegial, teacher-student, and familial relationships. Meeting the challenges of this task requires that we manage our stress (A. R. Martin, 1986; McCue, 1982; Quill & Williamson, 1990; Vincent, 1983) to levels that allow us to be free to be present for others. This requires the development of true collegiality, where personal respect is the norm and where authority is collaborative rather than autocratic or violent (i.e., by being manipulative, coercive, or punitive; Haring, 1975). In these ways, faculty will model personal and relational values that demonstrate how to treat oneself, one's family, and one's students.

As Diana McLain Smith reminded us, a common direction that we are all seeking is from unilateral to joint control, from win/lose or up/down to authentic, collaborative relationships. It is from valuing results to valuing the process-as-result. It is from linear to systemic thinking, from insight to action.

THE ACTION PLAN

From Insight to Action

The symposium culminated in moving from thought to a plan of action. The action that most represented our collective thoughts and energies was the foundation of a consortium that would continue to meet and conduct interuniversity research to put into action what we had discovered through our dialogue. This consortium (which has called itself the Calgary Consortium) agreed (in our second meeting) that it is open to new members, membership being defined by an active contribution to the collaborative research of the consortium. This has resulted in three and possibly four department of family medicine chairs in Canada and the United States supporting the activity of this research venture. Several other departments are considering following this lead. Several meetings have taken place since the Calgary meeting, and a research proposal is being developed. The group intends to define the "stuck" clinical situation through qualitative research, and to design a family intervention for a common medical problem, likely diabetes. This intervention will be introduced into teaching and nonteaching settings and its educational and clinical impact will be studied.

A number of other issues were defined as areas in which action would further the agenda of incorporating the family into family medicine. For instance, we agreed that it is important to identify clinical problems where the existing management is not satisfactory and where family intervention would improve patient care. Once identified, these specific areas can become the focus of family interventions designed (through qualitative research) and tested (through combined qualitative and quantitative methods as well as innovative research approaches). It is important to identify illnesses that promise to be medical conditions likely to benefit from a family approach. We should also confirm those conditions that we already know are helped through family intervention. We must develop and test problem-specific protocols for family interventions. It will also be beneficial to conduct controlled studies of multiple-family psychoeducational interventions and compare them with individual/single-family interventions. There is also a clear need to promote practice organization and financing that will support family-oriented care.

The consortium agreed that we should identify the richness that currently exists in the practice setting. This current activity needs to be tapped with some good research in order to establish the experiential base for family intervention.

It is clear that we must do qualitative research. It is through qualitative research that we maximize the chances of understanding the meaning of our patients' worlds, through listening to their stories and learning how to understand and evaluate them. Through a combination of qualitative and quantitative methods, we will come to discern patterns in our interactions that can be articulated to create new understandings: of patients, the doctor-patient relationship, the therapeutic triangle (doctor-patient-family relationship), and the healing relationship. Qualitative methods allow us to observe family physicians who integrate family. We also need to study patients who do well with family approaches and those who do not, as a way of evaluating the innovations that are introduced.

Some of the group have begun to learn about and develop research methods that describe what exemplars and practitioners do. This includes qualitative methods such as action science and process tracing. From these kinds of studies will evolve family medicine models of families and family physicians. Theory construction will be an evolving process grounded in actual clinical practice. New models will be contrasted with existing ones. Theory will include ethical considerations and the observer as part of the model.

As Donald Ransom has suggested, benefit will be gained by shifting research design and analysis to include person- and family-centered constructs that are meaningful to clinicians. It will be of benefit to give learners opportunities to experience guided observation of exemplar family practitioners. We will gain from a discussion of our students' observations. Studies need to be done to describe "authentic" family thinking, feeling, and behaviors of physicians who believe they are doing family-oriented care and get feedback from their patients. These descriptions can ground theoretical constructs and modes of thinking. Qualitative studies in this area will clarify the elements of doctor-patient-family interactions.

We must ensure that the learning environment models the caring that we expect learners to provide their patients. It would be valuable to study how differences between U.S. and Canadian academic practice modes relate to differences in the doctor-patient-family relationship.

THE FUTURE:
WHICH VISION WILL WE CHOOSE?

It is my belief that the coming decade will present us with a number of choices that could alter significantly the way primary care medicine is practiced. The present has been shaped by the marvelous accomplishments of science and technology. In North America, the path to the present was primarily set in motion by the Flexner Report, which was written in 1910 (see Perkin, Chapter 17, this volume). This report led to the needed shift to the sciences as the foundation of medical practice as well as the flourishing of specialization.

However, the needs of today are not the same as the needs of Flexner's day. In fact, as a result of the tremendous advances in medicine (among other factors), we now live longer, and because of our increased lifespan we (as a population) have more chronic illness. Given these factors, as well as the cost of our sophisticated technology, we also have upwardly spiraling costs that have become a major concern. Limited resources are now an important factor in deciding the course of action in some critical medical situations.

The science and philosophy that have been the foundation of the medical model (with its mind/body duality, reductionism, and Newtonian physics) have made their contribution. Systems theory, existentialism, phenomenology, relativity, and our glimpse into the subatomic world have changed our understanding of reality.

Western medicine, from its earliest beginnings in Greece, has always been an art as well as a science. This art involves skill in human relationships as well as the ability to make "good" decisions (Pellegrino & Thomasma, 1981; Wulff, Pedersen, & Rosenberg, 1986). It has always involved, and will always involve, values (Pellegrino & Thomasma, 1981).

The present time may be the window of opportunity for a shift in the direction of the development of medicine. Resources for ever-expanding technology may have reached their zenith. We have witnessed the fall of the great Soviet empire, something unthinkable only a short while ago. In its fall, we see the poverty and misery of a people whose basic needs have not been met because of a bureaucratic system that placed technology and military might ahead of human beings.

We are learning that we are all interconnected. Our interconnection with nature itself is becoming more important and obvious as we make decisions about how we use or misuse our natural resources. However, we have built two cultures that are badly in need of dialogue with each other. On the one hand is the culture, perhaps even the "god," of science and technology. On the other is the culture that includes our humanity—our spirituality, beliefs, and values. At times these two cultures seem divorced from each other. There needs to be more cooperation between these two, more collaboration throughout society. It is only in this way that we will get our priorities right. It is, in my opinion, humankind's highest priority to develop the essence of what it is to be human, to be a person. It is with this priority in place that medicine may make the decisions necessary to shape its future.

AN ETHICAL BASIS FOR THE PRACTICE OF SYSTEMIC FAMILY/PRIMARY CARE MEDICINE

Ethics is a branch of philosophy that discusses the goodness of our actions. Theories that affect our understanding of what it is to know something (epistemology) also have an impact on what ethical behavior looks like. I will now discuss some of the ethical implications of theoretical developments in family therapy. It is not my intent to present an exhaustive discussion, but to touch on a few important points. As primary care clinicians and theorists, we cannot loose sight of the fact that the end of our art is the good of our patients. We can learn much in this area from those clinicians and theorists who have blazed the trail of systemic thinking and intervention: the family therapists.

Family therapy was originally developed by psychoanalysts. It was initially developed to deal with patient populations that did not respond to extant therapies. Its initial ethical concerns were with the boundaries between the therapist and the patient/family. With the advent of systems theory, human behavior became understandable as a function of either system structure (family architecture) or feedback cybernetics (homeostasis). Therapists became active agents in determining healthy versus unhealthy family systems and in changing social structure and blocking feedback. Among the ethical concerns this raised was the issue of which is the client, the individual or the family (Goolishian & Anderson, 1991)? This same issue must be addressed by primary care in adopting a systemic approach, although it is usually clear who the patient is. But, further, does beneficial change for the family always benefit the individual?

Ethical issues regarding therapist competence required that therapists be skilled in moving into and altering a family's interactional patterns by the use of certain techniques, such as paradox, directives, reframing, and cybernetic conceptualization. Concerns in the primary care application of these skills involved a recognition that medical clinicians needed much training beyond the residency level to be competent to use these skills. The development of the "levels of involvement with families" concept by Doherty and Baird (1986) helped avert an outright rejection (by some) of trying to integrate the family into primary care by defining skill levels that could be attained by primary care clinicians. There is a major qualitative difference between the skills and methods of intervention between family therapists and others who have not had specific training to become competent therapists.

The postmodern era (since the early 1970s) has brought with it second-order cybernetics, in which therapists view themselves as part of the system that must change (Hoffman, 1990), and constructivism, in which families had become the distinctions made by observing therapists who were now seen as part of the family system (see Doherty, Chapter 4; McWhinney & Patterson, Chapter 5, this volume). More recently, social constructionist theory has defined competent and ethical family therapy to mean dialogue and shared meaning in which there is collaboration rather than an expert who is at the pinnacle of a hierarchy (see Doherty, Chapter 4, this volume). These changes have challenged the notion of natural foundational principles.

> The hope of discovering universal truths characteristic of human systems and human problems has now been abandoned. . . . shared understandings and situated interpretations replace ferretable facts. . . . meaning becomes an intersubjective matter. (Goolishian & Anderson, 1991, pp. 7-8)

Therapy itself changes

> from a therapy that is interventionist, relying on the strategic skill of the therapist, to a therapy that is mutual and relies on the expertise and integrity of our clients . . . from a therapy based on concepts of pathology and disease to a therapy that is simply dialogical and semantic in nature . . . [to] a conversational art. (Goolishian & Anderson, 1991, p. 8).

These changes have seen concepts such as family pathology and generational issues that have provided ethical constraints give way to

> local discourse and problem definition . . . [with the] frightening ethical prospects of relativism, nihilism, and solipsism (reality is all an irrational and subjective fantasy). . . . Ethical and competent therapy is being translated into a multi-colored tapestry of ideas, beliefs and meaning. This pluralism leaves us with no single hue, no pattern, or method to guide us. In the post modern era of therapy there is not a single or universal ethic. Instead, there is a multi-layered, complex set of ethical considerations that change from conversation to conversation, from context to context. For the post-modern therapist there is nothing inside to guide us except what we create in conversation with each other. There are no criteria other than that which we have created in conversation with each other in the course of constructing our mutual social practices. There are no external standards in moral and rational action free of obedience to our own socially constructed conventions. Constraints to potential meaning represent the consensus of the cultural conversational community, which is always changing. Ethics in therapy become very different than applying external criteria or conceptualizing the therapist as the skilled convener of expert methodology. (Goolishian & Anderson, 1991, pp. 8-9)

Medical clinicians are immediately accountable for their actions. They are entrusted with the responsibility of deciding who is free from societal obligations due to sickness, who is competent mentally to stand trial or manage their own affairs, and who is in danger of being abused and thus in need of protection by the state. Each of these responsibilities requires the comparison of an individual case with a norm. The clinician works within a set of norms that are universal (allowing for exceptions and difference in individual application of technologies, for instance, calibrating a specific value in a given laboratory). This is because science uses nature (anatomy and physiology, for instance) as its norm.

In order for primary care to understand and conduct dialogue with its colleagues in the social sciences and with family clinicians, a mutual understanding of the different ways of thinking appropriate to each is essential (see Sawa, Chapter 12, this volume). An ethic that is applicable in all fields of human interaction and intervention is most useful, if not desirable. There are several other proposals for an ethic for family therapy that should be mentioned.

Doherty (1991) suggests that family therapy adopt an ethical system in which virtue, in particular the virtue of the person of the therapist/clinician, be adopted. This would involve a focus on the moral qualities of the person of the therapist, instead of a focus on ethical principles, values, guidelines, and actions. This position supports Pellegrino and Thomasma's (1988), which revives Aristotle's concept of virtue with the addition to Aristotle's thinking of the concepts of social context and tradition. Doherty (1991) names benevolence or caring (a disposition to enhance the welfare of the client/family as agents of their own lives), justice (a disposition toward fair treatment of persons and groups, with special sensitivity to the vulnerable and disenfranchised), courage (an ability to remain nonreactive in the face of tension, to face one's personal issues, and to take risks for the welfare of the client/family), truthfulness (a disposition toward honest expression of beliefs and a disinclination toward deception), and prudence (an ability to balance competing needs, to act from reflection and consultation) as the basic virtues for family therapists. Pellegrino and Thomasma (1988) describe the virtues required of the physician.

A third possible source of ethical theory derives from the conjunction of social justice and family therapy. A lack of clarity between the kinds of thinking proper to the "mechanical" and the "systemic" ways of thinking (see Chapter 12, this volume) had prompted family therapists to use the mechanical way of thinking in search of causes and cures in the family domain, as if people's therapeutic problems were entities in themselves (like viruses, bacteria, and antibiotics). However, this endeavor tended to separate therapeutic problems from the social and cultural contexts out of which they developed. It is by moving into a systemic way of thinking in which one is able to "construct" the story of a person, family, or culture that we move beyond the restrictions of the mechanical way of thinking into the realm of personal and collective meaning. From this new perspective, "good therapy engages authentically with people's woven pattern of meaning, and then in appropriate ways weaves new threads of resolution and hope that blend with, but nevertheless change, the problem-centred design" (Waldegrave, 1990, p. 19). The importance of this is brought into strong relief by therapists working in multicultural settings, such as the Family Centre in New Zealand, which has learned to work with Maori and Samoan families as well as white Anglo-Saxons (Waldegrave, 1990). It also highlights the importance of spirituality as a part of each person's and culture's meaning.

> In our work with Maori people we have found it quite impossible to carry out successful therapy without acknowledging the wairua (spiritual) side. It is not uncommon for the realization of the significance of a dream to change the whole family system. This is because spirituality in many cultures is an integral and essential part of their meaning patterns. (Waldegrave, 1990, p. 19)

This model of family therapy offers, alongside the pathological meanings ascribed to sickness, a responsible and self-determining perspective to events, which emphasizes that central to practically all therapeutic problems is meaning (i.e., the personal). And meaning, which is a created pattern, determines the manner in which a problem is responded to. The therapeutic relationship has the potential to change the person's or family's meaning web, and therefore the way the person or family views the problem. Thus simply providing information about an illness without helping the sufferer(s) to gain some sense of meaning (and possible transcendence) that helps the patient cope may be an incomplete intervention, because the patient or family lacks a sense of purposeful or transcendent meaning.

Meaning or coherence is a powerful coping mechanism in itself (Antonovsky, 1979, 1987). Social justice family therapy deals with the reality context of the client or family.

> The teaching of therapy in practically all academic institutions has been mono-cultural. Concepts deeply embedded in modern North American and Western European societies have been presented as the international and intercultural ways of therapy. Further, the social context of those most in need of health and welfare resources, such as housing, employment and

adequate income, seldom affects the therapeutic task. It is neatly confined to some other worker or institution, leaving the therapist free to get on with the "real" therapeutic task. It is the culture of the particular person, however, which probably determines more than any other factor, the underlying structure of their meaning system. Inevitably, people's ability to access resources like food and housing significantly influences their construction of reality. (Waldegrave, 1990, p. 15)

In this context, the Family Centre in New Zealand intervened by setting aside resources to provide employment for the cultures that were discriminated against by the larger society, affirmed the therapeutic processes that these cultures already had, exchanged knowledge, and tailored family therapy approaches to the particular communities involved. Thus, in this case, family therapy expresses in a model a sense of responsibility (ethical involvement) about larger systems (political, cultural, economic, spiritual) in which persons find their meaning.

By reflecting on the ethical implications involved in applying some systems and family theories to clinical practice, we recognize that primary care must apply theoretical models that complement its theoretical foundations. The "personal way of thinking" grounds primary care in an ethical system that is complemented by the concept of virtuous persons and social justice. The usefulness of systemic thinking is obvious, as is the need for the personal way of thinking.

Implications

The rapid changes in the epistemology (how we know what we know; Anderson & Goolishian, 1990; Atkinson & Heath, 1990; Auerswald, 1985, 1987; Falzer, 1986; Golann, 1988; Held & Pols, 1985; Keeney, 1979; Willi, 1987) of family therapy as it broke away from the scientific framework and was affected by changes in theoretical models have had a profound, albeit confusing (Auerswald, 1987) effect on its clinicians. As it broke away and established its own unique identity, its relationship to biomedicine became blurred. If one assumed that the underlying ontology (the underlying essence of things) of one or the other was the "correct" one, then the relationship would become strained. However, practitioners and academics who continued to work in both "camps" throughout these transitions have borne witness to an opportunity for the enrichment of both disciplines (through dialogue).

On the one hand, family therapy has recognized the therapeutic value of moving beyond the problems of people to the meanings that they attach to those problems. These meanings also potentially unite those who share them. The use of this therapeutically can help physicians move beyond their therapeutic impasses. On the other hand, biomedicine is required to remain stable in its epistemological and ethical foundations, because it is the gatekeeper for society with respect to social responsibility and accountability. The commonsense (grounded in accountability and experience) approach to clinical problems that medicine must adopt can serve as an anchor for family therapy and related clinical fields, such as social work, especially when family workers are involved in issues related to physical health. In these areas one must be able to use and relate to the mechanical way of thinking (see Sawa, Chapter 12, this volume). The McMaster model of family functioning was designed to be applied by physicians, and it provides a language that can be used by both family therapists and medical clinicians (Epstein et al., 1978).

Also, family therapy can help medical practitioners to recognize the power they exercise in labeling and diagnosing illness (particularly emotional/psychiatric and family problems). This refers also to the potential harm that can be done by attributing or reinforcing negative or judgmental (and stigmatizing) meaning to therapeutic problems. This may lead to less "diagnosing" or "medicalizing" (by normalizing). This is most important in situations where diagnosis is not relevant to the intervention. Rather, in many instances, helping patients to find meaning in their illnesses and existential situations may be far more therapeutic.

Also, following the example of social justice models of family therapy, primary care medicine may choose to recognize that unjust or destructive "larger systems," including the organizations within which health care is taught and delivered, must be altered to provide collaborative, empowering, and hopeful environments in which men and women may be encouraged to contribute their talents and develop themselves, as well as produce specific products or services. I will now discuss this point at some length.

"TRANSFORMED" ORGANIZATIONAL MODELS

The Learning Organization

The impact of the shift in thinking in society brought about by the application of systems theory to social systems, along with existential (Kierkegaard, 1962) and phenomenological (Searle, 1987) thinking, has been felt in organization theory. It is beyond the scope of this book to do more than point out some potential implications of these developments for primary health care.

The traditional organization is hierarchical. Motivation is based on behaviorist theory—reward and punishment. Leadership is autocratic and noncollaborative. The goals of the organization are some product and some profit, usually to the benefit of the few, usually not the members of the organization themselves. While this model has had its successes, it also has its price. Power can be used to manipulate, and coercion can be violent, insofar as authority uses force to impose its views on those in lesser authority. There is no commonly shared vision that motivates members of the organization.

Influenced by systems theory, theology, and existential and phenomenological philosophy, the "new" models motivate through a shared vision that members of the organization strive to realize. Accomplishing the vision becomes the mission of the organization, and all involved are engaged in collaboration. Some have termed this model a "learning organization" (Senge, 1990). In this model, systems thinking is incorporated in terms of the shared "meaning" of the enterprise as well as the application of systems theory to provide an understanding of the organization and to provide techniques for systemic change. Systems thinking is further utilized to build a shared vision, where goals, values, and missions bind people together around a common identity. A third ingredient is the promotion of the ideal of personal mastery, which involves a lifelong commitment to learning and a continual clarifying and deepening of a personal vision, including our highest aspirations. The roots of this discipline are seen in both Eastern and Western spiritual traditions. The final principle is team learning, which begins with dialogue in which team members suspend assumptions and enter into a genuine "thinking together." At the heart of this model of a learning organization is a

> shift of mind . . . from seeing ourselves as separate from the world to connected to the world, from seeing problems as caused by someone or something "out there" to seeing how our own actions create the problems we experience. A learning organization is a place where people are continually discovering how they create their own reality. (Senge, 1990, pp. 12-13)

A learning organization involves not only adaptive learning but generative learning (see Smith, Chapter 10, this volume), which enhances our capacity to create.

Appreciative Management and Leadership

> Where there is no vision the people get out of hand or perish. (Proverbs 29:18)

Academic departments of family medicine can be driven by negative control, or they may choose to adopt affirmative/positive control (Atkinson, 1990; Cooperrider, 1990) and collaboration. Mood, cognition, and action tend to create feedback loops of amplifying intensity. High negative affect may be associated with enhanced experience of life stress, deficient cognition, learned helplessness, and the breakdown of social bonds. Positive affect, on the other hand, is associated with creative problem solving, more effective decision making and judgment, and increased learning activity (Cooperrider, 1990).

This model takes advantage of the therapeutic value of positive affect and positive imagery. Positive imagery appears to trigger in the perceiver an increased capacity to perceive the success of others, to access from memory positive rather than negative aspects of others, and to perceive the positive rather than the negative possibilities of ambiguous situations (Cooperrider, 1990). It also is based on the assumption that systems project ahead of themselves horizons of expectations that bring the future into the present in a causal manner. Cognition is seen as an internal dialogue that the mind carries on with itself. Positive imagery and dialogue are seen to arise when the environment encourages a belief in an open and influenceable future, values creative imagination mixed with philosophical questioning and freedom of speech, and encourages creative thinking. A hypothesis about human systems that this model utilizes is "that human systems have an observable tendency to macro-deterministically evolve in the direction of those positive images that are the brightest and boldest, most illuminating and promising" (Cooperrider, 1990, p. 113). Positive images of the future are proposed

> to generate in organizations an affirmative ecology that strengthens people's readiness and capacity to recall the positive aspects of the past, to selectively see the positive in the present, and envision new potentials in the future . . . [and to] . . . catylize an affirmative emotional climate, for example of heightened optimism, hope, care, joy, altruism, and passion . . . [and to] . . . provoke confident and energized action. (Cooperrider, 1990, p. 117)

In this postbureaucratic environment, the central executive task is to nourish the appreciative soil from which affirmative actions grow.

This model will be difficult to implement, however, since among the contraindications to a collaborative process are included when "one stakeholder has the power to take unilateral action . . . [and when] . . . one or more groups of stakeholders cannot establish representation" (Gray, 1989, p. 255). This style of leadership thus requires that those in authority actually relinquish their power to the collaborating parties, of which they are only one stakeholder.

Affirmative organizations are propelled by positive images and the presence of hope (Marcel, 1962), but also by self-knowledge and self-transformation. Self-knowledge is important, because the more we know about ourselves, the more of reality we can perceive.

Physician, Heal Thyself!

It is clear that any transformations in the larger system will have to begin with ourselves, the only system over which we have control. In an excellent 1972 prospective study carried out in New England, Vaillant, Sobowale, and McArthur found that physicians, particularly those who are most directly involved in primary care, had poorer or less supportive childhoods than those in the control group of nonphysicians. Not surprisingly, as time progressed, those physicians who experienced emotional impairment—as defined by alcohol and drug dependency, unhappy marriages, and psychiatric treatment—had significantly poorer or more insecure childhoods than their healthy physician colleagues. It is when the physician from a barren childhood becomes overly burdened by the demands of his or her dependent patients that trouble arises (Vaillant, Sobowale, & McArthur, 1972).

The insecure physician has an excessive need to be needed, valued, appreciated, loved, and accepted, and is at risk for overwork, fatigue, and exhaustion. From these may follow alcoholism (Brewster, 1986) and drug dependency (Pond, 1991), probably in a frequency similar to their numbers in the entire population (Brewster, 1986); marital conflicts (Gabbard, Menninger, & Coyne, 1987), which respond well to therapy (Glick & Borus, 1984); depression (M. J. Martin, 1981); and even suicide (Vincent, 1983). Thus primary care physicians in particular must be aware of the effects of stress on themselves and their practices (A. R. Martin, 1986; McCue, 1982) and must develop healthy approaches to combat it (Clements & Paine, 1981; Quill & Williamson, 1990) as well as strategies to care for their own families (Robertson, 1986).

Change from the old model to the new one also involves a shift to a collaborative model on the part of the physician in dealing with patients and students. Again, a surrender of power is required. For all of us, it is important to take time to get to know ourselves. There is now an excellent literature designed to give us insight into our personality makeup (Beesing, Nogosek, & O'Leary, 1984; James & Jongeward, 1973; Kiersey & Bates, 1984; Riso, 1987) and to help us gain insight into the impact (personal and clinical) of growing up in the particular families we grew up in (Coopersmith, 1980; Crouch, 1987; Crouch & Davis, 1987; Sawa, 1985; Thrower, Bruce, & Walton, 1982).

A major error, in my opinion, in any attempt to build a new model, would be to fail to recognize that the main purpose of human labor is not monetary profit, which would position persons in organizational systems as tools for material gain, but rewards that reflect values that transcend the material, including human dignity and respect. For such an enterprise to succeed, leadership must itself be virtuous, healthy, and nurturing.

While the corporate world is experimenting in these directions to improve productivity, our motivation is to foster the development of compassionate and effective physicians. We are well advised also to take the steps necessary to see to it that both we and our students make our growth and fulfillment as persons, and the nurturance we give and receive in our own families, our highest priority. It seems to me that we have no choice but to move in this direction. Technology has produced the knowledge and skills that allow us to intervene effectively in many conditions that formerly were nontreatable. However, we now have a society in which people live longer, and we experience health care systems that cannot afford the treatments we have devised. While our patients often demand prompt service in the "McDonald's" world of consumerism we have created, the need for refuge, solace, and understanding, and for caring, has never been so great. As family/primary care physicians we have the opportunity to lead the way in the evolution of a truly healing profession.

The symposium that led to the development of this book, and its sequelae, has resulted in a truly exciting time for everyone involved. I hope that we have been able to convey some of that excitement to you, the reader, through the pages of this book. Together, with some of the insights found in these pages, we may look toward the twenty-first century with hopes for a more humane world.

References

Abramson, H., & Peshkin, H. (1979). Psychological group therapy with parents of children with intractable asthma: The Peters family. *Journal of Asthma Research, 16,* 103-117.

Ader, R. (Ed.). (1981). *Psychoneuroimmunology.* New York: Academic Press.

Agar, M. H. (1980). *The professional stranger: An informal introduction to ethnography.* New York: Academic Press.

Agar, M. H. (1986). *Speaking of ethnography.* Beverly Hills, CA: Sage.

Aiken, L., Lewis, C., Craig, J., et al. (1979). The contribution of specialists to the delivery of primary care. *New England Journal of Medicine, 300,* 1363-1370.

Ainsworth, M. D. S. (1982). Attachment: Retrospect and prospect. In C. M. Parkes & J. Stevenson-Hinde (Eds.), *The place of attachment in human behavior.* New York: Basic Books.

Ainsworth, M. D. S., Blehar, M. C., Waters, E., & Wall, S. (1978). *Patterns of attachment: The psychological study of the strange situation.* Hillsdale, NJ: Lawrence Erlbaum.

Aldous, J. (1978). *Family careers: Developmental change in families.* New York: John Wiley.

Alpert, J. J. (1964). Broken appointments. *Paediatrics, 34,* 127-132.

Alpert, J. J., & Charney, E. (1973). *The education of physicians for primary care* (DHEW Publication No. HRA 74-3113). Washington, DC: Government Printing Office.

American Academy of Family Physicians. (1975, April 18). [Letter]. Kansas City, Missouri.

American Association of Marriage and Family Therapy. (1986). *Membership requirements*. Washington, DC: Author.

American Medical Association, Ad Hoc Committee on Education for Family Practice. (1966). *Meeting the challenge of family practice*. Chicago: American Medical Association.

American Psychiatric Association. (1980). *Diagnostic and statistical manual of mental disorders* (3rd ed.). Washington, DC: Author.

Anderson, C. M. (1983). A psychoeducational program for families of patients with schizophrenia. In W. R. McFarlane (Ed.), *Family therapy in schizophrenia* (pp. 99-116). New York: Guilford.

Anderson, C. M., Hogarty, G., Bayer, T., et al. (1984). Expressed emotion and social networks of parents of schizophrenic patients. *British Journal of Psychiatry, 144,* 247-255.

Anderson, C. M., Reiss, D. J., & Hogarty, G. E. (1986). *Schizophrenia and the family: A practitioner's guide to psychoeducation and management*. New York: Guilford.

Anderson, H., & Goolishian, H. A. (1990). Beyond cybernetics: Comments on Atkinson and Heath's "Further thoughts on second-order family therapy." *Family Process, 29*(2).

Antonovsky, A. (1979). *Health, stress, and coping: New perspectives on mental and physical well-being*. San Francisco: Jossey-Bass.

Antonovsky, A. (1987). *Unraveling the mystery of health: How people manage stress and stay well*. San Francisco: Jossey-Bass.

Arbogast, R. C., Scralton, J. M., & Krick, J. P. (1978). The family as patient: Preliminary experience with a recorded assessment scheme. *Journal of Family Practice, 7,* 1151-1157.

Argyris, C., Putnam, R., & Smith, D. M. (1985). *Action science*. San Francisco: Jossey-Bass.

Argyris, C., & Schon, D. (1974). *Theory in practice*. San Francisco: Jossey-Bass.

Armondino, N., & Walker, J. (1977). *The primary care physician: Issues in distribution* (Research Series, No. 7). Hartford: Connecticut Health Services.

Association of American Medical Colleges, Committee on Medical Schools. (1968). Planning for comprehensive and continuing care of patients through education. *Journal of Medical Education, 43,* 751-759.

Atkinson, B. J., & Heath, A. W. (1990). The limits of explanation and evaluation. *Family Process, 29,* 164-167.

Atkinson, P. E. (1990). *Creating culture change: The key to successful quality management*. London: IFS Ltd.

Auerswald, E. H. (1985). Thinking about thinking in family therapy. *Family Process, 24,* 1-12.

Auerswald, E. H. (1987). Epistemological confusion in family therapy and research. *Family Process, 26,* 317-330.

Babbott, D., & Halter, W. D. (1983). Clinical problem-solving skills of internists trained in the problem-oriented system. *Journal Medicine of Education, 58,* 947-953.

Balint, M. (1964). *The doctor, his patient and the illness*. London: Pitman.

Baranowski, T., Nader, P. R., Dunn, K., & Vanderpool, N. A. (1982, Summer). Family self-help: Promoting changes in health behavior. *Journal of Communications,* pp. 161-170.

Barbarin, O. A., & Tirado, M. (1984). Family involvement and successful treatment of obesity: A review. *Family Systems Medicine, 2,* 37-45.

Barden, G., & McShane, P. (1969). *Towards self-meaning*. Dublin: Gill & MacMillan.

Barrows, H. S., Norman, G. R., Neufeld, V. R., & Feightner, J. W. (1982). The clinical reasoning of randomly selected physicians in general medical practice. *Clinical Investigative Medicine, 5,* 49-54.

Barsky, A. (1988). The paradox of health. *New England Journal of Medicine, 318,* 414-418.

Bartholomew, B. D., & Schneiderman, L. J. (1982). Attitudes of patients toward family care in a family practice group. *Journal of Family Practice, 15,* 477-481.

Bartrop, R. W., Luckhurst, E., Lazarus, L., Kiloh, L. G., & Penny, R. (1977). Depressed lymphocyte function after bereavement. *Lancet, 1,* 834-836.

Bauman, M. H., & Grace, N. T. (1974). Family process and family practice. *Journal of Family Practice, 1,* 24-26.

Beautrais, A. L., Fergusson, D. M., & Shannon, F. T. (1982). Life events and childhood morbidity: A prospective study. *Pediatrics, 70,* 935-940.

Beck, F. (1965). The family's part in caring for the patient. *International Nursing Review, 12,* 31-50.

Beesing, M., Nogosek, R., & O'Leary, P. (1984). *The enneagram: A journey of self-discovery*. Denville, NJ: Dimension.

Bell, L. G., & Bell, D. C. (1982). Family climate and the role of the female adolescent: Determinants of adolescent functioning. *Family Relations, 31,* 519-527.

Belmont, J. M. (1989). Cognitive strategies and strategic learning. *American Psychologist, 44,* 142-148.

Benbassat, J., & Bachar-Bassan, E. (1984). A comparison of initial diagnostic hypotheses of medical students and internists. *Journal of Medical Education, 59,* 951-956.

Berger, P. L., & Luckmann, T. L. (1966). *The social construction of reality*. Garden City, NY: Doubleday.

Berner, E. S., Hamilton, L. A., & Best, W. R. (1974). A new approach to evaluating problem-solving in medical students. *Journal of Medical Education, 49,* 666-672.

Bidney, D. (1947). Human nature and the cultural process. *American Anthropologist, 49,* 375-399.

Bishop, D., Byles, J., & Horn, D. (1984). Family therapy training methods. *Journal of Family Therapy, 6,* 323-334.

Bishop, D. S., & Epstein, N. B. (n.d.). *Family therapy and the family physician: Where to family medicine, where to family training*. Unpublished manuscript.

Bishop, D. S., & Epstein, N. B. (1985). Response to Hochheiser and Chapados. *Family Systems Medicine, 3,* 481-485.

Bishop, D. S., Epstein, N. B., Gilbert, R., van der Spuy, H. I. J., Levin, S., & McClemont, M. A. (1984). Training family physicians to treat families: Unexpected compliance problems. *Family Systems Medicine, 2,* 380-386.

Blake, R. L. (1988). The effects of stress and social support on health: A research challenge for family medicine. *Family Medicine, 20,* 19-24.

Blake, R. L. (1989). Integrating quantitative and qualitative methods in family research. *Family Systems Medicine, 7,* 411-427.

Bloch, D. A. (1989). Illness and family systems: A co-evolutionary model. In C. N. Ramsey (Ed.), *Family systems in medicine* (pp. 321-333). New York: Guilford.

Block, J. (1961). *The Q-sort method in personality assessment and psychiatric research*. Springfield, IL: Charles C Thomas.

Blumer, D. (1982). Chronic pain as a variant of depressive disease: The pain-prone disorder. *Journal of Nervous and Mental Disease, 170,* 381-406.

Borysenko, J. (1984). Psychoneuroimmunology. In J. D. Matarazzo, S. M. Weiss, J. A. Herd, & N. E. Miller (Eds.), *Behavioral health: A handbook of health enhancement and disease prevention* (pp. 248-256). New York: John Wiley.

Boss, P. G. (1988). *Family stress management.* Newbury Park, CA: Sage.

Boss, P. G., Doherty, W. J., LaRossa, R., Schumm, W. R., & Steinmetz, S. K. (Eds.) (1992). *Sourcebook of family theories and methods: A contextual approach.* New York: Plenum Press.

Bowen, M. (1978). *Family therapy in clinical practice.* New York: Jason Aronson.

Bracher, K. D. (1973). *Totalitarianism.* In P. P. Wiener (Ed.), *Dictionary of the history of ideas* (pp. 406-411). New York: Scribner's.

Brackett, T. (1984). The emotional care of a person with a spinal cord injury. *Journal of the American Medical Association, 252,* 793-795.

Bradshaw, M. (Ed.). (1988). *Nursing of the family in health and illness: A developmental approach.* Norwalk, CT: Appleton & Lange.

Brennan, M. (1981). A study of patients with psychosocial problems in a family practice. *Journal of Family Practice, 13,* 837-843.

Brewster, J. M. (1986). Prevalence of alcohol and other drug problems among physicians. *Journal of the American Medical Association, 255,* 1913-1920.

Broadhead, W. E., Kaplan, B. H., James, S. A., Wagner, E. H., Schoenback, V. J., Grimson, R., Heyden, S., Tibblin, G., & Gehlbach, S. H. (1983). The epidemiologic evidence for a relationship between social support and health. *American Journal of Epidemiology, 177,* 521-537.

Broderick, C., & Smith, J. (1979). The general systems approach to the family. In W. R. Burr, R. Hill, F. I. Nye, & I. L. Reiss (Eds.), *Contemporary theories about the family* (Vol. 2). New York: Free Press.

Brodsky, C. (1983). "Allergic to everything": A medical subculture. *Psychosomatics, 24,* 731-742.

Brody, H. (1987). *Stories of sickness.* New Haven, CT: Yale University of Press.

Brown, G. W., Birley, J., & Wing, J. K. (1972). Influence of family life on the course of schizophrenic disorders: A replication. *British Journal of Psychiatry, 121,* 241-258.

Brown, G. W., Monck, E. M., Carstairs, G. M., & Wing, J. K. (1962). The influence of family life on the course of schizophrenic illness. *British Journal of Preventive Social Medicine, 16,* 55-68.

Brown, J. B., Weston, W. W., & Stewart, M. A. (1989). Patient centred interviewing: Part II. Finding common ground. *Canadian Family Physician, 35,* 153-157.

Brown, P., & Levinson, S. (1978). Universals in language usage. In E. N. Goody (Ed.), *Questions and politeness.* Cambridge: Cambridge University Press.

Brownell, K. D., Heckerman, C. L., Westlake, R. J., Hayes, S. C., & Monti, P. M. (1978). The effects of couple training and partner cooperativeness in the behavioral treatment of obesity. *Behaviour Research and Therapy, 16,* 323-333.

Brownell, K. D., Kelman, J. H., & Stunkard, A. J. (1983). Treatment of obese children with and without their mothers: Changes in weight and blood pressure. *Pediatrics, 71,* 515-523.

Browner, C. H., Ortiz de Montellano, B. R., & Rubel, A. J. (1988). A methodology for cross-cultural ethnomedical research. *Current Anthropology, 29,* 681-689 (commentaries and reply, pp. 689-702).

Buber, M. (1958). *I and thou.* New York: Scribner Library.

Buchwald, D. (1987). Frequency of "chronic active Epstein-Barr virus infection" in a general medical practice. *Journal of the American Medical Association, 257,* 2303-2307.

Burbeck, T. W. (1979). An empirical investigation of the psychosomatogenic family model. *Journal of Psychosomatic Research, 23,* 327-337.

Calabrese, J. R., Kling, M. A., & Gold, P. W. (1987). Alterations in immunocompetence during stress, bereavement and depression: Focus on neuroendocrine regulation. *American Journal of Psychiatry, 144,* 1123-1134.

Califano, J. A. J. (1979). *Healthy people: The surgeon general's report on health promotion and disease prevention* (DHEW Publication No. 79-55071). Washington, DC: Government Printing Office.

Campbell, T. L. (1986). The family's impact on health: A critical review and annotated bibliography. *Family Systems Medicine, 4,* 135-328.

Canter, D. (Ed.). (1985). *Facet theory: Approaches to social research.* New York: Springer-Verlag.

Carmichael, L. P. (1976). The family in medicine: Process or entity? *Journal of Family Practice, 5,* 562-563.

Cauthen, D. B., Turnbull, J. M., Lawler, W. R., & Friedman, P. C. (1979). A teaching program in family dynamics. *Journal of Family Practice, 9,* 954-955.

Chrisman, N. J. (1977). The health seeking process: An approach to the natural history of illness. *Culture, Medicine and Psychiatry, 1,* 351-377.

Chrisman, N. J., & Maretzki, T. W. (Eds.). (1982). *Clinically applied anthropology: Anthropologists in health science settings.* Boston: D. Reidel.

Christie, R. J., & Hoffmaster, C. B. (1986). *Ethical issues in family medicine.* New York: Oxford University Press.

Christie-Seely, J. (1981). Teaching the family system concept in family medicine. *Journal of Family Practice, 13,* 391-401.

Christie-Seely, J. (1984a). Prevention or health promotion. In J. Christie-Seely (Ed.), *Working with the family in primary care: A systems approach to health and illness.* New York: Praeger.

Christie-Seely, J. (Ed.). (1984b). *Working with the family in primary care: A systems approach to health and illness.* New York: Praeger.

Christie-Seely, J., & Guttman, H. (1984). The relevance of the family to medical outcomes. In J. Christie-Seely (Ed.), *Working with the family in primary care: A systems approach to health and illness.* New York: Praeger.

Chung, R., Langelluddecke, P., et al. (1986). Threatening life events in the onset of schizophrenia, schizophreniform psychosis and hypomania. *British Journal of Psychiatry, 148,* 680-685.

Clark, C. H., Schwenk, T. L., & Plackis, C. X. (1983). Patients' perspectives of behavioral science care by family practice physicians. *Journal of Medical Education, 58,* 954-961.

Clark, N. M., Feldman, C. H., Evans, D., Millman, E. J., Wailewski, Y., & Valle, I. (1981). The effectiveness of education for family management of asthma in children: A preliminary report. *Health Education Quarterly, 8,* 166-174.

Cleghorn, J. M., & Levin, S. (1973). Training family therapists by setting learning objectives. *American Journal of Orthopsychiatry, 43,* 439-446.

Clements, W. M., & Paine, R. (1981). The family physician's family. *Journal of Family Practice, 13,* 105-112.

Clover, R. D., Abell, T., Becker, L. A., Crawford, S., & Ramsey, C. N., Jr. (1989). Family functioning and stress as predictors of influenza B infection. *Journal of Family Practice, 28,* 535-539.

Cohen, F. (1981). Stress and bodily illness. *Psychiatry Clinic of North America, 4,* 269-285.

Cohen, S., & Syme, S. L. (Eds.). (1985). *Social support and health.* Orlando, FL: Academic Press.

Connors, M., Johnson, C., & Stuckey, M. (1984). Treatment of bulimia with brief psychoeducational group therapy. *American Journal of Psychiatry, 141,* 1512-1516.

Constantine, L. C. (1986). *Family paradigms.* New York: Guilford.

Cooksey, F. (1954). The social adjustment of the physically handicapped [in comment]. *Proceedings of the Royal Society of Medicine, 47,* 735.

Cooperrider, D. L. (1990). Positive image, positive action: The affirmative basis of organizing. In S. Srivastva & D. L. Cooperrider (Eds.), *Appreciative management and leadership* (pp. 91-125). San Francisco: Jossey-Bass.

Coopersmith, E. (1980). The family floor plan: A tool for training, assessment and intervention in family therapy. *Journal of Marital and Family Therapy, 6,* 141-145.

Council on Scientific Affairs. (1983). Dietary and pharmacologic therapy for lipid risk factors. *Journal of the American Medical Association, 250,* 1873-1879.

Cowen, D. L., & Sbarboro, J. A. (1972). Family-centered health care—a viable reality: The Denver experience. *Medical Care, 10,* 164-172.

Coyne, J. C., & Anderson, B. J. (1988). "Psychosomatic family" reconsidered: Diabetes in context. *Journal of Marital and Family Therapy, 14,* 113-123.

Crouch, M. A. (1987). Working with one's own family issues: A path for professional development. In M. A. Crouch & L. A. Roberts (Eds.), *The family in medical practice: A family systems primer* (pp. 193-208). New York: Springer-Verlag.

Crouch, M. A., & Davis, T. (1987). Using the genogram (family tree) clinically. In M. A. Crouch & L. A. Roberts (Eds.), *The family in medical practice: A family systems primer* (pp. 174-192). New York: Springer-Verlag.

Crouch, M. A., & McCauley, J. (1985). Family awareness demonstrated by family practice residents: Physician behavior and patient opinions. *Journal of Family Practice, 20,* 281-284.

Crouch, M. A., & McCauley, J. (1986). Interviewing style and response to family information by family practice residents. *Family Medicine, 18,* 15-18.

Crouch, M. A., & Roberts, L. A. (Eds.). (1987). *The family in medical practice: A family systems primer.* New York: Springer-Verlag.

Crouch, M. A., & Theidke, C. C. (1986). Documentation of family health history in the outpatient medical record. *Journal of Family Practice, 22,* 169-171.

Cummings, S. R., Phillips, S. L., Wheat, M. E., Black, D., Godsby, E. Wlodarczy, K. D., et al. (1988). Recovery of function after hip fracture: The role of social supports. *Journal of the American Geriatric Society, 36,* 801-806.

Curry, N. B. (1974). The family as our patient. *Journal of Family Practice, 1,* 71.

Curry, N. B., & Grant, S. W. (1973). Role of the family physician. In H. F. Conn, R. E. Rakel, & T. W. Johnson (Eds.), *Family practice* (pp. 42-53). Philadelphia: W. B. Saunders.

Dakof, G. A., & Mendelsohn, G. A. (1989). Patterns of adaptation to Parkinson's disease. *Health Psychology, 8,* 355-372.

Davidson, R. H. (1986). Transference and countertransference phenomena: The problem of the observer in the behavioral sciences. *Journal of Psychoanalytic Anthropology, 9,* 269-283.

Dell, P. F. (1985). Understanding Bateson & Maturana: Toward a biological foundation for the social sciences. *Journal of Marital and Family Therapy, 11,* 1-20.

Dell, P. F. (1986). In defense of lineal causality. *Family Process, 25,* 513-521.

de Mause L. (1982). *Foundations of psychohistory.* New York: Creative Roots.

Detchon, T., & Storm, C. L. (1987). Grabbing the brass ring: A study of referrals to family therapists by family physicians. *Family Systems Medicine, 5,* 504-511.

Devereaux, M. (1988, Spring). 1986 census highlights: Marital status. *Canadian Social Trends,* pp. 24-27.

Devereux, G. (1967). *From anxiety to method in the behavioral sciences.* The Hague: Mouton.

Devereux, G. (1980). *Basic problems of ethno-psychiatry* (B. M. Gulati & G. Devereux, Trans.). Chicago: University of Chicago Press.

Diamond, M. D., Weiss, A. J., & Grynbaum, B. (1968). The unmotivated patient. *Archives of Physical Medicine, 49,* 281-284.

Doane, J. A., Falloon, I. R. H., Goldstein, M. J., & Mintz, J. (1985). Parental affective style and the treatment of schizophrenia: Predicting course of illness and social functioning. *Archives of General Psychiatry, 42,* 34-42.

Doherty, W. J. (1991, Winter). Virtue ethics: The person of the therapist. *American Family Therapy Association Newsletter,* pp. 19-20.

Doherty, W. J., & Baird, M. A. (1983). *Family therapy and family medicine: Toward the primary care of families.* New York: Guilford.

Doherty, W. J., & Baird, M. A. (1986). Developmental levels in family-centered medical care. *Family Medicine, 18,* 153-156.

Doherty, W. J., & Baird, M. A. (Eds.). (1987a). *Family-centered medical care: A clinical casebook.* New York: Guilford.

Doherty, W. J., & Baird, M. A. (1987b). Family medicine and the biopsychosocial model: The road toward integration. In W. J. Doherty, C. E. Christianson, & M. Sussman (Eds.), *Family medicine: The maturing of a discipline.* New York: Hayworth.

Doherty, W. J., Baird, M. A., & Becker, L. A. (1987). Family medicine and the bio-psychosocial model: The road toward integration. *Marriage and Family Review, 10*(3-4), 51-69.

Doherty, W. J., & Campbell, T. L. (1988). *Families and health.* Newbury Park, CA: Sage.

Doherty, W. J., Schrott, H. G., Metcalf, L., & Iasiello-Vailas, L. (1983). Effect of spouse support and health beliefs on medication adherence. *Journal of Family Practice, 17,* 837-844.

Doherty, W. J., & Whitehead, D. (1986). The social dynamics of cigarette smoking: A family FIRO analysis. *Family Process, 25,* 453-459.

Donohue, J. F., & Shumway, J. M. (1983). A senior medical student seminar designed to promote problem-solving. *Journal of Medical Education, 58,* 425-427.

Draper, T. W., & Marcos, A. C. (Eds.). (1990). *Family variables: Conceptualization, measurement, and use.* Newbury Park, CA: Sage.

Dulcan, M. (1985). *Psychoeducational therapy with families of severely impaired children.* Paper prepared under NIMH Clinical Training Human Resource Development Grant.

Earp, J. L., Ory, M. G., & Strogatz, D. S. (1982). The effects of family involvement and practitioner home visit on the control of hypertension. *American Journal of Public Health, 72,* 1146-1153.

Eckert, J. K., & Galazka, S. S. (1986). An anthropological approach to community diagnosis in family practice. *Family Medicine, 18,* 274-277.

Eddy, D. M., & Clanton, C. H. (1982). The art of diagnosis: Solving the clinicopatholog-ical exercise. *New England Journal of Medicine, 306,* 1263-1267.

Eisenberg, L., & Kleinman, A. (Eds.). (1981). *The relevance of social science for medicine.* Boston: D. Reidel.

Elliot, D. L., & Hickam, D. H. (1987). Evaluation of physical examination skills: Reliability of faculty observers and patient instructors. *Journal of the American Medical Association, 258,* 3405-3408.

Elliott, S., & Herndon, A. (1981). Teaching family systems theory to family practice residents. *Journal of Medical Education, 56,* 139-141.

Elstein, A. S., Shulman, L. S., & Sprafka, S. A. (1978). *Medical problem solving: An analysis of clinical reasoning.* Cambridge, MA: Harvard University Press.

Engel, G. L. (1977). The need for a new medical model: A challenge for biomedicine. *Science, 8,* 129-136.

Epstein, N. B., & Bishop, D.S. (1981). Problem centred systems therapy of the family. *Journal of Marital and Family Therapy, 7,* 23-31.

Epstein, N. B., Bishop, D. S., & Baldwin, L. (1982). McMaster model of family functioning: A view of the normal family. In F. Walsh (Ed.), *Normal family processes.* New York: Guilford.

Epstein, N. B., Bishop, D. S., & Levin, S. (1978). The McMaster model of family functioning. *Journal of Marital and Family Therapy, 4,* 19-33.

Erickson, E. H. (1963). Eight ages of man. In E. H. Erickson, *Childhood and society* (pp. 247-274). New York: W. W. Norton.

Estes, H. E. (1977). *Primary care in medicine: Report of a task force.* Washington, DC: National Academy of Sciences.

Eustaugh, S., & Hatcher, M. (1982). Improving compliance among hypertensives: A triage criterion with cost benefit implications. *Medical Care, 20,* 1001-1017.

Falloon, I., & Liberman, R. (1983). Behavioral family interventions in the management of chronic schizophrenia. In W. R. McFarlane (Ed.), *Family therapy in schizophrenia* (pp. 141-152). New York: Guilford.

Falloon, I., Boyd, J., McGill, C., et al. (1985). Family management in the prevention of morbidity of schizophrenia. *Archives of General Psychiatry, 42,* 887-896.

Falzer, P. R. (1986). The cybernetic metaphor: A critical examination of ecosystemic epistemology as a foundation for family therapy. *Family Process, 25*(3).

Feletti, G. I., & Gillies, A. H. B. (1982). Developing oral and written formats for evaluating clinical problem-solving by medical undergraduates. *Journal of Medical Education, 57,* 874-876.

Fennell, M. L., & Warnecke, R. B. (1988). *The diffusion of medical innovations: An applied network analysis.* New York: Plenum.

Figley, C. R. (Ed.). (1989). *Treating stress in families.* New York: Brunner/Mazel.

Filsinger, E. E. (1990). Empirical typology, cluster analysis, and family-level measurement. In T. W. Draper & A. C. Marcos (Eds.), *Family variables: Conceptualization, measurement, and use.* Newbury Park, CA: Sage.

Filsinger, E. E., & Karoly, P. (1985). Taxonometric methods in health psychology. In P. Karoly (Ed.), *Measurement strategies in health psychology.* New York: John Wiley.

Fischer, D. (1977). *Growing old in America.* New York: Oxford University Press.

Fischman-Havstad, L., & Marston, A. R. (1984). Weight loss maintenance as an aspect of family emotion and process. *British Journal of Clinical Psychology, 23,* 265-271.

Fisher, L., Kokes, R. F., Ransom, D. C., Phillips, S. L., & Rudd, P. (1985). Alternative strategies for creating "relational" family data. *Family Process, 24,* 213-224.

Fisher, L., Ransom, D. C., Terry, H. E., & Burge, S. (in press). The California Family Health Project: IV. Family structure/organization and adult health. *Family Process.*

Fisher, L., Ransom, D. C., Terry, H. E., Lipkin, M., & Weiss, R. (1992). The California Family Health Project: I. Introduction and a description of adult health. *Family Process, 31*(2).

Fisher, L., Terry, H. E., & Ransom, D. C. (1990). Advancing a family perspective in health research: Models and methods. *Family Process, 29,* 177-189.

Flora, G. (1977). Problem solving in diagnostics and therapeutics of neurology: The treatment of seizure disorders. *South Dakota Journal of Medicine, 30,* 15-16.

Frank, K., Heller, S., & Kornfeld, D. (1979). Psychological intervention in coronary heart disease: A review. *General Hospital Psychiatry, 1,* 18-23.

Freeman, H., & Simmons, O. (1961). Feeling of stigma among relatives of former mental patients. *Social Problems, 8,* 312-321.

Freud, S. (1957). The future prospects of psycho-analytic therapy. In *The standard edition of the complete psychological works of Sigmund Freud* (J. Strachey, Trans.) (Vol. 11, pp. 139-151). London: Hogarth. (Original work published 1910)

Frowick, B., Shank, J. C., Doherty, W. J., & Powell, T. A. (1986). What do patients really want? Redefining a behavioral science curriculum for family physicians. *Journal of Family Practice, 23,* 141-146.

Fry, J. (1973). Information for patient care in office-based practice. *Medical Care, 11*(2, Suppl.), 35-40.

Fujikawa, L. S., Bass, R. A., & Schneiderman, L. J. (1979). Family care in a family practice group. *Journal of Family Practice, 8,* 1189-1194.

Gabbard, G. O., Menninger, R. W., & Coyne, L. (1987). Sources of conflict in the medical marriage. *American Journal of Psychiatry, 144,* 567-572.

Gaines, A. D. (1979). Definitions and diagnoses: Cultural implications of psychiatric help-seeking and psychiatrists' definitions of the situation in psychiatric emergencies. *Culture, Medicine and Psychiatry, 3,* 381-418.

Ganster, D. C., & Victor, B. (1988). The impact of social support on mental and physical health. *British Journal of Medical Psychology, 61,* 17-36.

Garfinkel, A. (1967). *Studies in ethnomethodology.* Englewood Cliffs, NJ: Prentice-Hall.

Garrison, V. (1978). Support systems of schizophrenic and non-schizophrenic Puerto Rican women in New York City. *Schizophrenia Bulletin, 4,* 561-596.

Geertz, C. (1973). *The interpretation of cultures: Selected essays.* New York: Basic Books.

Gergen, K. (1985). The social constructionist movement in modern psychology. *American Psychologist, 40,* 266-275.

Geyman, J. P. (1977). The family as the object of care in family practice. *Journal of Family Practice, 5,* 571-575.

Geyman, J. P. (1978). Family practice in evolution: Progress, problems, and projectives. *New England Journal of Medicine, 298,* 593-601.

Glaser, B. G., & Strauss, A. L. (1967). *The discovery of grounded theory: Strategies for qualitative research.* Chicago: Aldine.

Glaser, R. (1990). The reemergence of learning theory within instructional research. *American Psychologist, 45,* 29-39.

Glenn, M. L. (1984). *On diagnosis: A systemic approach.* New York: Brunner/Mazel.

Glick, I. D., & Borus, J. F. (1984). Marital and family therapy for troubled physicians and their families. *Journal of the American Medical Association, 251,* 1855-1858.

Glick, P. (1984). American household structure in transition. *Family Planning Perspectives, 16,* 205-211.

Golann, S. (1988). On second order family therapy. *Family Process, 27*(1).

Goldstein, M., Rodnick, E., Evans, J., et al. (1980). Drug and family therapy in the aftercare of acute schizophrenics. *Archives of General Psychiatry, 35,* 1169-1177.

Gonzales, S., Steinglass, P., & Reiss, D. (1987). *Family-centered interventions for people with chronic disabilities.* Washington, DC: George Washington University, Rehabilitation Research Center.

Gonzales, S., Steinglass, P., & Reiss, D. (1989). Putting illness in its place: Discussion groups for families with chronic medical illness. *Family Procedures, 28,* 69-88.

Good, B. J. (1977). The heart of what's the matter: Semantics and illness in Iran. *Culture, Medicine and Psychiatry, 1,* 108-138.

Good, B. J., & Good, M. D. (1981). The meaning of symptoms: A cultural hermeneutic model for clinical practice. In L. Eisenberg & A. Kleinman (Eds.), *The relevance of social science for medicine.* Boston: D. Reidel.

Good, M. J. D., Good, B. J., & Cleary, P. H. (1987). Do patient attitudes influence physician recognition of psychosocial problems in primary care? *Journal of Family Practice, 25,* 53-59.

Goolishian, H. A., & Anderson, H. (1991, Winter). An essay on changing theory and changing ethics: Some historical and post structural views. *American Family Therapy Association Newsletter,* pp. 6-10.

Gordon, M. (1978). Research traditions available to family medicine. *Journal of Family Practice, 7,* 59-68.

Gorlick, C., & Promfret, A. (1988). *The impact of social support on low income female parents.* Paper presented at a joint session of the Canadian Sociology and Anthropology Association and Canadian School of Social Work Learned Conference, University of Windsor.

Gottlieb, B. H. (1976). Lay influences on the utilization and provision of health services: A review. *Canadian Psychology Review, 17,* 126-136.

Gottlieb, B. H. (Ed.). (1988). *Marshaling social support: Formats, processes, and effects.* Newbury Park, CA: Sage.

Grace, N. T. (1977). Recognition of importance of family distinguishes family practitioner. *Family Practice News, 7,* 54.

Grace, N. T., Neal, E. M., Wellock, C. E., et al. (1977). The family-oriented medical record. *Journal of Family Practice, 4,* 91-98.

Grad, J., & Sainsbury, P. (1963). Mental illness and the family. *Lancet, 1,* 533-547.

Gray, B. (1989). *Collaborating: Finding common ground for multiparty problems.* San Francisco: Jossey-Bass.

Green, L. W., Eriksen, M., & Schor, E. (1990). Preventive practices by physicians: Behavioral determinants and potential intervention. In *Implementing preventive services* (pp. 108-110). New York: Oxford University Press.

Greeno, J. G. (1989). A perspective on thinking. *American Psychologist, 44,* 134-141.

Griffith, J. L., & Griffith, M. E. (1987). Structural family therapy in chronic illness. *Psychosomatics, 28,* 202-205.

Guba, E. G. (1981). Criteria for assessing the trustworthiness of naturalistic inquiries. *Education Communication and Technology Journal, 29,* 75-91.

Gustafsson, P. A., Kjellman, N. I., & Cederblad, M. (1986). Family therapy in the treatment of severe childhood asthma. *Journal of Psychosomatic Research, 30,* 369-374.

Gustafsson, P. A., Kjellman, N. I., Ludvigsson, J., & Cederblad, M. (1987). Asthma and family interaction. *Archives of Diseases of Childhood, 62,* 258-263.

Guttman, H., & Sigal, J. (1978). Teaching family psychodynamics in a family practice center: One experience. *International Journal of Psychiatric Medicine, 8,* 383.

Guttman, H., & Steinert, Y. (1987). Establishing parameters for teaching family systems in a family-practice centre. *Family Systems Medicine, 5,* 322-332.

Hammer, M. (1981). Social supports, social networks, and schizophrenia. *Schizophrenia Bulletin, 7,* 45-57.

Hampton, J. R., Harrison, M. J. G., Mitchell, J. R. A., Prichard, J. S., & Seymour, C. (1975). Relative contributions of history-taking, physical examination, and laboratory investigation to diagnosis and management of medical outpatients. *British Medical Journal, 2,* 486-489.

Hansen, J., Bobula, J., Meyer, D., Kushner, K., & Pridham, K. (1987). Treat or refer: Patients' interest in their psychosocial problems. *Journal of Family Practice, 24,* 499-503.

Harasym, P., Baumber, J., Bryant, H., Fundytus, D., Preshaw, R., Watanabe, M., & Wyse, G. (1980). An evaluation of the clinical problem-solving process using a simulation technique. *Medical Education, 14,* 381-386.

Haring, B. (1975). *Ethics of manipulation: Issues in medicine, behavior control and genetics.* New York: Seabury.

Hatfield, A. (1983). What families want of family therapists. In W. R. McFarlane (Ed.), *Family therapy in schizophrenia* (pp. 41-68). New York: Guilford.

Heath, D. B. (1976). Anthropological perspectives on alcohol: An historical review. In M. W. Everett, J. O. Waddell, & D. B. Heath (Eds.), *Cross-cultural approaches to the study of alcohol: An interdisciplinary perspective* (pp. 41-101). The Hague: Mouton.

Heath, D. B. (1980). A critical review of the sociocultural model of alcohol use. In T. C. Harford, D. A. Parker, & L. Light (Eds.), *Normative approaches to the prevention of alcohol abuse and alcoholism* (Research Monograph No. 3) (pp. 1-18). Rockville, MD: U.S. Department of Health, Education and Welfare.

Heider, K. G. (1988). The Rashomon effect: When ethnographers disagree. *American Anthropologist, 90,* 73-81.

Held, B., & Pols, E. (1985). The confusion about epistemology and "epistemology": What to do about it. *Family Process, 24*(4).

Henao, S., & Grose, N. (Eds.). (1985). *Principles of family systems in family medicine.* New York: Brunner/Mazel.

Henry, J. (1963). *Culture against man.* New York: Random House.

Henry, J. (1967). My life with the families of psychotic children. In G. Handel (Ed.), *The psychosocial interior of families* (pp. 30-46). Chicago: Aldine.

Henry, J. (1973). *Pathways to madness.* New York: Random House.

Hickam, D. H., Sox, H. C., Marton, K. I., Skeff, K. M., & Chin, D. (1982). A study of the implicit criteria used in diagnosing chest pain. *Medical Decision Making, 2,* 403-414.

Hill, R. (1958). Generic features of families under stress. *Social Casework, 39,* 139-159.

Hill, R. (1971, October 7). Modern systems theory and the family: A confrontation. *Social Science Information.*

Hochheiser, L., & Chapados, J. (1985). Training family physicians to treat families. *Family Systems Medicine, 3,* 476-480.

Hoebel, F. C. (1977). Brief family-interactional therapy in the management of cardiac-related high-risk behaviors. *Journal of Family Practice, 3,* 613-620.

Hoffman, L. (1990). Constructing realities: An art of lenses. *Family Process, 29*(2), 1-12.

Hogarty, G., Anderson, C., Reiss, D., et al. (1986). Family psychoeducation, social skills training and maintenance chemotherapy in the aftercare treatment of schizophrenia. *Archives of General Psychiatry, 43,* 633-642.

Holden, D., & Lewine, R. (1982). How families evaluate mental health professionals, resources and effects of illness. *Schizophrenia Bulletin, 8,* 626-633.

Holleb, A. I. (1985). Survey of physicians' attitudes and practices in early cancer detection. *Cancer, 35,* 197-219.

Holmes, C., Kane, R. L., Ford, M., & Fowler, J. (1978). Toward the measurement of primary care. *Milbank Memorial Fund Quarterly/Health Society, 56,* 231-251.

Holmes, T. H., & Rahe, R. H. (1967). The social readjustment scale. *Journal of Psychosomatic Research, 39,* 413-431.

House, J. S., Landis, K. R., & Umberson, D. (1988). Social relationships and health. *Science, 241,* 540-545.

Houts, P. S., & Leaman, T. L. (1983). *Case studies in primary medical care: Social psychological and ethical issues in family practice.* University Park: Pennsylvania State University Press.

Huygen, F. J. A., van den Hoogen, H. J. M., van Eijk, J. T. M., & Smits, A. J. A. (1989). Death and dying: Longitudinal study of their medical impact on the family. *Family Systems Medicine, 7,* 374-384.

Hymovich, D., & Barnard, M. (Eds.). (1973). *Family health care.* New York: McGraw-Hill.

Jackson, D. D. (1965). Family homeostasis and the family physician. *California Medicine, 103,* 239-242.

James, M., & Jongeward, D. (1973). *Born to win: Transactional analysis with Gestalt experiments.* Reading, MA: Addison-Wesley.

Janowski, D., et al. (1973). Provocation of schizophrenic symptoms by intravenous administration of methlphenidate. *Archives of General Psychiatry, 28,* 185-191.

Johnson, B. (1974). Before hospitalization: A preparation program of the child and his family. *Child Today, 3,* 18-21.

Johnson, D. J. (1990). The family's experience of living with mental illness. In H. P. Lefley & D. J. Johnson (Eds.), *Families as allies in treatment of the mentally ill* (pp. 31-64). Washington, DC: American Psychiatric Association Press.

Johnson, P. E. (1983). What kind of expert should a system be? *Journal of Medicine and Philosophy, 8,* 77-97.

Kane, R. L. (1977). Primary care: Contradictions and questions. *New England Journal of Medicine, 296,* 1410-1411.

Kanton, W. (1984). The prevalence of somatization in primary care. *Comprehensive Psychiatry, 25,* 208-215.

Kassirer, J. P., & Gorry, G. A. (1978). Clinical problem solving: A behavioral analysis. *Annals of Internal Medicine, 89,* 245-255.

Kassirer, J. P., Kuipers, B. J., & Gorry, G. A. (1982). Toward a theory of clinical expertise. *American Journal of Medicine, 73,* 251-259.

Keefe, S. E. (1984). Real and ideal extended familism among Mexican Americans and Anglo Americans: On the meaning of "close" family ties. *Human Organization, 43*(1), 65-70.

Keeney, B. P. (1979). Ecosystemic epistemology: An alternate paradigm for diagnosis. *Family Process, 18*(2).

Kellner, B. R. (1963). *Family ill health.* London: Tavistock.

Kelly, G. (1955). *Psychology of personal constructs.* New York: W. W. Norton.

Kerr, M., & Bowen, M. (1988). *Family evaluation: An approach based on Bowen theory.* New York: W. W. Norton.

Kiecolt-Glaser, J. K., Fisher, L. D., Ogrockl, P., Stout, J. C., Spelcher, C. E., & Glaser, R. (1987). Marital quality, marital disruption, and immune function. *Psychosomatic Medicine, 49,* 13-32.

Kiecolt-Glaser, J. K., Kennedy, S., Malkoff, S., Fisher, L. D., Spelcher, C. E., & Glaser, R. (1988). Marital discord and immunity in males. *Psychosomatic Medicine, 50,* 213-229.

Kierkegaard, S. (1962). *Works of love.* New York: Harper & Row.

Kiersey, C., & Bates, M. (1984). *Please understand me.* Del Mar, CA: Prometheus Nemesis.

Kirk, J., & Miller, M. L. (1986). *Reliability and validity in qualitative research.* Beverly Hills, CA: Sage.

Kleinman, A. (1980). *Patients and healers in the context of culture: An exploration of the borderland between anthropology, medicine, and psychiatry.* Berkeley: University of California Press.

Kleinman, A. (1983). The cultural meanings and social uses of illness: A role for medical anthropology and clinically oriented social science in the development of primary care theory and research. *Journal of Family Practice, 16,* 539-545.

Kleinman, A., & Good, B. (Eds.). (1985). *Culture and depression: Studies in the anthropology and cross-cultural psychiatry of affect and disorder.* Berkeley: University of California Press.

Kleinman, A., & Katon, W. (1981). Doctor-patient negotiation and other social science strategies in patient care. In L. Eisenberg & A. Kleinman (Eds.), *The relevance of social science for medicine.* Boston: D. Reidel.

Klos, M., Reuler, J. B., Nardone, D. A., & Girard, D. E. (1983). An evaluation of trainee performance in the case presentation. *Journal of Medical Education, 58,* 432-433.

Kobasa, S. C. (1979). Stressful life events, personality and health. *Journal of Personality and Social Psychology, 37,* 1-11.

Kog, E., Vandereycken, W., & Vertommen, H. (1985). The psychosomatic family model: A critical analysis of family interaction concepts. *Journal of Family Therapy, 7,* 31-44.

Kormos, H. R. (1984). The industrialization of medicine. In J. L. Ruffini (Ed.), *Advances in medical social science* (Vol. 2, pp. 323-339). New York: Gordon & Breach.

Korzybski, A. (1933). *Science and sanity.* Lancaster, PA: Science.

Kottgen, C., Sonnichsen, I., Mollenauer, K., et al. (1984). Group therapy with families of schizophrenic patients: Results of the Hamburg Camberwell Family Interview Study III. *International Journal of Family Psychiatry, 5,* 83-94.

Koukal, S., & Parham, E. (1978). A family learning experience to serve the juvenile patient with diabetes. *Journal of the American Diabetes Association, 72,* 411-413.

Kruskal, J. B., & Wish, M. (1978). *Multidimensional scaling.* Beverly Hills, CA: Sage.

Kuhn, T. S. (1962). *The structure of scientific revolutions.* Chicago: University of Chicago Press.

Kuhn, T. S. (1970). *The structure of scientific revolutions* (2nd ed.). Chicago: University of Chicago Press.

Kuriansky, J., Sharpe, L., & O'Connor, D. (1982). The treatment of anorgasmia: Long term effectiveness of a short term behavioral group therapy. *Journal of Sexual and Marital Therapy, 8,* 29-43.

Kushner, K. P., Mathew, H. E., Rodgers, L. A., & Hermann, R. L. (Eds.). (1982). *Critical issues in family practice: Cases and commentaries.* New York: Springer.

Kushner, K. P., & Meyer, D. (1989). Family physicians' perceptions of the family conference. *Journal of Family Practice, 28,* 65-68.

Kushner, K. P., Meyer, D., & Hansen, M. (1986). The family conference: What do patients want? *Journal of Family Practice, 23,* 463-467.

Kushner, K. P., Meyer, D., & Hansen, J. (1989). Patients' attitudes toward physician involvement in family conferences. *Journal of Family Practice, 28,* 75-78.

Kuzel, A. J. (1986). Naturalistic inquiry: An appropriate model for family medicine. *Family Medicine, 18,* 369-374.

La Barre, W. (1951). Appraising today's pressures on family living. *Social Casework, 32*(2), 51-57.

La Barre, W. (1968). *The human animal.* Chicago: University of Chicago Press.

La Barre, W. (1972). *The Ghost Dance: The origins of religion.* New York: Dell.

La Barre, W. (1978). The clinic and the field. In G. D. Spindler (Ed.), *The making of psychological anthropology* (pp. 258-299). Berkeley: University of California Press.

Laing, R. D. (1965). Mystification, confusion and conflict. In I. Boszormenyi-Nagy & J. Framo (Ed.), *Intensive family therapy.* New York: Harper & Row.

Laing, R. D. (1967). Individual and family structure. In P. Lomas (Ed.), *The predicament of the family.* London: Hogarth.

Lamb, H., & Oliphant, E. (1978). Schizophrenia through the eyes of families. *Hospital and Community Psychiatry, 29,* 803-806.

La Rue, A. (1985). Aging and mental disorders. In J. E. Birren & K. Schaie (Eds.), *Handbook of the psychology of aging* (2nd ed.). New York: Van Nostrand.

Lask, B., & Matthew, D. (1979). Childhood asthma: A controlled trial of family psychotherapy. *Archives of Disease in Childhood, 54,* 116-119.

Lawler, E., et al. (1985). *Doing research that is useful for theory and practice.* San Francisco: Jossey-Bass.

Lazarus, R. S., & Folkman, S. (1984). *Stress, appraisal, and coping.* New York: Springer.

Leahey, M., & Tomm, K. (1982). Evaluation of medical student training in family assessment. *Journal of Medical Education, 57,* 197-199.

Leff, J. (1989). Family factors in schizophrenia. *Psychiatric Annals 19,* 542-547.

Leff, J., Berkowitz, N., Shavit, N., et al. (1989). A trial of family therapy vs. a relatives group for schizophrenia. *British Journal of Psychiatry, 154,* 58-66.

Leff, J., Kuipers, L., Berkowitz, R., et al. (1982). A controlled trial of social intervention in the families of schizophrenic patients: Two year follow-up. *British Journal of Psychiatry, 140,* 594-600.

Leff, J., & Vaughn, C. (1980). The interaction of life events and relatives' expressed emotion in schizophrenia and depressed neurosis. *British Journal of Psychiatry, 136,* 146-153.

Leff, J., & Vaughn, C. (1985). *Expressed emotion in families.* New York: Guilford.

Lesser, A. L. (1981). The psychiatrist and family medicine: A different training approach. *Medical Education, 15,* 40-48.

Levenson, R. W., & Gottman, J. M. (1983). Marital interaction: Physiological linkage and affective exchange. *Journal of Personality and Social Psychology, 47,* 587-597.

Levenson, R. W., & Gottman, J. M. (1985). Physiological and affective predictors of change in relationship satisfaction. *Journal of Personality and Social Psychology, 49,* 85-91.

Levine, D. M., Green, L. W., Deeds, S. G., Chwalow, J., Russell, R. P., & Finlay, J. (1979). Health education for hypertensive patients. *Journal of the American Medical Association, 241,* 1700-1703.

Like, R. C., & Steiner, R. P. (1986). Medical anthropology and the family physician. *Family Medicine, 18,* 87-92.

Linn, N., Caffey, E., Klett, C., et al. (1979). Day treatment and psychotropic drugs in the aftercare of schizophrenic patients. *Archives of General Psychiatry, 36,* 1055-1066.

Lipowski, Z. J. (1987). Somatization: Medicine's unsolved problem. *Psychosomatics, 28,* 294-297.

Lipowski, Z. J. (1988). Somatization: The concept and its clinical application. *American Journal of Psychiatry, 145*(11), 28-32.

Lipton, F., Cohen, C. F. E., & Katz, S. (1981). Schizophrenia: A network crisis. *Schizophrenia Bulletin, 7,* 144-151.

Litman, T. J. (1966). The family and physical rehabilitation. *Journal of Chronic Diseases, 19,* 211-217.

Litman, T. J. (1974). The family as a basic unit in health and medical care: A social-behavioral overview. *Social Science and Medicine, 8,* 495-519.

Lloyd, G. (1986). Psychiatric syndromes with a somatic presentation. *Journal of Psychosomatic Research, 30,* 113-120.

Lonergan, B. (1967). Cognitional structure. In F. E. Crowe (Ed.), *Collection: Papers by Bernard Lonergan* (pp. 221-239). Montreal: Palm.

Lonergan, B. (1972). *Method in theology.* New York: Seabury.

Lorr, M. (1983). *Cluster analysis for social scientists.* San Francisco: Jossey-Bass.

Lown, B., Desilva, R. A., Reich, P., & Murawski, B. J. (1980). Psychophysiologic factors in sudden cardiac death. *American Journal of Psychiatry, 137,* 1325-1335.

Lutz, L. J., Schultz, D. E., & Litton, E. M. (1986). Diagnosis formulation by residents and physicians at different levels of experience. *Journal of Medical Education, 61,* 984-987.

MacMurray, J. (1933). *Interpreting the universe.* London: Faber & Faber.

Mannker, M. (1976). The family in medicine. *Proceedings of the Royal Society of Medicine, 69,* 115-124.

Marcel, G. (1962). *Homo viator: Introduction to the metaphysics of hope.* New York: Harper & Brothers.

Margolis, C. Z., Barnoon, S., & Barak, N. (1982). A required course in decision-making for preclinical medical students. *Journal of Medical Education, 57,* 184-190.

Marinker, M. (1976). The family in medicine. *Proceedings of the Royal Society of Medicine, 69,* 115-124.

Marshall, J. R. (1983). How we measure problem-solving ability. *Medical Education, 17,* 319-324.

Martin, A. R. (1986). Stress in residency: A challenge to personal growth. *Journal of General Internal Medicine, 1,* 252-256.

Martin, M. J. (1981). Psychiatric problems of physicians and their families. *Mayo Clinic Proceedings, 56,* 35-44.

Mattessich, P., & Hill, R. (1987). Life cycle and family development. In M. B. Sussman & S. K. Steinmetz (Eds.), *Handbook of marriage and the family.* New York: Plenum.

McCubbin, H. I., & Patterson, J. M. (1983). The family stress process: The double ABCX model of adjustment and adaptation. In H. I. McCubbin, M. B. Sussman, & J. M. Patterson (Eds.), *Social stress and the family: Advances and developments in family stress theory and research.* New York: Haworth.

McCue, J. D. (1982). The effects of stress on physicians and their medical practice. *New England Journal of Medicine, 306,* 458-462.

McDaniel, S. H., Campbell, T. L., & Seaburn, D. B. (1990). *Family-oriented primary care: A manual for medical providers.* New York: Springer-Verlag.

McDaniel, S. H., Campbell, T. L., Wynn, L. C., & Weber, T. (1988). Family systems consultation: Opportunities for teaching in family medicine. *Family Systems Medicine, 6,* 391-403.

McFarlane, W. R. (1983). Multiple family therapy in schizophrenia. In W. R. McFarlane (Ed.), *Family therapy in schizophrenia.* New York: Guilford.

McFarlane, W. R. (1990). Multiple family groups in the treatment of schizophrenia. In H. A. Nasrallah (Ed.), *Handbook of schizophrenia* (Vol. 4, pp. 167-189). Amsterdam: Elsevier.

McFarlane, W. R. (1991). Schizophrenia and psychoeducation. *Canadian Family Physician, 37,* 2457-2465.

McKenna, M. S., & Wacker, W. E. C. (1976). Do patients really want "family doctors"? *New England Journal of Medicine, 295,* 279-280.

McKeown, B., & Thomas, D. (1988). *Q methodology.* Newbury Park, CA: Sage.

McLean, P. D., & Miles, J. E. (1975). Training family physicians in psychosocial care: An analysis of a program failure. *Journal of Medical Education, 50,* 900-902.

McWhinney, I. R. (1986). Are we on the brink of a major transformation of clinical method? *Canadian Medical Association Journal, 135,* 873-878.

McWhinney, I. R. (1989). *A textbook of family medicine.* Oxford: Oxford University Press.

Mead, G. H. (1934). *Mind, self and society.* Chicago: University of Chicago Press.

Medalie, J. H. (Ed.). (1978). *Family medicine: Principles and application.* Baltimore: Williams & Wilkins.

Medalie, J. H., & Goldbourt, U. (1976). Angina pectoris among 10,000 men: Psychosocial and other risk factors as evidenced by a multifactorial analysis of a five year incidence study. *American Journal of Medicine, 60,* 910-921.

Medalie, J. H., Snyder, M., Groen, J. J., Neufeld, H. N., Goldbourt, U., & Ross, E. (1973). Angina pectoris among 10,000 men: Five-year incidence and univariate analysis. *American Journal of Medicine, 55,* 583-593.

Mendelsohn, G. A. (1979). The psychological consequences of cancer: The study of adaptation to somatic illness. *Cahiers d'Anthropologie, 2,* 53-92.

Mendelsohn, G. A., de la Tour, F., Coudin, G., & Raveau, F. H. M. (1984). A comparative study of the adaptation to breast cancer. *Cahiers d'Anthropologie, 4,* 71-96.

Mengel, M. (1987). The use of the family APGAR in screening for family dysfunction in a family practice center. *Journal of Family Practice, 24,* 394-398.

Merkel, W. T. (1983). The family and family medicine: Should this marriage be saved? *Journal of Family Practice, 17,* 857-862.

Mermelstein, R., Lichtenstein, E., & McIntyre, K. (1983). Partner support and relapse in smoking cessation programs. *Journal of Consulting and Clinical Psychology, 51,* 465-466.

Meyer, R. J., & Haggerty, R. J. (1962). Streptococcal infections in families: Factors altering individual susceptibility. *Paediatrics, 29,* 539-549.

Miller, J., & Janosik, E. (Eds.). (1980). *Family focused care.* New York: McGraw-Hill.

Milsum, J. H. (1984). *Health, stress, and illness: A systems approach.* New York: Praeger.

Minuchin, S. (1974). *Families and family therapy.* Cambridge, MA: Harvard University Press.

Minuchin, S., Baker, L., Rosman, B. L., Liebman, R., Milman, L., & Todd, T. C. (1975). A conceptual model of psychosomatic illness in children: Family organization and family therapy. *Archives of General Psychiatry, 32,* 1031-1038.

Minuchin, S., Rosman, B. L., & Baker, L. (1978). *Psychosomatic families.* Cambridge, MA: Harvard University Press.

Mitroff, I. I., & Featheringham, T. R. (1974). On systematic problem solving and the error of the third kind. *Behavioral Science, 19,* 383-393.

Morisky, D. E., Levine, D. M., Green, L. W., Shapiro, S., Russell, R. P., & Smith, C. R. (1983). Five year blood pressure control and mortality following health education for hypertensive patients. *American Journal of Public Health, 73,* 153-162.

Morley, P. C. (1988). From holistic anthropology to holistic health: A personal odyssey. *High Plains Applied Anthropologist, 8*(2), 12-28.

Moss, G. E. (1973). *Illness, immunity and social interaction: The dynamics of biosocial resonation.* New York: John Wiley.

Murata, P. J., & Kane, R. L. (1976). Do families get family care? *Journal of the American Medical Association, 257,* 1912-1915.

Murdock, G. P. (1949). *Social structure.* New York: Free Press.

Murdock, G. P. (1967). *Ethnographic atlas.* Pittsburgh, PA: University of Pittsburgh Press.

National Center for Health Statistics. (1984). *Health, United States* (DHHS Publication No. PHS 85-1232). Washington, DC: Government Printing Office.

National Center for Health Statistics. (1985). [Divorce statistics]. *Monthly Vital Statistics Report, 34*(9, Suppl.).

National Center for Health Statistics. (1991). *Health, United States, 1990.* Washington, DC: Government Printing Office.

National Heart, Lung and Blood Institute, Working Group on Health Education and High Blood Pressure Control. (1987). *The physician's guide: Improving adherence among hypertensive patients.* Washington, DC: Government Printing Office.

National Institute on Aging. (1986). *Resource data book* (DHHS Publication No. NIH 86-2443). Washington, DC: Government Printing Office.

National Centre for Health Statistics. (1985). *Monthly Vital Statistics Report, 34*(9, Suppl.).

Neuchterlein, K. H., & Dawson, M. (1984). A heuristic vulnerability/stress model for schizophrenic episodes. *Schizophrenia Bulletin, 10,* 300-312.

Neufeld, V. R., Norman, G. R., Feightner, J. W., & Barrows, H. S. (1981). Clinical problem-solving by medical students: A cross sectional longitudinal analysis. *Medical Education, 15,* 315-322.

Newberger, C. (1986). The American family in crisis: Implications for children. *Current Problems in Paediatrics, 16,* 674-721.

Nisbett, R., & Ross, L. (1980). *Human inference: Strategies and shortcomings of social judgement.* Englewood Cliffs, NJ: Prentice-Hall.

Norton, A. (1986). One parent families: A social and economic profile. *Family Relations, 35,* 9-17.

Norton, P. G., Stewart, M., Tudiver, F., Bass, M. J., & Dunn, E. V. (1991). *Primary care research: Traditional and innovative approaches.* Newbury Park, CA: Sage.

Nuckolls, K. B., Cassel, J., & Kaplan, B. H. (1972). Psychosocial assets, life crisis and the prognosis of pregnancy. *American Journal of Epidemiology, 95,* 431-441.

Oakes, W., Ward, J. R., Gray, R. M., Klouber, M. R., & Moody, P. M. (1970). Family expectations and arthritis: Patient compliance to a hand resting splint regimen. *Journal of Chronic Diseases, 22,* 757-764.

Obetz, N., Swenson, W., McCarty, C., Gillchrist, J. E., & Burget, E. (1980). Children who survive malignant disease: Emotional adaptation of the children and families. In J. Schulman & M. Kupst (Eds.), *The child with cancer.* Springfield, IL: Charles C Thomas.

Olson, D. H., McCubbin, H. I., Barnes, H., Larsen, A., Muxen, M., & Wilson, M. (1983). *Families: What makes them work.* Beverly Hills, CA: Sage.

Olson, D. H., Russell, C. S., & Sprenkle, D. H. (1983). Circumplex model of marital and family systems: Theoretical update. *Family Process, 22,* 69-84.

Olson, D. H., Sprenkle, D. H., & Russell, C. S. (1979). Circumplex model of marital and family systems: I. Cohesion and adaptability dimensions, family types, and clinical applications. *Family Process, 18,* 3-28.

Osterweis, M., Solomon, F., & Green, M. (Eds.). (1984). *Bereavement: Reactions, consequences, and care.* Washington, DC: National Academy Press.

Parker, A. W., Walsh, J. M., & Coon, M. (1976). A normative approach to the definition of primary health care. *Milbank Memorial Fund Quarterly/Health Society, 54,* 415-438.

Patterson, J. M. (1988). Families experiencing stress: The family adjustment and adaptation response model. *Family Systems Medicine, 5,* 202-237.

Patterson, J. M., & McCubbin, H. I. (1983). Chronic illness: Family stress and coping. In C. F. Figley & H. I. McCubbin (Eds.), *Stress and the family: Vol. 2. Coping with catastrophe.* New York: Brunner/Mazel.

Pattison, E., Llama, R., & Hurd, G. (1979). Social network mediation of anxiety. *Psychiatric Annals, 9,* 56-67.

Pearce, J. W., LeBow, M. D., & Orchard, J. (1981). Role of spouse involvement in the behavioral treatment of overweight women. *Journal of Consulting and Clinical Psychology, 49,* 236-244.

Pearlin, L. (1977). Marital status, life-strains and depression. *American Sociological Review, 42,* 704-715.

Pearse, I. H., & Crocker, L. (1943). *The Peckham experiment: A study in the living structure of society.* London: Allen & Unwin.

Pellegrino, E. D., & Thomasma, D. C. (1981). *A philosophical basis of medical practice.* New York: Oxford University Press.

Pellegrino, E. D., & Thomasma, D. C. (1988). *For the patient's good: The restoration of beneficence in health care.* New York: Oxford University Press.

Penn, P. (1983). Coalitions and binding interactions in families with chronic illness. *Family Systems Medicine, 1,* 16-25.

Perkin, R. I. (1991, November). Family revisited. *Canadian Family Physician, 37.*

Perls, F. S. (1970). *Gestalt therapy verbatim.* New York: Bantam.

Plattner, S. (1989). Ethnographic method. *Anthropology Newsletter* (American Anthropological Association), *30*(1), 32, 21.

Pless, I. B. (1984). The family as a resource unit in health care: Changing patterns. *Social Science and Medicine, 19,* 385-389.

Podrasky, P. (1986). The family perspective of the cured patient. *Cancer, 58,* 522-523.

Polanyi, M. (1967). *The tacit dimension*. Garden City, NY: Doubleday.

Pond, R. A. (1991). Abuse of drugs in the health professional. *Canadian Family Physician, 37*, 1755-1758.

Population Reference Bureau. (1987, February). *Juggling jobs and babies: America's child care challenge* (Publication No. 12). Washington, DC: Author.

Pratt, L. (1976). *Family structure and effective health behavior: The energized family*. Boston: Houghton Mifflin.

Pridham, K. F., & Hansen, M. F. (1980). An observation methodology for the study of interactive clinical problem-solving behavior in primary care settings. *Medical Care, 18*, 360-375.

Quill, T. E., & Williamson, P. R. (1990). Healthy approaches to physician stress. *Archives of Internal Medicine, 150*, 1857-1861.

Rabkin, J. G., & Streuning, E. L. (1976). Life events, stress and illness. *Science, 194*, 1013-1020.

Rachlis, M. (1989). *Second opinion: What's wrong with Canada's health care system and how to fix it*. Toronto: Collins.

Raiffa, H. (1968). *Decision analysis: Introductory lectures on choices under uncertainty*. Reading, MA: Addison-Wesley.

Ramsey, C. N., Abell, T. D., & Baker, L. C. (1986). The relationship between family functioning, life events, family structure, and the outcome of pregnancy. *Journal of Family Practice, 22*, 521-527.

Ransom, D. C. (1981). The rise of family medicine: New roles for behavioral science. *Marriage and Family Review, 4*(1/2), 31-72.

Ransom, D. C. (1983). Random notes: The family as patient—what does this mean? *Family Systems Medicine, 1*, 99-103.

Ransom, D. C. (1986a). Random notes: On the absence of role models in family practice training. *Family Systems Medicine, 4*, 123-128.

Ransom, D. C. (1986b). Random notes: Research on the family in health, illness and care—state of the art. *Family Systems Medicine, 4*, 329-336.

Ransom, D. C. (1987). Random notes: On light versus electron microscopes in family research. *Family Systems Medicine, 5*, 383-390.

Ransom, D. C., Fisher, L., Phillips, S., Kokes, R. F., & Weiss, R. (1990). The logic of measurement in family research. In T. W. Draper & A. C. Marcus (Eds.), *Family variables: Conceptualization, measurement, and use*. Newbury Park, CA: Sage.

Ransom, D. C., & Vandervoort, H. E. (1973). The development of family medicine: Problematic trends. *Journal of the American Medical Association, 225*, 1098-1102.

Reeb, K. G., Graham, A. V., Zyzanski, S. J., & Kitson, G. C. (1987). Predicting low birthweight and complicated labor in urban black women: A biopsychosocial perspective. *Social Science and Medicine, 25*, 1321-1327.

Reiss, D. (1981). *The family's construction of reality*. Cambridge, MA: Harvard University Press.

Reiss, D., & De-Nour, A. K. (1989). The family and medical team in chronic illness: A transactional and development perspective. In C. N. Ramsey (Ed.), *Family systems in medicine*. New York: Guilford.

Reiss, D., Gonzales, S., & Kremer, N. (1986). Family process, chronic illness and death. *Archives of General Psychiatry, 43*, 795-807.

Reiss, D., & Klein, D. (1987). Paradigm and pathogenesis: A family-centered approach to problems of etiology and treatment of psychiatric disorders. In T. Jacob (Ed.),

Family interaction and psychopathology: Theories, methods, and findings (pp. 203-255). New York: Plenum.

Research note: Young adults choose alternatives to marriage, remain single longer. (1991). *Family Planning Perspectives, 23,* 45-47.

Reynolds, R. E. (1975). Primary care, ambulatory care, and family medicine: Overlapping but not synonymous. *Journal of Medical Education, 50,* 893-895.

Richards, A. (1956). *Chisungu.* London: Faber & Faber.

Richardson, H. B. (1945). *Patients have families.* New York: Commonwealth Fund.

Riso, D. R. (1987). *Personality types.* Boston: Houghton Mifflin.

Ritzer, G., & Walczak, D. (1986). The changing nature of American medicine. *Journal of American Culture, 9,* 43-51.

Robertson, R. G. (1986). How can we as physicians care for our own families? *Journal of Family Practice, 23,* 165-166.

Rogers, C. R. (1961). *On becoming a person.* Boston: Houghton Mifflin.

Rogers, E. M., & Shoemaker, F. F. (1971). *Communication of innovations: A cross-cultural approach.* New York: Macmillan.

Rogers, J. C., & Cohn, P. (1987). Impact of a screening family genogram on first encounters in primary care. *Family Practice, 4,* 291-301.

Rogers, J. C., & Durkin, M. (1984). The semi-structured genogram interview: I. Protocol; II. Evaluation. *Family Systems Medicine, 2,* 176-186.

Rolland, J. S. (1984). Toward a psychosocial typology of chronic and life-threatening illness. *Family Systems Medicine, 2,* 245-263.

Rolland, J. S. (1987a). Chronic illness and the life cycle: A conceptual framework. *Family Process, 26,* 203-221.

Rolland, J. S. (1987b). Family illness paradigms: Evolution and significance. *Family Systems Medicine, 5,* 482-503.

Rosenberg, M. (1965). *Society and the adolescent self-image.* Princeton, NJ: Princeton University Press.

Rosman, B. L., & Baker, L. (1988). The psychosomatic family reconsidered: Diabetes in context—a reply. *Journal of Marital and Family Therapy, 14,* 125-132.

Ross, C. (1983). Dividing work, sharing work, and in-between: Marriage patterns and depression. *American Sociological Review, 48,* 809-823.

Ryan, M. (1987). Loneliness in the elderly. *Journal of Gerontological Nursing, 13,* 6-12.

Saccone, A. J., & Israel, A. C. (1978). Effects of experimental versus significant other-controlled reinforcement and choice of target behavior on weight loss. *Behavior Therapy, 9,* 217-278.

Sagan, L. A. (1987). *The health of nations: True causes of sickness and well-being.* New York: Basic Books.

Salit, I. (1985). Sporadic post infectious neuromyasthenia. *Canadian Medical Association Journal, 133,* 659-663.

Sander, F. M. (1979). *Individual and family therapy: Toward an integration.* New York: Jason Aronson.

Sawa, R. J. (1985). *Family dynamics for physicians: Guidelines to assessment and treatment.* Lewiston, NY: Edwin Mellen.

Sawa, R. J. (1986). Assessing interviewing skills: The simulated office oral. *Journal of Family Practice, 23,* 567-571.

Sawa, R. J. (1988). Incorporating the family into medical care. *Canadian Family Physician, 34,* 87-93.

Sawa, R. J., & Goldenberg, S. (1988, February 28). *Teaching family practice residents to work with families: An outcome study.* Paper presented at the Family in Family Medicine Conference, Society of Teachers of Family Medicine, Amelia Island.

Sawa, R. J., Henderson, E. A., Pablo, R. Y., & Falk, W. A. (1985). Family practice impact of a teaching curriculum in family dynamics. *Family Systems Medicine, 3,* 50-59.

Sawa, R. J., Jennett, P., & Elford, R. W. (1991). Reducing the risk of coronary artery disease. *Canadian Family Physician, 37,* 651-654.

Scherger, J. E., Gordon, M. J., Phillips, T. J., & LoGerfo, J. P. (1980). Comparison of diagnostic methods of family practice and internal medicine residents. *Journal of Family Practice, 10,* 95-101.

Schleifer, S. J., Keller, S. E., Camerino, M., Thornton, J. C., & Stein, M. (1983). Suppression of lymphocyte stimulation following bereavement. *Journal of American Medical Association, 250,* 374-377.

Schmidt, D. D. (1978). The family as the unit of medical care. *Journal of Family Practice, 7,* 303-313.

Schmidt, D. D. (1987). [Letter to the editor]. *Family Systems Medicine, 5,* 377-379.

Schon, D. (1983). *The reflective practitioner.* New York: Basic Books.

Schon, D. (1987). *Educating the reflective practitioner.* San Francisco: Jossey-Bass.

Schroder, K. H., Casadaban, A. B., & Davis, B. (1988). Interpersonal skills training for parents of children with cystic fibrosis. *Family Systems Medicine, 6,* 51-68.

Schwartz, D., Wang, M., Zeitz, L., & Goss, M. (1962). Medication errors made by elderly, chronically ill patients. *American Journal Public Health, 52,* 2018-2029.

Schwartz, L., Marcus, R., & Condon, R. (1978). Multidisciplinary group therapy for rheumatoid arthritis. *Psychosomatics, 19,* 289-293.

Schwenk, T. L., Clark, C. H., Jones, G. R., Simmon, R. C., & Coleman, M. L. (1982). Defining a behavioral science curriculum for family physicians: What do patients think? *Journal of Family Practice, 15,* 339-345.

Seagull, E. (1987). Social support and child maltreatment: A review of the evidence. *Child Abuse and Neglect, 11,* 41-52.

Searle, J. (1987). What is an intentional state? In H. L. Dreyfus (Ed.), *Husserl intentionality and cognitive science.* Cambridge: MIT Press.

Senge, P. M. (1990). *The fifth discipline: The art and practice of the learning organization.* Garden City, NY: Doubleday.

Shands, H. C. (1971). *The war with words: Structure and transcendence.* The Hague: Mouton.

Shapiro, W. (1989a). Ritual kinship, ritual incorporation and the denial of death. *Man, 23,* 275-297.

Shapiro, W. (1989b). Thanatophobic man. *Anthropology Today* (Royal Anthropological Institute, London), *5*(2), 11-14.

Shorter, E. (1975). *The making of the modern family.* New York: Basic Books.

Shorter, E. (1986). *Bedside manners: The troubled history of doctors and patients.* New York: Simon & Schuster.

Shorter, E. (1989). Einige demographische Auswirkungen des postmodernen Familienlebens. *Zeitschrift für Bevolkerüngswissenschaft, 15,* 221-233.

Shorter, E. (1992). *From paralysis to fatigue: A history of psychosomatic illness in the modern era.* New York: Free Press.

Shye, S. (Ed.). (1978). *Theory construction and data analysis in the behavioral sciences.* San Francisco: Jossey-Bass.

Silver, H. K., & McAtee, P. R. (1975). A descriptive definition of the scope and content of primary health care. *Paediatrics, 56,* 957-959.

Silverman, D., Gartrell, N., Aronson, M., Steer, M., & Edbril, S. (1983). In search of the biopsychosocial perspective: An experiment with beginning medical students. *American Journal of Psychiatry, 140,* 1154-1159.

Simpson, D. E., Gjerdingen, D., Dalgaard, K. A., & O'Brien, D. K. (1982). *Data utilization in diagnostic reasoning: A comparison of family physicians and internists.* Unpublished manuscript.

Slater, E., & Roth, M. (Eds.). (1977). *Mayer-Gross Slater and Roth clinical psychiatry* (3rd ed.). London: Balliere Tindall.

Smilkstein, G. (1978). The family APGAR: A proposal for a family function test and its use by physicians. *Journal of Family Practice, 6,* 1231-1235.

Smith, D. M. (1986a). *The problem with problem-solving: Some common understandings and rules brought to problems.* Paper presented at the Educational Leadership Conference, Seton Hall, NJ.

Smith, D. M. (1986b). *In the pursuit of meaning: Coming face to face with practice worries* (Research findings on a study of consultants and therapists). Newton, MA: Action Design Associates.

Smith, D. M. (1986c). *The risk of getting caught in the middle: Some dilemmas in covering conflict* (Research findings on a study of journalists covering conflict, in conjunction with the Harvard Negotiation Project). Newton, MA: Action Design Associates.

Smith, D. M. (1987a). *Reflection manual: Mapping theories of action.* Newton, MA: Action Design Associates.

Smith, D. M. (1987b). *Reflections on a program for the instruction of lawyers* (Research findings on a training program in negotiations). Newton, MA: Action Design Associates.

Smith, D. M. (1988). *Training managers for the 21st century: Some thoughts on a management development program* (Research findings on a corporate training program for managers). Newton, MA: Action Design Associates.

Smith, D. M. (1989). *On modelling an intervention practice.* Unpublished manuscript, Action Design Associates, Newton, MA.

Smith, D. M., & Putnam, R. (1989). *Toward a map of teaching negotiation* (Research findings on training corporate personnel how to negotiate). Newton, MA: Action Design Associates.

Smith, R. C. (1984). Teaching interviewing skills to medical students: The issue of "countertransference." *Journal of Medical Education, 59,* 582-588.

Smith, R. C., & Stein, H. F. (1987). A topographical model of clinical decision-making and interviewing. *Family Medicine, 19,* 361-363.

Snider, G., & Stein, H. F. (1987). An approach to community assessment in medical practice. *Family Medicine, 19,* 213-219.

Spiegel, C. T., Kemp, B. A., Newman, M. A., Birnbaum, P. S., & Alter, C. L. (1982). Modification of decision-making behaviour of third-year medical students. *Journal of Medical Education, 57,* 769-777.

Spiegel, D., & Yalom, I. (1978). A support group for dying patients. *International Journal of Group Psychotherapy, 28,* 233-245.

Spiegel, J. (1971). *Transactions: The interplay between individual, family, and society.* New York: Science House.

Spiro, M. E. (1979). *Gender and culture.* Durham, NC: Duke University Press.

Spiro, M. E. (1982a). *Buddhism and society: A great tradition and its Burmese vicissitudes* (2nd ed.). Berkeley: University of California Press.

Spiro, M. E. (1982b). *Oedipus in the Trobriands.* Chicago: University of Chicago Press.

Spiro, M. E. (1986). Cultural relativism and the future of anthropology. *Cultural Anthropology, 1,* 259-286.

Spradley, J. P. (1979). *The ethnographic interview.* New York: Holt, Rinehart & Winston.

Stamm, I. (1987). *Countertransference in hospital treatment: Basic concepts and paradigms* (Occasional Paper No. 2). Topeka, KS: Menninger Foundation.

Starfield, B. H. (1979). Measuring the attainment of primary care. *Journal of Medical Education, 54,* 361-368.

Stein, H. F. (1974). Where seldom is heard a discouraging word: American nostalgia. *Columbia Forum, 3*(3), 20-23.

Stein, H. F. (1982a). The annual cycle and the cultural nexus of health care behaviour among Oklahoma wheat farming families. *Culture, Medicine and Psychiatry, 6,* 81-99.

Stein, H. F. (1982b). The ethnographic mode of teaching clinical behavioral science. In N. J. Chrisman & T. W. Maretzki (Eds.), *Clinically applied anthropology: Anthropologists in health science settings* (pp. 61-82). Boston: D. Reidel.

Stein, H. F. (1983a). An anthropological view of family therapy. In D. Bagarozzi, A. Jurich, & B. Jackson (Eds.), *New perspectives in marriage and family therapy: Issues in theory, research and practice* (pp. 262-294). New York: Human Sciences Press.

Stein, H. F. (1983b). The case study method as a means of teaching significant context in family medicine. *Family Medicine, 15,* 163-167.

Stein, H. F. (1984). Family dynamics, family therapy, and anthropology. In J. L. Ruffini (Ed.), *Advances in medical social science* (Vol. 2, pp. 289-321). New York: Gordon & Breach.

Stein, H. F. (1985). *The psychodynamics of medical practice.* Berkeley: University of California Press.

Stein, H. F. (1986). Social role and unconscious complementarity. *Journal of Psychoanalytic Anthropology, 9,* 235-268.

Stein, H. F. (1987a). One's self in clinical relationships. *Family Medicine, 19,* 7-8.

Stein, H. F. (1987b). Polarities in the identity of family medicine: A psychocultural analysis. In W. J. Doherty, C. E. Christianson, & M. B. Sussman (Eds.), *Family medicine: The maturing of a discipline* (pp. 211-233). New York: Haworth.

Stein, H. F. (1990). *A meaning-centered approach to exploring family influences on health-related decision-making.* Paper presented at the International Symposium on the Family in Primary Care, Calgary, Alberta.

Stein, H. F., & Apprey, M. (1985). *Context and dynamics in clinical knowledge* (Series in Ethnicity, Medicine and Psychoanalysis, No. 1). Charlottesville: University Press of Virginia.

Stein, H. F., & Apprey, M. (1987). *From metaphor to meaning: Papers in psychoanalytic anthropology* (Series in Ethnicity, Medicine and Psychoanalysis, No. 2). Charlottesville: University Press of Virginia.

Stein, H. F., & Pontious, J. M. (1985). Family and beyond: The larger context of non-compliance. *Family Systems Medicine, 3,* 179-189.

Stein, R. E., & Jessop, D. J. (1982). A non-categorical approach to chronic childhood illness. *Public Health Report, 97,* 354-362.

Steinberg, H., & Durell, J. (1968). A stressful social situation as a precipitant of schizophrenia. *British Journal of Psychiatry, 114*, 1097-1105.

Steinert, Y., & Rosenberg, E. (1987). Psychosocial problems: What do patients want? What do physicians want to provide? *Family Medicine, 19*, 346-350.

Steinglass, P. (1987a). Psychoeducational family therapy for schizophrenia: A review essay. *Psychiatry, 50*, 14-23.

Steinglass, P. (1987b). A systems view of family interaction and psychopathology. In T. Jacob (Ed.), *Family interaction and psychopathology: Theories, methods and findings*. New York: Plenum.

Steinglass, P., Bennett, L. A., Wolin, S. J., & Reiss, D. (1987). *The alcoholic family*. New York: Basic Books.

Steinglass, P., & Horan, M. E. (1988a). Families and chronic illness. In F. Walsh & C. M. Anderson (Eds.), *Chronic disorders and the family*. New York: Haworth.

Steinglass, P., & Horan, M. E. (1988b). Families and chronic medical illness. *Journal of Psychotherapy and the Family, 3*, 127-142.

Steinglass, P., Temple, S., Lisman, S. A., & Reiss, D. (1982). Coping with spinal cord injury: The family perspective. *General Hospital Psychiatry, 4*, 259-264.

Stephens, G. G. (1984). The medical supermarket: Futuristic or decadent? Part II. *Continuing Education for the Family Physician, 19*, 600-610.

Stephenson, M. J., & Bass, M. J. (1983). Creativity in management in family medicine. *Journal of Family Practice, 16*, 347-350.

Stephenson, W. (1953). *The study of behavior*. Chicago: University of Chicago Press.

Stewart, A. L., Greenfield, S., Hays, R. D., Wells, K., Rogers, W. H., Berry, S. D., et al. (1989). Functional status and well being of patients with chronic conditions. *Journal of American Medical Association, 262*, 907-913.

Stewart, D. (1985). Psychiatric assessment of patients with "20th century disease" ("Total allergy syndrome"). *Canadian Medical Association Journal, 133*, 1002-1006.

Stewart, D. (1987). Total allergy syndrome: A critical overview of the 20th century disease. *Psychiatry in Canada, 1*, 51-56.

Stewart, M. A., Brown, J. B., & Weston, W. W. (1989). Patient centred interviewing: Part III. Five provocative questions. *Canadian Family Physician, 35*, 159-161.

Strain, J. J., Pincus, H. A., Gise, L. H., & Houpt, J. (1986). Mental health education in three primary care specialties. *Journal of Medical Education, 61*, 958-966.

Straus, S. (1985). Persisting illness and fatigue in adults with evidence of Epstein-Barr virus infection. *Annals of Internal Medicine, 102*, 1-6.

Taerk, G. S. (1987). Depression in patients with neuromyasthenia asthenia (benign myalgic encephalomyelitis). *International Journal of Psychiatry in Medicine, 17*, 49-56.

Tarrier, N., Barrowclough, C., Vaughn, C., et al. (1988). The community management of schizophrenia: A controlled trial of behavioral intervention with families to reduce relapse. *British Journal of Psychiatry, 153*, 532-542.

Taylor, S. E. (1983). Adjustment to threatening events: A theory of cognitive adaptation. *American Psychologist, 41*, 1161-1173.

Tecce, J., & Cole, J. (1976). The distraction-arousal hypothesis, CNV and schizophrenia. In D. I. Mostofsky (Ed.), *Behavior control and modification of psychological activity*. Englewood Cliffs, NJ: Prentice-Hall.

Thacker, S., Salber, B., Osborne, C., et al. (1972). Primary care in Durham County: Who gives care to whom? *Medical Care, 17*, 69-85.

Thorne, S. A., & Robinson, C. A. (1989). Guarded alliance: Health care relationships in chronic illness. *Image: Journal of Nursing Scholarship, 21.*

Thornton, A. (1983). The changing American family. *Population Bulletin, 38*(4).

Thrower, S. M., Bruce, W. E., & Walton, R. F. (1982). The family circle method: Integrating family systems concepts in family medicine. *Journal of Family Practice, 15,* 451-457.

Tolsdorf, C. (1976). Social networks, support and coping: An exploratory study. *Family Process, 15,* 407-417.

Tomm, K. (1987a). Interventive interviewing: Part 1. Strategizing as a fourth guideline for the therapist. *Family Process, 26,* 3-13.

Tomm, K. (1987b). Interventive interviewing: Part 2. Reflexive questioning as a means to enable self-healing. *Family Process, 26,* 167-183.

Tomm, K. (1988). Interventive interviewing: Part 3. Intending to ask circular, strategic, or reflexive questions? *Family Process, 27,* 1-15.

Totman, R. (1979). *Social causes of illness.* New York: Pantheon.

Trostle, J. A., Hauser, W. A., & Susser, I. S. (1983). The logic of noncompliance: Management of epilepsy from the patient's point of view. *Culture, Medicine and Psychiatry, 7,* 35-56.

Tudiver, F., Hilditch, J., & Permaul, J. (1991). *A comparison of psychosocial characteristics of new widowers and married men.* Unpublished manuscript.

Turk, D. C. (1979). Factors influencing the adaptive process with chronic illness. In S. I. Spielberger & C. Spielberger (Eds.), *Stress and anxiety* (pp. 291-311). Washington, DC: Hemisphere.

Vachon, M. S. L., Lyall, W. A. L., Rogers, J., Freedman-Letofsky, K., & Freeman, S. J. (1980). A controlled study of self-help intervention for widows. *American Journal of Psychiatry, 137,* 1380-1384.

Vaillant, G., Sobowale, N. C., & McArthur, C. (1972). Some psychologic vulnerabilities of physicians. *New England Journal of Medicine, 287,* 372-375.

Vaughn, C., & Leff, J. (1976). The influence of family and social course of psychiatric illness: A comparison of schizophrenic and depressed neurotic patients. *British Journal of Psychiatry, 129,* 125-137.

Venters, M. (1981). Familial coping with chronic and severe childhood illness: The case of cystic fibrosis. *Social Science of Medicine, 15,* 289-297.

Venters, M. (1986). Family life and cardiovascular risk: Implications for the prevention of chronic disease. *Social Science of Medicine, 22,* 1067-1074.

Verbrugge, L. M. (1977). Marital status and health. *Journal of Marriage and Family, 7,* 267-285.

Vincent, M. O. (1983). Some sequelae of stress in physicians. *Psychiatric Journal of the University of Ottawa, 8*(3), 120-124.

Voytovich, A. E., Rippey, R. M., & Suffredini, A. (1985). Premature conclusions in diagnostic reasoning. *Journal of Medical Education, 60,* 302-307.

von Bertalanffy, L. (1969). *General system theory: Essay on its foundation and development* (rev. ed.). New York: George Braziller.

Waldegrave, C. (1990). Just therapy. *Dulwich Centre Newsletter, 1,* 5-20.

Walsh, F. (1982). *Normal family processes.* New York: Guilford.

Ware, J., Brook, R. H., Davies-Avery, A., Williams, K. N., Stewart, A. L., Rogers, W. H., Donald, C. A., & Johnston, S. A. (1984). *Conceptualization and measurement of health for adults in the health insurance study: Vol. 1. Model of health and methodology* (Publication No. R:1987/1-HEW). Santa Monica, CA: RAND Corporation.

Watzlawick, P., Weakland, J., & Fisch, R. (1974). *Change.* New York: W. W. Norton.

Weiner, J. P., & Starfield, B. H. (1983). Measurement of primary care relief office-based physicians. *American Journal of Public Health, 73,* 666-671.

Weinberger, D. (1987). Implications of normal brain development for the pathogenesis of schizophrenia. *Archives of General Psychiatry, 44,* 660-670.

West, D. (1986). The effects of loneliness: A review of the literature. *Comprehensive Psychiatry, 27,* 351-363.

Westhead, J. (1985). Frequent attenders in general practice: Medical, psychological and social characteristics. *Journal of the Royal College of General Practitioners, 35,* 337-340.

Weston, W. W. (1987). Family therapy and the family physician: Reflections after 15 years. *Family Systems Medicine, 5,* 357-363.

Weston, W. W., Brown, J. B., & Stewart, M. A. (1989). Patient centred interviewing: Part I. Understanding patients' experiences. *Canadian Family Physician, 35,* 147-151.

White, K. L. (1967). Primary medical care for families: Organization and evaluation. *New England Journal of Medicine, 277,* 847-852.

Whitehead, D., & Doherty, W. J. (1989). Systems dynamics in cigarette smoking: An explanatory study. *Family Systems Medicine, 7,* 264-273.

Wigton, R. S., Hoellerich, V. L., & Kashinath, D. P. (1986). How physicians use clinical information in diagnosing pulmonary embolism: An application of conjoint analysis. *Medical Decision Making, 6,* 2-11.

Willi, J. (1987). Some principles of an ecological model of the person as a consequence of the therapeutic experience with systems. *Family Process, 26*(4).

Williams, J. T., & Leaman, T. L. (1973). Family structure and function. In H. F. Conn, R. E. Rakel, & T. W. Johnson (Eds.), *Family practice* (pp. 3-18). Philadelphia: W. B. Saunders.

Williamson, J. W., German, P. S., Weiss, R., Skinner, E. A., & Bowes, F. (1989). Health science information management and continuing education of physicians: A survey of U.S. primary care practitioners and their opinion leaders. *Annals of Internal Medicine, 110,* 151-160.

Williamson, P., McCormick, T., & Taylor, T. (1983). Who is the patient? A family case study of a recurrent dilemma in family practice. *Journal of Family Practice, 17,* 1039-1043.

Wilson, G. T., & Brownell, K. (1978). Behavior therapy for obesity: Including family members in the treatment process. *Behavior Therapy, 9,* 943-945.

Wulff, H. R., Pedersen, S. A., & Rosenberg, R. (1986). *Philosophy of medicine: An introduction.* Oxford: Blackwell Scientific.

Yaffe, F. M., & Stewart, M. A. (1986). Patients' attitudes to the relevance of nonmedical problems in family medicine care. *Journal of Family Practice, 23,* 241-244.

Yalom, I. D. (1980). *Existential psychotherapy.* New York: Basic Books.

Yarrow, M., Clausen, J., & Robbins, P. (1955). The social meaning of mental illness. *Journal Social Issues, 11,* 33-48.

Young, D. A. (1981). Communications linking clinical research and clinical practice. In E. B. Roberts, R. I. Levy, S. N. Finkestein, J. Moskowitz, & E. J. Sondik (Eds.), *Biomedical innovation.* Cambridge: MIT Press.

Zarit, J., & Zarit, S. (1982). Families under stress: Interventions for caregivers of senile dementia patients. *Psychotherapy: Theory, Research and Practice, 16,* 461-471.

Zborowski, M. (1969). *People in pain.* San Francisco: Jossey-Bass.

Zola, I. K. (1972). Studying the decision to see a doctor. *Psychosomatic Medicine, 8,* 216-236.

Index

About the Authors

Macaran A. Baird, M.D., a family physician and certified family therapist, is Professor and Chairman of the Department of Family Medicine, SUNY Health Science Center at Syracuse, New York, and Director of Medical Education, St. Joseph's Hospital Health Center, Syracuse. Prior to moving to Syracuse, he served as Residency Director, Department of Family Medicine at the University of Oklahoma, Oklahoma City. A native Minnesotan, he received his B.A. degree from Macalester College and his M.S. from the University of Minnesota School of Environmental Health. After receiving his M.D. degree from the University of Minnesota at Minneapolis-Saint Paul, he completed his residency in family practice at Bethesda Lutheran Hospital, Saint Paul. He completed his family therapy training at the University of Minnesota and earned an M.S. in family practice. He was in private practice in Wabasha, Minnesota, from 1978 to 1983. His research and practice interests include family therapy and chemical dependency. He is a nationally known expert in family therapy, as it relates to family practice, and in the area of chemical dependency, particularly alcoholism, in relation to family therapy and family practice. His numerous publications include two books coauthored with William Doherty, Ph.D.: *Family Therapy and Family Medicine* (1983) and *Family Centered Care: A Clinical Casebook* (1987).

Lorne A. Becker, M.D., is Associate Professor in the Department of Family and Community Medicine at the University of Toronto, and Chief of the Department of Family and Community Medicine at the Toronto Hospital. He received his M.D. from the University of Western Ontario Medical School in 1969. He has certification by The College of Family Physicians of Canada and the American Board of Family Practice. Dr. Becker has been a Fellow in the American Academy of Family Physicians since 1980, and in the College of Family Physicians of Canada since 1991. His current research is focused on ways in which families adapt to a chronic health problem in a family member. One of these is investigating family predictors of functional status after coronary angioplasty or bypass surgery. A second looks at the impact of family factors on perceived self-efficacy in patients with a newly discovered elevation of serum cholesterol.

Thomas L. Campbell, M.D., received his undergraduate degree from Harvard College (1974) and his M.D. in 1979 from Harvard Medical School. He completed his family practice residency and fellowship in psychosomatic medicine at the University of Rochester School of Medicine and Dentistry. Currently he is an Associate Professor of Family Medicine and Psychiatry at the University of Rochester, where he codirects the Family Systems Medicine Fellowship and psychosocial training for the Family Medicine Residency Program with Susan McDaniel, Ph.D. He has written extensively on the role of the family in medical practice and on the influence of the family on physical and mental health. His National Institute of Mental Health monograph *Family Impact on Health* has been an influential review of the current research in this area. Other books he has coauthored include *Families and Health* (with William Doherty, Ph.D.) and *Family-Oriented Primary Care: A Manual for Medical Providers* (with Susan H. McDaniel, Ph.D., and David B. Seaburn, M.S.). He is board certified in family practice and a clinical member of the American Association of Marriage and Family Therapy.

William J. Doherty, Ph.D., is Professor of Family Social Science at the University of Minnesota, and Director of Graduate Studies. He is also a Lecturer in the Department of Family Practice and Community Health at the University of Minnesota. He has coauthored or coedited five books in the area of families and health. He also conducts research on the health implications of divorce. He received his Ph.D. from the University of Connecticut in 1978.

William R. McFarlane, M.D., is the Director of the Biosocial Treatment Research Division and also Director of the Fellowship in Public Psychiatry and of Family Therapy Training at New York State Psychiatric Institute and Columbia University Department of Psychiatry. He is a graduate of Columbia University College of Physicians and Surgeons in New York. Currently he is an Associate Clinical Professor of Psychiatry at Columbia University and the Director of the Training Program in Family Psychoeducation for the New York State Office of Mental Health. He has more than 20 years' experience working with families with schizophrenic members and is an expert in multiple-family group treatment. He is the editor of *Family Therapy in Schizophrenia*.

Ian R. McWhinney, M.D., FCFP, FRCGP, is Professor of Family Medicine at The University of Western Ontario in London, Ontario, Canada. He graduated from Cambridge University in 1949 and was awarded an M.D. by thesis by Cambridge in 1959. He became a member of the Royal College of Physicians in 1954 and was elected to a fellowship in 1986. After 14 years in general practice in Britain, he was appointed Chairman of the Department of Family Medicine at the University of Western Ontario in 1968, a position he held until 1987. From 1986 through 1991 he was Medical Director of the Palliative Care Unit, Parkwood Hospital, London, Ontario. His most recent book, *A Textbook of Family Medicine*, was published by Oxford University Press in 1989.

Joan M. Patterson, Ph.D., is an Assistant Professor of Maternal and Child Health in the School of Public Health and Director of Research, Center for Children with Chronic Illness and Disability, at the University of Minnesota. Using a biopsychosocial paradigm, she focuses in her research on examining the reciprocal impacts of childhood chronic illness and family functioning. She is particularly interested in the development and evaluation of interventions for preventing psychosocial problems in individuals and families coping with chronic physical illness. She is also interested in the development of family assessment measures; theory building in the area of family stress, coping, and adaptation; and training health and education providers in family assessment and intervention. She completed her doctoral studies in family social science at the University of Minnesota.

Reg L. Perkin, M.D., CCFP, FCFP, FRCGP (Hon.), FRACGP (Hon.), is Executive Director of the College of Family Physicians of Canada, in Mississauga, Ontario, Canada. Prior to taking this position in 1985, he was a practicing family physician in Mississauga for 29 years and a Professor in the Department of Family and Community Medicine at the University of Toronto for 16 years. He was the first Chairman of the University of Toronto Department of Family and Community Medicine, and held the position of Residency Program Director for 12 years. He was head of the Department of Family Practice at the Mississauga Hospital from 1967 to 1975. He was President of the College of Family Physicians of Canada in 1981-1982.

Donald C. Ransom, Ph.D., is Professor of Family and Community Medicine at the University of California at San Francisco and Coordinator of Behavioral Science Training in the Family Practice Residency Training Program at Community Hospital in Santa Rosa, California. For the last decade, he and Lawrence Fisher, Ph.D., have conducted the California Family Health Project, a longitudinal study of family and health relationships supported by the National Institute of Mental Health and the Health Institute of the New England Medical Center. Educated at Harvard and the University of California at Berkeley, he has been a steady contributor to the field of family medicine for more than 20 years. His interest in family measurement and developing methods for studying families in primary care led to his receiving the Weatherby Award for Outstanding Clinical Research in Primary Care from the North American Primary Care Research Group and the Society of Teachers of Family Medicine in 1989.

John C. Rogers, M.D., MPH, is Associate Professor of Family Medicine and Director of the Predoctoral Section, Department of Medicine, at the Baylor College of Medicine, Houston, Texas. He received his M.D. degree from the University of Iowa and his MPH from the University of Washington. He completed a family practice residency at the University of North Carolina at Chapel Hill and a preventive medicine residency at the University of Washington. He is board certified in both family practice and public health/general preventive medicine. He has been Chair of the Research Committee of the Society of Teachers of Family Medicine and now chairs the Society's Special Committee on Clinical Policies. His primary areas of teaching and research have been clinical prevention, medical decision making, mental health, and family care. He recently integrated his interests to develop a Clinical Performance Laboratory that assesses and assures competence of current medical students and investigates ways of improving clinical performance.

Walter W. Rosser, M.D., CCFP, MRCGP, FCFP, is Professor and Chairman of the Department of Family and Community Medicine at the University of Toronto. He has previously held similar positions at the University of Ottawa and McMaster University in Hamilton. His research interests have spanned behavioral change in patients around smoking cessation issues and methods of improving delivery of preventive services in family practice. He also has an ongoing interest in prescribing patterns and critical appraisal.

Russell J. Sawa, M.D., CCFP, received his undergraduate degree in philosophy from Gonzaga University (1968) and his M.D. in 1975 from The University of Western Ontario. After his family practice residency in Toronto he completed a fellowship year in Family Therapy at McMaster University (1978) and has been a clinical member of the American Association of Marriage and Family Therapy since 1979. Currently he is an Associate Professor of Family Medicine at the University of Calgary. His career-long interest has been the integration of the whole person and family into all levels of medical teaching and medical care. He authored the textbook *Family Dynamics for Physicians* (1985). His current research concerns the assessment of family function and a family approach to the prevention of coronary artery disease.

Edward Shorter, Ph.D., is Hannah Professor of the History of Medicine in the Faculty of Medicine of the University of Toronto. A social historian of medicine, he has published widely on the history of obstetrics and gynecology, the history of the doctor-patient relationship (in *Bedside Manners: The Troubled History of Doctors and Patients*; Simon & Schuster, 1986), and the history of psychiatry. His most recent book is *From Paralysis to Fatigue: A History of Psychosomatic Illness in the Modern Era* (Free Press, 1992). He received his Ph.D. from Harvard University in 1968.

Diana McLain Smith, Ed.D., is a partner in Action Design Associates (ADA Consulting), a research-based consulting firm that specializes in organizational learning. At present, she is a Lecturer on Organizational Behavior and Consulting Theory and Practice at Boston College's Carroll School of Management. She is the author of numerous articles and manuals on intervention practice, and coauthor of *Action Science* (with Chris Argyris and Robert Putnam; Jossey-Bass, 1985). She is especially interested in how professionals learn within the constraints imposed by the organizations in which they work. She received her doctoral degree in consulting psychology from Harvard University.

Howard F. Stein, Ph.D., is Professor of Family Medicine at the University of Oklahoma Health Sciences Center, Oklahoma City. He serves as Balint Group Coordinator in the Oklahoma City Program and directs behavioral science teaching at the Enid Family Medicine Clinic, a community-based, rural-oriented residency training program in northwest Oklahoma. A medical and psychoanalytic anthropologist, psychohistorian, and political psychologist, he received his Ph.D. from the University of Pittsburgh in 1972. From 1980 to 1988, he was editor of the *Journal of Psychoanalytic Anthropology*. He is the author of more than 150 scholarly and clinical papers, and his recent books include *American Medicine as Culture, Clinical Stories and Their Translations* (with Maurice Apprey) and *Maps from the Mind* (coedited by William Niederland). He is currently writing about the culture of Oklahoma and about psychodynamically oriented consultation with organizations.

Peter Steinglass, M.D., is Director of the Ackerman Institute for Family Therapy in New York City, a position he assumed in July 1990. He previously was Professor of Psychiatry and Behavioral Sciences and Director of the Center for Family Research at the George Washington University School of Medicine in Washington, D.C. His research and teaching interests have focused on the relationship between family interaction and chronic psychiatric and medical conditions. He is also currently editor of the journal *Family Process* and has authored numerous scientific papers and books, including *The Alcoholic Family,* which outlines his research and conceptual ideas about alcoholism and the family. He received his M.D. degree from Harvard Medical School.

Maurine H. Venters, Ph.D., is a Program Director in Academic Administration, University of Minnesota. She received her Ph.D. in health care administration from the University of Minnesota in 1980, and received her J.D. degree in 1991. She has published several articles on various family health issues using both sociological and epidemiological approaches. While serving as Coordinator of the Family Medicine Faculty Development Program at the University of Minnesota, she took part in teaching and scholarly presentations and published articles that integrated research about family health behavior/family care and the practice of family medicine.